AF619243

To Soda Lake

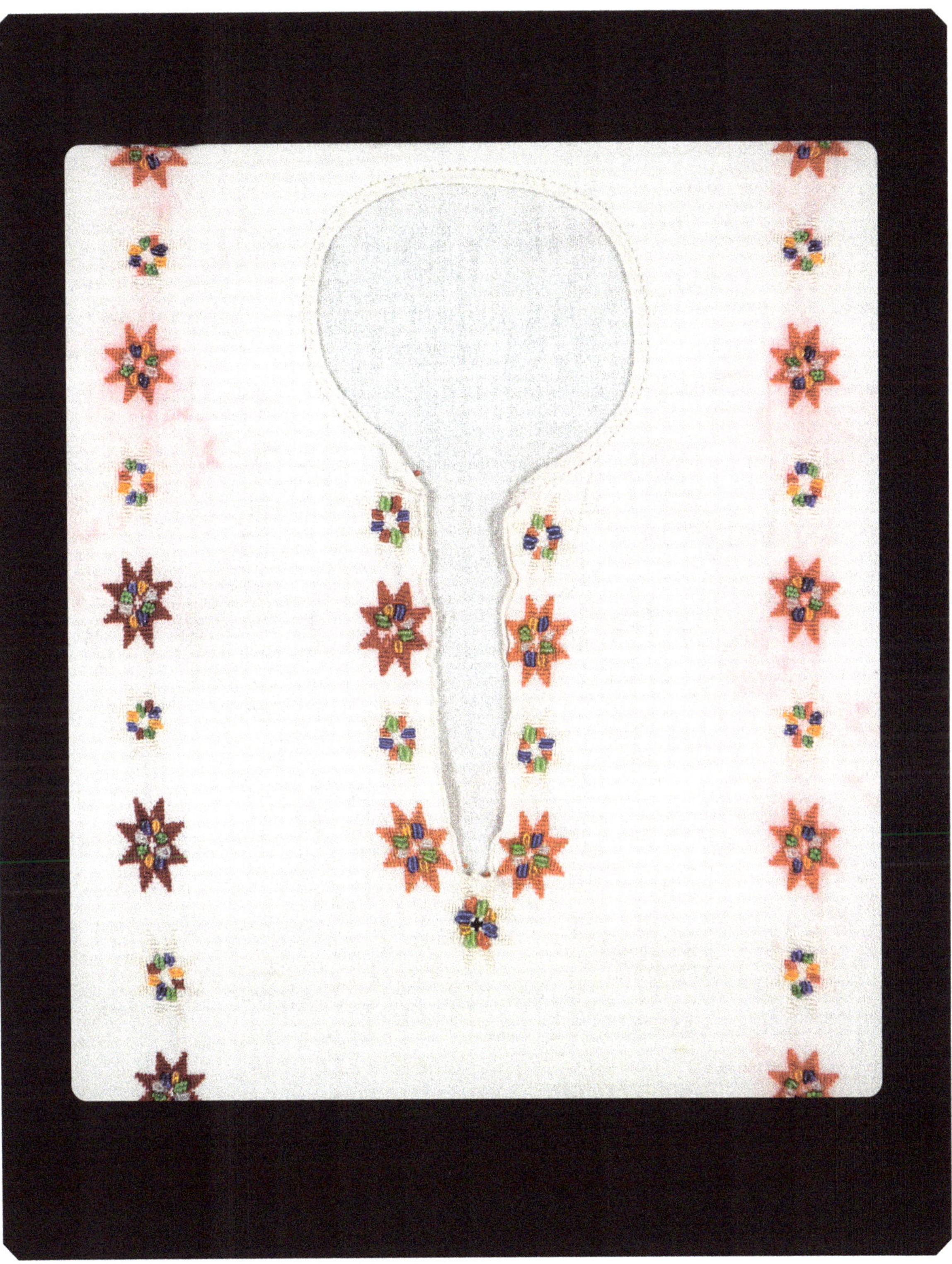

Copyright © 2024 by Monica Kindraka Jensen, Ph.D.
Book design: Don McCartney Design
Cover Art: "Among Women," original quilt using a commercial fabric panel based on Matisse paintings, hand appliquéd, hand and machine quilted.

Photos: Unless otherwise stated, all photos and graphics are property of the author.

All rights reserved. No part of this book may be reproduced by any mechanical, photographic or electronic process—other than for "fair use" as brief quotations embodied in articles, reviews or for educational and academic purposes—without prior written permission from the author.

Catalog-in-Publication Data is on file at the Library of Congress.

Softcover ISBN: 979-8-9858079-4-3

Published by Penn&Ink [pennandink.us]

Printed in the USA
Published December, 2024
Distributed by Ingram-Spark

Among Women

What was passed down
from mother to daughter
among five generations of one
Ukrainian-Canadian-American
family, my own.

A Personal History
By

Monica Kindraka Jensen, Ph.D.

*"In spite of biblically ancient warnings,
we don't think of our choices...as contaminating
or blessing not only ourselves but also our children."*

—Leaving Before the Rain Comes, 129.

Table of Contents

Ropchan Quilt

CHAPTER 1

To Begin

I know this story well, because I have been stuck inside it. I have lived with its causes and effects, its details and indelible lessons, my entire life.... And if I ever hope to leave this place, I must tell what I know.

— ***Shot In the Heart*** [1]

I FELL silent and slipped into a kind of shock. I had been speaking to a gallery full of eager museum goers who were hoping to learn more about the spectacular and enigmatic Al Held painting covering the wall before them. At the time, I was curating at a troubled art museum in Texas. For the eight years that preceded this moment, I had spoken with ease in front of museum groups. There is nothing so satisfying as to communicate why you love something to someone else so that they begin to love the thing too.

I stood at a vantage point, on the top step of the second gallery looking out over a packed main floor gallery, and observed myself with mounting horror. I had everything to say, a mind full of affection and information for each object in the gallery and the intelligence to talk about the pieces knowingly and clearly. I couldn't speak. Instead, I backed into my mind, observing myself observing myself, an endless hall of mirrors. It seemed hours before I nudged myself back into voice. Somehow I heard myself say to myself, "just talk about something really simple and then work out from there." This, I was able to do.

That was the day my art museum career ended.

How had it come to this? The willing years of graduate school, the eager visits to art museums to "learn" their collections, the hopeful job search, the broadening work experience at a number of small and ambitious art museums, getting to know and keeping in touch with museum "professionals" at conferences in Washington, D.C. or San Francisco. My energy had been directed to growing excellence in "the museum field."

The decision to end my museum career was not made lightly, though it was made quickly. When I handed my letter of resignation to the museum's director, he was surprised. His surprise surprised me, for he had considered me suspect from my first days at the museum. To his way of thinking, states like Indiana did not produce curators of merit and understandably he had wanted the best for his art museum. "To think, she's from Indiana," he would exclaim when I had organized a memorable exhibition. But I did not leave for any reason connected to his biases.

It was not a defeat. At least at the time, it did not seem so. I somehow had the good sense to remove myself from the track that was leading me to a breakdown. The voices of others were not merely drowning me out; they were drowning me. These voices were exclusively the voices of women. Every position in the museum—save those in Accounting and Building & Grounds—was filled by a female. Curatorial. Museum Education. Registrar. Publicity. Development. Art School. Assistants. Receptionists. What with a male director, it was nearly a harem.

I was pressed to fight for territory at every turn. I did not know how to mobilize and campaign among these women. I dissembled and gave ground. I isolated myself and gave ground. What began as a clear voice of good humor and openness devolved into a stuttering, hesitant mumble. Here and there I rallied in a scrambled kind of way, but for the most part, I retreated. I grew more silent. I disappeared. Why did I regard these women as dangerous creatures?

Seeking answers—submitting to therapy, launching into travel, slowing for deep introspection, it became obvious to me that I was not a normal person, especially among women. My particular anguish, the anguish that has frustrated and blocked me from myself, throughout my life has been my inability to trust women. It began with the women in my family, but extends far beyond them. Women have angered me and frightened me, pushed me into corners and silenced and on occasion driven me into a ravening froth. Truly. My husband likes to recount, humorously, the evening I returned from the publishing company where I worked and, suffering from an excruciatingly frustrating set of encounters with fellow females, hurled a large chef's knife into the kitchen wall, screaming. The question burned: why should it prove so difficult to secure balance with the females around me?

This book attempts to answer that question. My primary focus is on female relatives. They inadvertently led me to dark places. Around them, I carry a sense of dread like a favorite shoulder purse. For $150-an-hour, the shrinks confidentially tell me that safety and trust go hand in hand. Trust, however, was not something that the ladies of my bloodline passed forward. Never having been part of their own life experience, it simply never occurred to them. No doubt this deficit of trust contributes to my neuroses or post-traumatic stress disorder or all-around-twitchiness—whatever label the next psychologist or psychiatrist will enthusiastically attach to me.

Trust, in my experience, is for losers. This is not what I believe, but what I have observed. In my life, personally and professionally, my interchange with women—individuals whom I hoped would like me, help me, teach me, ask me to join them, or God forbid, understand me—has rarely worked. A door swings shut. I back away and quietly close my own door.

On the one occasion when I met Gloria Steinem—it was a book-signing event—I was struck by how naturally and gracefully she encouraged me. I'd confessed that I was trying to write a book about the women in my life. Everything in her manner was enthusiastic for my success. Her sentiments seemed genuine. She could have uttered something trite, flashed a defensive side with a "how dare you even suggest you could be a writer like me," and dismissed me, but she didn't. At the time, I was startled by the unfamiliarity of being treated as a near-equal and offered sincere hope.

I am smart, insightful, well informed, reasonably attractive and many more positive things—I do my homework— but I inevitably come away with a negative label— a label that ranges somewhere between unconventional and peculiar. There are days when I think I should restrict my wardrobe to all-black, the sophisticated power color. Perhaps that would help my inner and outer image. But I am too much in love with every other color to be able to embargo myself in this last way.

Give and take among women is something my mother didn't model. She was no wimp, but she withdrew from the battles with her five sisters—her confederation. It wasn't a matter of taking higher ground, hers was a conscious and grudging withdrawal. The worse Mother was treated, the more she gloried in it. Half in light and half in darkness, my *chiaroscuro* mother. To her last days, the Lord and Lady Willingdon Medal that she was awarded for achieving the highest high school marks of any senior in all of Alberta—it was a first for the province for she was a female and a Ukrainian female to boot—lay interred among other forgotten mementos in a steamer trunk in the attic. I was astonished to learn of this medal from Mother's older sister, Katherine. Mother waved it off. What was so powerful that she would commit herself, and by extension me to an insular community of distressed women? I still don't truly understand it.

Generally speaking, when things aren't working, one tries to find out why and does something about it. One packs one's bags and heads out in search of answers—Ian Frazier, John McPhee, William Least Heat Moon are among the illustrious on my bookshelves who had this insight. And so began a quest. In the 1990s, I decided to hit the road. I'd always been drawn to land-based quests—get out the *Federal Writers' Guide* for Indiana or Illinois and follow the Lincoln Highway, Highway 40; travel through Mississippi and Baton Rouge to New Orleans along that Delta blues yellow-brick road—that particular April, in the track of a drenching hurricane that brought white caps to the inside floor of my rusted VW Beetle—yes, Highway 61; retrace the Overland Trail backwards from California to Reno, east; camp through The Forty Mile Desert in Nevada.

There are no guides for the route I wanted to take; this only heightened the adventure. I zig-zagged the United States and western Canada, touching each of the living family members whom I could find: from sister to sister and brother to brother, seeking out remote cousins and former neighbors—often complete strangers to me. I collected recollections and observations. I got closer to things. In the process, I realized that I was going to have to confront the Ukrainian part of many of the narratives I had. In the 1890s, my family immigrated to Canada from what is now western Ukraine—then, the Austrian-Hapsburg crown province of Bukovyna. Once upon a time, they all shouted and laughed and wept with each other, always in Ukrainian. To me, Ukraine was one big mystery.

So I settled in for a long haul. How could I possibly understand my family without living where they lived and learning about the culture that they took for granted, a culture that was alien to me. I signed on, yet again, for graduate school, this time in Canada. I would be studying Ukrainian culture and, yes, factoring "roots" into my studies—absorbing the flux from those attached to the family tree. I opted for a PhD degree at the University of Alberta, Edmonton, sixty miles, as it turns out, from the quarter-sections of my mother's family and most of her elders, now scattered about in tidy prairie cemeteries. It made sense to be near their bones.

In Canada, there was Edmonton and Calgary, Andrew, Mundare, Vegreville, Hairy Hill, Two Hills, Willingdon and the homestead lands—corners of wilderness prairie in Alberta. There was—on my father's side in Saskatchewan—Saskatoon, Yorkton, Melville, Birmingham and more homestead lands. Pausing in living rooms, dining rooms and the lounges of senior care facilities, I logged hundreds of tape hours. I rambled through flora and observed fauna-in-the-wild—at Elk Island Provincial Park, a buffalo, angry because our dachshund "Quark" barked at him through the car window, raced after our necessarily accelerating vehicle. I weathered Edmonton's Arctic days of -37° C or F—deep cold, equivalent on both scales—stomping my feet to keep them warm, while waiting for the absolutely on-time #9, #43 or the #50 bus. The busses always pulled over, no matter how packed. This was a municipal and humanitarian kindness.

Modest success in Canada led me further afield. I ventured to Ukraine. This meant I was able to drown my *perohe* (пероги, potato and cheese dumplings) in sour cream on both sides of the Atlantic. I traveled through the 18th and 19th centuries, while seated in classrooms and libraries. I visited ancestral villages. I visited research archives. I collected images, more observations, adventures, friends and not-friends. I tried to pursue the few facts I had at my command. I studied the language and floundered in it and on rare occasions communicated felicitously and wonderfully well.

L'viv, Striy, Chernivtsi and Chornivka in Ukraine were important stops along my course. I nearly succumbed to heat stroke in one of those little *marshroutkas* (маршрутка, passenger van) that ply L'viv's cobbled streets. Windows must be tightly sealed against drafts, perversely on ninety-degree days: folk fantasy has it that drafts cause illness. Meanwhile, every day of my interviewing, studying, traveling—at the bottom of it all—I sought to understand what happened to the women in my family, all of them or at least as many as I knew. I thought that if I knew about them, then I would know about me.

It was in Ukraine where I met Larysa; she begins this narrative. We're speaking non-fiction here. She nearly burned my wagon to the ground. I met wonderful souls like Oksana, who encouraged me to pursue Ukrainian, and Liuda and Andriy who artfully handled fire extinguishers. My journeying led to a fuller understanding of my mother's sisters, my mother, my grandmothers and great-grandmothers—that bloodline littered with unhappiness and, as I was to discover, blood.

Cruel things happened to the women to whom I am related. In order to exhale, they—knowingly and unknowingly—did cruel things to one another. It was a tightly sealed, pressure-filled container in which they lived. I assume that a kind of free-floating ancestral memory of abuse—something carried at a cellular level—afflicted them all. Where does abuse and cruelty come from? Where does it go?

For me, it is my female antecedents who represent the darkest, most complex, confusing, and thus, most fascinating part of the family's never-ending discourse.

In the pages that follow, I give you five generations of daughters, sisters, mothers and grandmothers, and a miscellany of catalysts. I trust these women will answer this question. I trust you will come to embrace them as I now do.

---

1 Mikal Gilmore, *Shot In the Heart*, xi.

CHAPTER 2

L'viv: Larysa and Me
Лариса

"I've said I want to die on Mars, just not on impact."
***—Elon Musk*[1]**

THE summer I spent with Larysa was the second worst of my life. The much earlier first-prize summer was the one that passed after my springtime hysterectomy: pain, good drugs like Morphine, bladder infections, depression, that sort of thing. In terms of scale, comparing Larysa to major abdominal surgery—and in 1978, when I had that surgery, it was *major*—says something. What made the time living with Larysa in her dark, rancid flat so bad was her desire to inflict pain at every turn. It had little to do with me. Yet I have often thought back to that horrid May and June and July of 2001. I engineered an exit from her apartment and her "lessons" by August. Why I allowed myself, for the most part, to become Larysa's victim troubles me still.

L'viv, in western Ukraine is a city, a somewhat tarnished gem, I now regard with great fondness, but not because of Larysa. I was in L'viv hoping to learn the rudiments of Ukrainian. The deal with Larysa was blithely set up by a dissertation advisor, whom I'll call "M." He and Larysa had on occasion been research colleagues. I needed to acquire Ukrainian, fast; Larysa needed the money. Pretty straightforward. She did not speak English, I spoke no Ukrainian, so the summer was going to be an exercise in total immersion, quite gonzo. Several friends in the department warned me that Larysa was a bit paranoid, but they would go no further than that. Letters and permissions passed back and forth and on May 22nd, I flew from Chicago to Zurich; on May 24th I flew from Zurich to Kiev and took the train west to L'viv.

As for train travel in Ukraine, the Kiev-L'viv train works something like this. You board it at about 7:30pm, find your "cabin"—in my case, I had paid for a relatively private cabin that I would be sharing with one other person, of course a stranger— tuck your suitcase under the couch-bed, show your ticket and passport to the conductress, purchase clean bed linens, have a bit of tea, try to chat, make your bed and then settle down to sleep through the 340 noisy miles. I am not a good travel-sleeper.

Around 5:30 am, the train arrived in L'viv. Blunted by sleeplessness and dazed by the exoticism of the place, I looked, and there she was, unmistakable by virtue of her thick, thigh-length strawberry blond hair. She wore it straight, though on occasion she wore it in one long, thick-as-a-rattlesnake, braid. A single, whopper braid down a woman's back is the stuff of Ukrainian Cossack legend: the true, pure Ukrainian maiden wears that braid—tradition demands that the hair of such a classic beauty be black, her eyebrows black, her skin white and her eyes blue. My great grandmother was just such a beauty. When the fair-haired Yulia Tymoshenko was a candidate for the Office of President, she suddenly sported that Cossack braid, which she wrapped around her head like a wreath. Ukrainians knew exactly what it signified.

Larysa, the peaches and cream color of her skin, with its tendency to freckle, was in accord with that Titian blond mane. In her youth, documented in a photo she later shared with me, her features were pert, her lips a perfect cupid's bow, her chin line fine and delicate. She had been uncommonly pretty and she knew it. But with time, her nose lengthened and sharpened and her face took on a severe set, desiccated. The loss of a tooth did not help her infrequent smile. Still, at forty-eight, Larysa showed only a bit of grey at her temples and from the back, looked much younger than she was.

I knew I was in trouble when I stepped off of the train. Brown-eyed and unsmiling, she greeted me and made me to understand that I should follow her. I was struck by her lack of warmth, but was too weary to think on it. Then she pivoted on her heels, speed-walking to a taxi. She did not turn to engage me or to check to see if I was behind her. It was as if she were trying to lose me in all of the pedestrian traffic of a good-sized city. Most of my early photos of L'viv street scenes show Larysa twenty to thirty feet out on some sidewalk or another.

Her apartment was on the fourth floor of a stately-looking 19th century building. When the taxi stopped she raced from it to the building's open-to-the-air inner courtyard and speed-climbed up the dimly lit spiral of a creaking wooden staircase. Finally, she stopped at a pair of French doors, wood and glass coated entirely in bittersweet chocolate brown paint; these doors comprised the entrance to her suite of rooms. We were standing near a finely carved banister finial, an incongruously elegant pineapple, at the top level of the staircase. On Larysa's doors, a battery of locks waited to be wrestled with, their secrets known only to her.

Once inside the actual apartment, I was unnerved by its gloom. A long airless hallway—its floor cluttered by standing coat racks and scattered worn shoes—flanked by darkened French doors extended before me. It frightened me. My thoughts raced to Anna Akhmatova in the 1920s, starving and freezing in such an apartment in St. Petersburg. Hallway narrowness and the twelve-foot high ceiling exacerbated the hall's tunnel-like, claustrophobic quality. When the dimmest of ceiling lights, approximately one-candle power, was switched on, a rather battered tiled parquet floor appeared.

Larysa's father, a Communist party-functionary, had been, according to her, a poet and a painter. Sunrise to sunset, his ghoulish erotic oil on canvas of a nude woman vanquished by a nude vampire sulked and smoldered in the former parlor, now my room. He secured or was awarded the walk-up situated in this once graceful building on *Vinnichenka* Street (Винниченка): French doors opening from room to room, deep casement windows that looked into mature oaks and lindens, high white ceilings decorated with floral stucco garlands. In its youth, it must have been delightfully sun-filled. But at some point, the expansive whole was unceremoniously divided among neighbors, so that Larysa retained the parlor, her father's study, a bedroom, and then a tiny box of a kitchen that sided an adjacent sink-bathtub cubicle, both created out of something else. Inside, just to the right of the front door, as you were entering the blackness of the hallway, was a nasty water closet with a pull-chain toilet. Mid-summer, inexplicably Larysa removed the toilet seat from the contraption and left it off, but by then our relationship had taken a nose-dive.

The windowless kitchen provided barely enough room for a miniature four-burner stove and a three-quarters refrigerator, yet it held five large tropical fish tanks, lit at odd hours of the day or evening. One burner of the gas stove was always aflame, set on "low." Over it, Larysa placed a brick-like stone. On the stone she warmed big pots of water for the fish tanks. The heated brick also kept the air in the kitchen humid. Later I was to discover that Larysa frequently slept in the kitchen on the padded bench below her gurgling fish tanks.

Plavati (плавати) was one of the first verbs I learned from Larysa that actually stuck. It means "to swim." All day long, her tropical fish were plavae. They swam with particular vigor when she fed them the squirming hair-like worms that she cut up with a razor blade on a broken piece of glass. (Illustration 2.1) She kept the worms, diligently acquired every week from a particular vendor at the open-air *Krakivs'kiy* (Краківський, Cracow) market—it was once on the road to Cracow—in her pungent refrigerator. The process of slicing them up was akin to a ritual. Indeed, from my perspective, she took more care with the worms than with any meal she ever prepared, never flinching at their windings and thrashings.

A heavy drape hung over the kitchen door and blocked light that might come from the parlor, that is, the room directly across the hallway from the kitchen. When the fish were sleeping, Larysa wanted no sliver of light to disturb them. But then, light did not escape from room to room or into the hallway. Although the room I lived and worked in should have been awash in natural light from the soaring street-facing windows, it was dark like the rest of Larysa's rooms. Tangles of ill-kept house plants blocked out sunlight, as well as a view of the cobbled *Vinnichenka* below.

Lessons began with the two of us sitting at the oriental-carpet covered round table in the ex-parlor. During the day, I worked at the dictionary-strewn table or wrote in the worn ochre armchair because it had broad arm rests, good for supporting the anemic table lamp, a cup of hot tea and my notebooks.

Perhaps Larysa and I, tutor-tutoree, would have reached some common comfortable ground together in her home, if it had not been for the expedition to Bulgaria. It was something "Z" helped to orchestrate, originally for himself and other colleagues. From his desk in Edmonton, Alberta, he and a cohort in Sweden, and another in England, and another from somewhere else put together a proposal to study indigenous Vlach gypsy dance in Bulgaria. The proposal got funded. Two ethnology scholars, a mother and daughter team in Sofia, made the arrangements. They found rooms in the Sofia sports club complex "Champion," (Шампион, *Shampion*), rented a van and a driver, scoped out two villages—Хърлец (*Kh'rlets*) and Лилияч (*Liliiach*), notified officials, mapped out a route, and the anthropological-ethnological-terpsichorean rolling mini-bus tour of northeastern Bulgaria became reality.

"Z" had to back out of the trip. He funded Larysa. I paid for myself. On day-four in Larysa's parlor, I learned with a jolt that that very evening at 11:45pm, we would board a train bound for Sofia. Mistakenly I thought the Bulgaria trip would not come so quickly. I simply did not understand all that Larysa told me. I had acquired little Ukrainian at this point.

There we were, rolling south through the rest of Ukraine, through all of Romania and across the Danube into Bulgaria, parsing sentences together, attaching vocabulary to what was out the train car window—дика квітка (*dika kvitka*) "wild flower," дика нарцис (*dika nartsis*) "wild iris." Somewhere in Romania, as I stood in the rail car hallway studying the fields and attendant meadows, a fellow traveler asked me for the time. "О сьомій годині (*O s'omiy hodyni*)," I said, that is, "the 7th hour or 7:00pm." I was hugely proud that I understood his question and had responded promptly with an actual and accurate number. "Perfect Ukrainian," I thought. "Bravo!"

Not so. Larysa disagreed with a kind of smirk and a headshake. First of all, the gentleman did not understand me because he was speaking Russian and I Ukrainian. "But," I protested, "I understood him." Secondly, I should not have used the preposition "O" before the numeral. Furthermore, the Locative case of the preposition was incorrect. It was not in Larysa to say, "good job" for the parts I did well. This is rather typical of Ukrainian pedagogy and not just Larysa: no rewards.

As the expedition unfolded in Sofia and later in Хърлец (*Kh'rlets*) and Лилияч (*Lili-*

iach), Larysa developed gnarly ticks. Our little group consisted of two Americans, two Bulgarians, a Swede, an Icelandic couple, an Italian, a Brit and Larysa-the-Ukrainian. By default, the agreed upon language was English. This placed Larysa at a disadvantage, for she understood English only sparsely and my level of Ukrainian was not sufficient to bridge the void. The multi-lingual group leader spoke English, German, Russian and nearly everything else. Technically, Larysa was not out of the loop.

She began to hang back when the group strolled from place to place, idly picking up leaves or plucking flowers, a bit like the mad Ophelia. At one of our mini-van stops, I was chided by another group member for "allowing" Larysa to wander off and hold the rest of the group hostage. One never knew when she would reappear. At group meals—in Sofia we had a favorite café that served luscious salads of fresh tomatoes and cucumbers (шопський салат, *Shops'kiy salat*), sensational coffee, good red wine, sturdy bread, Larysa would willfully ignore our leader's assistance in ordering. (2.2) In the Mediterranean heat, we grew genuinely concerned about her collapsing, she was eating and drinking so little: an Espresso for breakfast, a bag of potato chips for lunch. I wondered if I should be buying food for her and offered to do so to no avail.

Atypically, Larysa started to bobby-pin curl her hair at night, then slouch silently at meals smoking thin cigars and looking for all the world like a Berthold Brecht version of Shirley Temple. In Sofia, there was a snarling fit *chez* Larysa when, dividing the inconsequential fare, four of us decided to take a taxi back to the sports club-hotel. We covered Larysa's fare. She simply refused to spend a Bulgarian *lev*, yet the expedition was covered for her by $600 Canadian and I had handed Larysa $2,000 US in cash for the summer.

In both *Kh'rlets* and *Liliiach*, our group became a kind of festive event. Not only did we observe and record unfamiliar folk dances performed for us outside in the grass and shade, we visited private homes with front door plaques honoring Stalin, tasted home-canned roasted red peppers—as common in Bulgaria as is blueberry jam in Minnesota, joined a wedding party for toasts, toured a local wood workshop where the seasoned craftsman, lit cigarette hanging from his mouth, turned out wooden spoons, spatulas and forks— incendiary woodchips flying all around him. There were all-village sit-down dinners accompanied by *sopilka* playing (сопилка, flute) and dancing. One evening, Dina, Theresa and I took turns protecting each other from "the polkaing ass-grabber," our name for the guy. Seated alone, back against the wall at our emptied out table, Larysa, the stone maiden, refused to dance when even the flatware on the cloth was in motion. All languages-be-damned, she would not be drawn out or into the whirl and merriment. Her hidden agenda, expressed in tight-lipped defiance and a steely-eyed slow burn, was hard to ignore. Later, Theresa was to observe that Larysa interacted with the group only when it was convenient for her.

When our train lurched north, headed for the Danube, I felt a mixture of relief and sadness. The toilet at the end of our rail car seemed positively heavenly. One can grasp a wall hand-hold and lean back towards the toilet and even flush it by stepping on a release pedal, whereupon the contents pour onto the railroad track bed. Back in *Kh'rlets* and *Liliiach*, positioning one's feet on the two bricks at the side of that triangular hole in the concrete floor of the outhouse—"the Turkish-style bathroom," Bulgarians say— and squatting and trying to keep one's clothing off of anything, avoiding spiders, swatting flies and mosquitoes, fishing the toilet paper out of one's pocket, it's a challenge. As we clicked along the rails I wondered whether anyone has written a scholarly paper about the symbolism of the triangle and the Turkish toilet: the mystical isosceles triangle, the number three, etc., *ad absurdum*. Mini-van group members were going to be writing scholarly papers about the dances we saw and the music we heard, but probably not about waterclosets. I was going to miss them, the mini-van group that is.

As the train chugged through Romanian fields and skirted rivers, Larysa and I tried to talk, but the conversation was rather dark. She suggested that the Bulgarian expedition organizer was taking a 10% cut of everything we'd been paying. This I could not imagine, particularly because Anna had been uniquely generous and thoughtful regarding Larysa. The accusation was disheartening. I sliced up an apple for us to share, peeling the skin off because the apple had not been washed. Larysa refused the apple, then ate the peel.

Back in L'viv, my lessons resumed. Wrapped in sweaters, huddled under the 40-watt study lamp with my textbook, I wrote out or verbally drilled noun-pronoun-adjective declensions and cases, verb conjugations and the bedeviling endings that goad a student of Ukrainian. Outside it rained; inside, the days were dusky grey. On the rare occasion when Larysa and I ventured out, say to the *Krakivs'kiy* market for tomatoes, cucumbers, bread, butter, cheese, cabbage, frozen fish, garlic, yellow cherries and always worms, I usually misjudged the outside temperature. Leaving the cave-flat with its constant 55°- 60°F temperature, sweater-clad, I was almost embarrassed; I did not need all those layers, and certainly not a sweater. What's more, it came as a surprise to me on market days that, in addition to the multiple exterior locks, Larysa secured every door inside her apartment—that is, the door to the kitchen, the door to the parlor, the door to the study, the door to her bedroom, the door to the water closet—when she stepped out.

The difficulty of keeping up with Larysa as we moved towards any of the several markets—*Krakivs'kiy, Halits'kiy*, also reasserted itself. Head locked forward—never did she look around her—Larysa took long steps, walking fast, and changed from one side of a street to another idiosyncratically, keeping twenty to forty paces ahead of me at all times. In the maze of venerable lanes and avenues, I never knew quite which way we would turn. The sidewalks and streets themselves were paved with huge cobblestones, rounded, slippery, tricky to negotiate at Larysa's brisk pace. For me, compounding the challenge of following Larysa, vehicular traffic showed no concern for pedestrians. I needed three eyes to watch out for myself: one for the walking surface, the second to keep my guide in view, a third to avoid trams, vans and cars. There were rarely moments to study the surroundings, the countless steepled or onion-domed churches peppering the skyline, the icing-cake apartment buildings with their bosomy caryatids, the Neptune or Apollo or Diana fountains that didn't work. It seemed that Larysa wanted to interact with the beautiful L'viv and its coffee house culture as little as possible, and somehow that being on the streets, among people, was hazardous.

Our uneasy routine continued to unfold. Work, then breakfast. Breakfasts (обід, obid) consisted of hot black tea and an open-faced sandwich—dark bread spread with cheese or butter, covered by a sliced cucumber topped with salty fish eggs. After breakfast there was more work, then lunch (сніданок, *snidanok*) around 1:00pm. For lunch we often had more bread and tea and Larysa's *borshcht* (борщт), Ukrainian vegetable soup with beets. Unfortunately, Larysa used commercial bullion powder as the base for her *borshcht*, so my face and arms acquired the familiar rash that is my reaction to heavy salts. Breakfast and lunch took place in semi-dark: Larysa wanted the fish to rest. "Shhhh," she would caution. "The fish are sleeping" (Риба спить, *Riba spit'*).

In the afternoon, I had free time, mostly for homework. The Spanish soap operas (dubbed in Ukrainian) started at 4:00pm. These were a *must*, for I could actually "get" the dialogue of the dragon-mother destroying the lives of her married daughters. Evening news at 6:00pm was followed by supper (вечеря, *vecheria*). The dinner menu was variable, lean on vegetables, heavy on potato- or sauerkraut-filled dumplings, which I aptly named "little toughies," covered with sour cream. "*Smetana*" (смета́на, *smetána*), the Ukrainian word for sour cream, brought the name of that great Czech composer down a notch for me. While the t.v. was on and Larysa chopped onions, I would read aloud dialogues from my textbook, these, immediately corrected for pronunciation, inflection and pacing. Meal moths flickered in the lit kitchen. Theirs was a healthy population. Evidently, the tropical fish were not partial to them. Usually I wrote in my journal before rolling myself into the parlor couch-bed.

I was a low creature. Larysa was not pleased with the way I fumbled pronouncing the Ukrainian hard and the soft "l" [л]. A lesson would go something like this. The Ukrainian spelling of L'viv is Львів, which is transcribed into *L'viv*. That little apostrophe or the tiny "ь" means that the preceding consonant is soft. Now in a word like "light fixture," that is to say, лампа (*lampa*), there is no little "ь" after the "l." This means that the "l" is a hard "l." For a hard "l," the tongue is further forward; for a soft "l," the tongue is further back and slightly arched. It's a subtle distinction that comes with practice, much practice. For Larysa, I never got there. Then there was my trouble distinguishing the "kh" sound from "h." I endlessly confused the adjectives "hungry" (голодний, *holodniy*) and "cold" (холодний, *kholodniy*). We would drill and drill and drill, and in spite of the work, my tongue would be forward and not back and arched, "kh" and "h" remained inscrutably the same sound to my ear and my accent inevitably fell on the wrong syllable—I would say "keyhole" (замóк, *zamók*), when I meant "castle" (зáмок, *zámok*).

Larysa would fly into a rage—she would leave the room and fix herself a cup of tea—over my inability to understand, let alone remember grammatical terms such as "Masculine case noun" or "Feminine case noun," "Imperfective verb" or "Perfective verb." In my first year of language study in Canada, these terms were neither mentioned, nor used. Needless to say, Larysa had a base opinion of how Ukrainian was being taught on the other side of the big water. Naturally, her low opinion attained to the caliber of the North American language student, too.

By mid-June, if the day were sunny, a great rarity, I would use my free time in the afternoon to wander about L'viv alone. I would try to read billboards—cigarette ads were a great favorite, for they usually featured American imagery like Yosemite's Half Dome or a Bald Eagle or a cigarette box wearing a Bruce Springstein-like t-shirt alluding to the message, "American Summer" (Американське літо, *Amerikans'ke lito*). I guess if you smoked that cigarette brand, you would be enveloped in an American summer, as opposed to a Ukrainian one, where the men did not look like "The Boss." Usually, I would buy post cards. I memorized how to get to the post office and how to purchase postage stamps. Returning to the fourth-floor flat, I would find Larysa asleep under the fish tanks in her dank, inky-black kitchen.

On one of those free-time afternoons, I spotted a bilingual—Ukrainian/English—guidebook to L'viv, chock-a-block with helpful photos and maps. I paid $45 US for the treasure without blinking. How else was I going to familiarize myself with L'viv? Larysa was shocked by the purchase. Whereas before the guidebook, she had been cool towards me, frequently shrill around my language gaffes, quite suddenly she moved into another behavioral mode: outright hostility. She refused to dine with me. It had to do with that book. Perhaps it was the expense of the book that set her off. We were nearly age-equals and I'd bought one book for more than she lived on in a month. Then again, "M" slept in that parlor on a number of occasions and he certainly flashed his expenditures around. Perhaps, in Larysa's mind, he was supposed to buy stuff because he was a professor or a male. Or perhaps Larysa was thinking, "Well, now you have your guidebook, so you don't need me. Therefore, I'll vacate myself from you." In truth, I had no idea what was going on in her mind.

After one of my early guidebook outings, Larysa warned that I was an easy mark—alone, reading a guidebook on the city streets. "There are many people here who want to steal money and will stop at nothing. They even resort to using a spray can so that a victim passes out," she said. At least my language comprehension was improving. Indeed, I was approached several times by strangers, once by a young man who wanted to give me a $1.00 (5 гривня, *hryvnia*) history tour of "Market Square," (Площа Ринок, *Plosh-cha Rinok*)—the old Medieval, then Renaissance center of the town. I declined his offer. Days later, a rather shy woman came up wanting to tell me something. With my broken Ukrainian, her perfect Ukrainian and her broken English, I learned that she was one of the graphic artists for the guidebook. We turned to page 213 and collectively studied her drawing. She then pulled the original out of her leather briefcase. There was no mistaking her pleasure—her drawing was in a being-used guidebook. I came away glad that she had pointed out what she had done and charmed for her autographing the page, "From Galina Zimina to Monika."

But at Larysa's, animus reigned. There were the cherries, the lovely golden-yellow cherries in season at *Krakivs'kiy* Market. I'd bought a kilo of them for the two of us to share. Larysa refused to touch one. When I had to toss some of the cherries out as spoiled, she hissed at me: "If you hadn't bought so many and if you'd eaten them faster, they'd not be spoiled!" Then she counted the days since the purchase as if to underscore the transgression. She had been watching and waiting for a way to use those cherries as rancorous fodder. The contagion spread to bananas, then to the tomatoes I purchased for "the house."

Barriers popped up overnight like toadstools. The bathtub and bathroom sink, kept free weeks earlier, now filled with big pots of water and dirty filters-to-be-cleaned, the impedimenta necessary to maintain five tanks of fish. No effort was made to clear the assortment so that bathing could take place. Perhaps my putting two "s'es" into Odessa— the Russian way of spelling the city name, as opposed to "Odesa," the Ukrainian way—the previous day caused this fit of pique. Then the toilet seat disappeared. Was this due to my fractured declension skills? I just couldn't understand how the city of Chernivtsi must be declined as a plural noun, whereas the village of Chornivka was always declined as singular. Toilet paper! I'd already given up on expecting to see it. Quietly, I bought my own.

In the greater world outside of Larysa's, Pope John Paul II, ethnically Polish, was going to be visiting Ukraine. It was a big deal, way beyond the rapprochement between Catholicism and Orthodoxy. Almost before history, Poles and Ukrainians were enemies: Poles drifted into the "empty lands" of now-western Ukraine and "enticed" the peasants, mostly Ukrainians, to work for them. Consequently, in the 18th and 19th centuries the area around L'viv was awash in insurrections—local and murderous— and gorgeous Polish estates of jaw-dropping size and architectural sophistication. In the summer of 2001, bygones were bygones, the populace of L'viv prepared for the papal visit with warmth and enthusiasm. Never mind the torrential rains that fell nearly every day.

Late June and out of the murk of declining nouns—every one of which was an exception to the rule, Larysa announced that we'd been invited to a Hutsul wedding in the Carpathians and that we were going. Ukrainians are fervent about the Hutsuls. Think American cowboys or Woody Guthrie. Today, Hutsuls are a marker of national identity.

The great Ukrainian filmmaker, Paradjanov secured world fame with his magical *Shadows of Forgotten Ancestors* (1960) by interweaving actual scenes of Hutsul life in the Carpathians with a Romeo and Juliet plot. More recently, the mane-tossing, leggy Ukrainian pop star, Ruslana, won the EuroVision song competition in 2004 with "Wild Dances." Her blowout performance began with musicians trumpeting the eight- or ten-foot long Hutsul horns, трембита (*trembita*). After that, Ruslana's crew switched to Cossack kettle drums—never mind that the Cossacks appropriated this percussion instrument from the Ottoman Turks. Ukrainians went wild about Ruslana's references.

Whereas the early traditions of the Boikos, the Lemkos, the Podillians, or the Polissians more-or-less evaporated—in present-day Ukraine there is much folk-culture reconstruction based on hearsay, not on fact, Hutsul culture survives. Tucked away in their difficult-to-reach mountain aerie for centuries, the Hutsuls managed to avoid the wars and pogroms that repeatedly swept through the low land peoples, who understandably and consequently scattered.

After the Hutsul wedding, we'd also be swinging by my ancestral village—the carrot on the end of the stick. Larysa knew I wanted to see it, but my heart sank at the thought of more travel with her, the insisted upon deprivations. I repeatedly dialed the phone number "M" had given me "just in case" I needed an exit. Naturally, no one picked up the phone.

Finally, the sun came out on one of the last days of the Pope's visit to L'viv. I was hurrying along *Prospect Svbody* (*Boulevard Freedom*) to *Svitoch*, the fine old candy emporium, to buy chocolates for the Hutsuls. Crowds were thick along the boulevard, so I figured that the Pope was near. Sure enough, he wootled past us, waving from his white Pope-mobile. He seemed so matter-of-fact and observant; leaving water-logged L'viv he was quoted saying, "For you, rain falls, so that (your) children grow" (Для того, дощ падає, шоб діти росли. *Dlia toho, doshch padaie, shob dity rosly.*). That wise old man, the audacity and rightness of his visit, cheered me up. Even Larysa, unrelenting when it came to the use of the Ukrainian language, gave the Pope points for speaking Ukrainian better than Ukraine's president, whom she justifiably considered a scoundrel.

That evening, Larysa and I were again headed south via train on the 9:00pm to 6:30am "special," this time to Kolomiya in the foothills of the Carpathians and this time, accompanied by Roman (Роман), a folklore studies colleague of Larysa's. It came as no surprise that instead of a semi-private cabin with a closeable door and two or four pallets for sleeping, Larysa had booked the basic-everyman model, six to eight pallets climbing the walls of an unenclosed space, open to the flow of traffic and to noise, heat, and body odor. In those days, most Ukrainians, including Larysa, thought that deodorant was a Western contrivance foisted on them to destroy Ukrainian identity. Appropriately, a rooster was trying to screw a chicken at the threshold of our vaporous steel alcove.

As it turned out, Roman was thankfully logorrheic. He chattered away, never minding my mistakes. My Ukrainian skills spiked. Finally, a young soldier, who had a bunk in our area, told Roman to quiet down, he wanted to sleep. Sleep? For me there was no such thing. Apart from the banging and jerking of the train and the danger of sliding off of, or rather of being propelled off of, the hard leather pallet, there was the din in the car interior. At 1:30am a rollicking group of summer campers, Ukraine's youth, climbed aboard and partied 'til around 3:00am. At 4:30am, Roman awoke us, thinking that we were near Kolomiya. We weren't. He woke us again at 5:30am. We arrived an hour later and stumbled onto our first bus, Kolomiya to Kosiv. If I'd slept for two hours on the train, I'd be surprised.

At Kosiv, we waited in the dusty parking lot of a decrepit station for an hour-and-a-half to board our next bus, Kosiv to Verkhovina further up the mountains. This second bus, a little thing designed to carry about twenty passengers, was inundated by more than thirty souls, not including the quacking, clucking, honking ones. It was a mad push to get on and to find three adjacent seats. Unfortunately, we found them at the back of the bus. More unfortunate, my seat was on the blaring-sun side, the bus was poorly ventilated, and like being in the tail seat on an airplane during air turbulence, our communal back seat rocked and slammed its way up the mountain nearly independent of the bus.

A number of passengers were traveling to Verkhovina's farmer's market. Usurping two seats, a no-holds-barred woman juggled five huge baskets of strawberries, leaving other riders to stand, clinging to hand-holds along the aisle. Then there was the young man with goslings in a box with holes, but the box was tied into a plastic bag. When the *cognoscenti* heard the alarmed pitch of the goslings, there was a small uprising of concern: "Untie it! Untie it, or they will suffocate!" they shouted. The young man was much chastened by his bit of ignorance and the goslings survived, at least to market.

This traveling circus would have been a treat, the scenic ride into the mountains a joy had it not been for my exhaustion. The sun, the overcrowding, the diesel exhaust fumes, the caroming up a rutted and pot-holed road, my thirst—I wanted it to end. I clung to the hope that it would end. When we attained Verkhovina, I bought myself a bottle of water. It was a wise choice, I was to discover.

Foolish me! I thought that the Hutsuls who had invited us to a family wedding lived in Verkhovina. We began to walk, along a dirt road that narrowed to one lane, up, up and up, sharing the weight of three heavy pieces of luggage. Larysa and Roman were hauling video cameras and other recording equipment to document the rustics and the up-coming "authentic Ukrainian" wedding. Fit, strong, Roman began to joke that Larysa was sadistic, for we were exhausted to begin with and here we were climbing in the heat of mid-day, burdened by the bags. For my part, I enjoyed hearing the term "sadistic" pronounced crisply in Ukrainian. For her part, Larysa, her authority questioned, abruptly took off into the ever-near woods, leaving Roman and me dumbfounded, unsure of our destination, and waiting for forty minutes. It reeked of Larysa's Bulgarian behavior. When she reappeared, Larysa brightly twitted that she'd been studying wildflowers. She had wound a garland of flowers around her snake braid.

We lingered, resting a bit longer at the spot where Larysa rejoined us. (2.3) As we sat, a lone pedestrian, picking her way down the path towards us gradually took shape. When close, Larysa recognized her and she, Larysa. The conversation was animated. "We're on our way to the wedding," Larysa chirped. "No," the woman gasped. "It's not for another month!" Even I understood the Hutsul lady. Thus, the steely perfection that is Larysa had confused the dates: the wedding was not on June 28th, it was taking place on July 28th. With little choice, Roman and I resumed our plod. Larysa dawdled at the rear playing fairy flower princess. Here and there she disappeared completely.

Our Hutsul destination—a house, a barn, sheds, a well, an outhouse, beehives, a second house under construction— was on the down-slope side of the mountain, the walking path we traveled was parallel to and above the cluster of buildings. I was the first, Roman the second, in our rag-taggle line of uninvited and unannounced visitors. Thus, I had the opportunity to watch our host, who happened to be out in the sun scything a meadow for his growing haystack, as he spotted Larysa. His face fell, a look of annoyance ruffled his features. I could hear this mountain stalwart thinking, "Oh no! Not her! Not now!"

The Hutsul family consisted of our host, whose name I never heard mentioned, thus lamentably can only refer to as "host," his wife Paraska, their two adult sons, two grandsons, ten and eight respectively—Andriy and Yurko who were spending their summer away from mom in Kiev, our host's mother and an unrelated farmhand, a desperately afflicted stutterer. It was one of the two adult sons who was getting married at the end of July. Probably Paraska's daughter, the mother of Andriy and Yurko, would be coming from Kiev for the wedding. I fell in easily with Paraska and the two little boys, who marveled at my poor Ukrainian and without hesitation filled in my many blanks.

They were an efficient and likeable bunch. Their mountain-farm worked. Its meadows were green as spinach. The log buildings were strong and organized so that they interacted with ease. Rainstorm or snowstorm, the kitchen, the barn and the woodworking shop were all close. A line of apple trees accompanied the dining room's windowed wall. A grape arbor shaded the trafficked walkway to the one-holer. That outhouse was remarkable, the most exuberant and welcoming I'd encountered—with a tightly fitting wooden hole-plug to keep odor down; port hole windows allowing the user to gaze across the valley; interior walls papered with entertaining magazine clippings—a dazed father holding his triplets, a model with her bottom bared, a florid rooster, outlandish hair styles, Japanese ikebana arrangements; and wonder of wonders, a tidy felted wool cloth nailed around the seat for warmth and comfort.

The afternoon of our arrival, Roman and I found a shaded grassy spot near the unfinished house our host and his sons were slowly building and promptly lay down and slept. Meanwhile, playing out some fantasy, completely ignoring the rhythm of the household, Larysa banished all from the kitchen and insisted on fixing a time-consuming dinner. No doubt sensing that rain was on its way, our host and his haying crew did not stop their scything and raking until nearly 8:00pm. They were tired, ready to eat. The children needed to be fed. Roman and I had not eaten in 24-hours. Paraska quickly put down soup and bread, which were ravenously received. The host then brought out his homemade honey-brandy and we waited.

Larysa did not possess the secret for making thin, light dough. Even my brother, a thrice-removed Ukrainian who lives near Milwaukee, Wisconsin, knows how to make excellent, near-transparent dumpling dough. She was determined to serve her potato and brinza-filled dumplings—"*perohe*" or "*vareneky*" or "*pierogis*" or "little toughies," choose your favorite term. By 11:00pm, two bowls of Larysa's leathery bombs sat glowering on the table. Save for Larysa, no one was interested in them. We all tried to be polite and picked at them. The small boys, lucky they, were already tucked into bed.

Before sunset, while the haying proceeded, I helped Paraska assemble a makeshift bedroom in the solidly roofed, but still unglazed construction project. The newer building sat beside the current home, at a distance of perhaps fifty feet. A wooden runway with cross-slats underneath connected the two. Back and forth across the gangplank system, we carried bedding from the one structure to the other, fixing up a cot and a double-bed in a spacious room with window openings facing snow-capped mountains. Somewhere below, a cascade bounded *a capella* towards the Cheremosh River.

That night, Larysa burned the last bridge to my regarding her as sane. Thereafter, I dedicated myself to getting away from her, from her attempts at total control, from her lacerating lessons, from her morose apartment—all of it.

It was 1:00am when we left the table. Entering the room that Paraska and I put together, Larysa loudly announced to Roman and me that the cot was hers. She leapt into it and pulled the coverlet over her head. Certainly I, and possibly Roman, assumed that he would take the cot and Larysa and I, the double bed. (2.4) Thankfully there was no broom in the room, for had there been one, I was sufficiently angry to have grabbed it and with it wacked the cot, the coverlet and Larysa. Instead, I said to myself, "I've already packed for Kiev. Enough is enough!" Fully clothed, I slumped into the double bed. Roman took the other side and did the same. We needed sleep. When we opened our eyes in the morning, it was steadily pouring.

With rain and no wedding to film, we three were at loose ends. Larysa established a beachhead in the kitchen. Roman wandered inside and out, making a study of door-latches and the shapes of pitchforks. I was mildly interested in Roman's observations, but much more interested in the scrap book that eight-year-old Yurko created—page after page of *horilka* bottle labels. Russians call it "vodka," Ukrainians call it "*horilka*." The liquid has the same effect. The fanciful labels range from images of Cossack hetmen or of the most famous Cossack, *Bohdan Khmel'nyts'kyi*, to landmark Ukrainian churches, to Kiev's medieval gates, to highly regarded Ukrainian plays and playwrights, to the Dante and Shakespeare of the Ukrainian language, Taras Shevchenko. *Horilka* bottles are an opportunity to market Ukraine to Ukrainians or for that matter, to anyone who likes to drink the firewater. Fingering through the pages of Yurko's scrapbook, I remarked that he drank a lot. Both little boys were transported into gales of laughter. The joke was good for an entire downpour of an afternoon.

Between cold gusts of rain, I took strolls up the road. The air was perfumed by damp grasses and wild flowers. There was a life-list orchid growing from a water drainage ditch at the base of a hill—imagine an orchid by the side of the road like a dandelion. It was some variety of our Purple Fringed Orchid (*Platanthera psycodes*). Then there were the equally welcoming Heinz 57 meadow flowers, Toadflax, Blue Dicks, Ox Eye Daisies, Yarrow, Camas, Larkspur. Slightly further afield, I explored a cemetery pleasantly inhabited by metal and wooden crosses decorated with tinsel, colored paper and cloth flowers. The crosses were well-tended. On a high spot sat a tiny chapel covered with doily-lace cut tin. The structure, all filigree and high gables, seemed a happy haunt for mountain spirits.

After three days in the mountains, we wrapped up our non-wedding celebration. Larysa and I bid *adieu* to Roman at the Kolomiya train station and ventured on to Chernivtsi so that we might visit the *oblast* archive. Ultimately, she and I took another night train north, Chernivtsi to L'viv, whereupon I made a new discovery inside the apartment on *Vinnichenka* Street. If Larysa traveled out of the city, she would hide the interior door handles. Each had to be laboriously reattached and the door unlocked before any unpacking or settling-in could take place. If earlier I thought Larysa mad, I was now assured of it.

To thicken the stew, Gunther-the-German showed up on a Sunday. Larysa had never spoken of him. I knew she had been married once and that she despised her ex, but that was the extent of my knowledge about Larysa and men. The fiftyish Gunther was a short, blocky fellow, grayish-red-haired and red skinned. He was hot for Larysa. He brought Champagne. Larysa fixed him "little toughies" stuffed with cherries. He sat eating in the steaming kitchen stripped to the waist and sweating, his gold necklaces catching light from the aquariums. From their dialogue, I learned that Gunther's business travels landed him in L'viv occasionally. He rented an apartment in the city to which he sporadically tried to entice the coy Larysa, this she confided later.

To extricate himself from the kitchen after the cherry dumplings, Gunther insisted that we all go out for a beer. In a blink I was ready. Ten minutes, twenty minutes passed. I stayed in my room and wrote postcards. Gunther continued his kitchen sauna. Finally Larysa emerged from her room: nylons, silver-colored flats, white mini-skirt, white jacket, revealing white lace-trimmed elastic top, Lady Godiva hair. (2.5) I had never seen her so dressed up. Gunther went orgiastic. Larysa pretended not to notice; he was a helpless gnat caught in Ms. Larysa's web.

The minute I knew her to be in L'viv, I called a young professor from my Canadian *alma mater*. To my utter amazement and relief, she answered the phone: yes, I could join her intensive Ukrainian class. Yes, she'd work on another living arrangement—her sister had a colleague who had a cousin. Within two days, she called back to say "No hot water. $150 a month." I said, "Absolutely yes!" That is how I met the delightful young couple, Liuda and Andriy.

Moving into Liuda and Andriy's 9th floor apartment above *Striy* (Стрий) Boulevard, windows and doors open to east and west balconies, fragrance on the breeze from the Lindens blooming in *Striy* Park, was like entering the Garden of Eden. When I stepped out of the battered three-person elevator with my suitcase, Liuda was on the landing to greet me—smiling. I wanted to burst into tears.

The bedroom that she'd fixed for me had pale yellow wallpaper with a Milky Way of tiny, flocked blue stars that glowed when you turned out the lights after dark. Quite out of nowhere, I remembered the small plastic crosses we kids would receive annually for attending Vacation Bible School or for surrendering our penny-filled Lenten boxes to Father McCormick. Hanging from its purple tassel on the nightstand lamp, my cross would shine like the moon—a comforting pale glow—after I switched off the light.

By the end of July, I was "family." Indeed now, every July 30th, we—Liuda, Andriy and I, celebrate their wedding anniversary via emails. I may miss other events, but not their anniversary. Without Larysa, I would never have met them. But no, I don't want to even think of them and Larysa together in the same paragraph. Liuda and Andriy were the beginning of my falling in love with Ukraine.

After the fact, I shudder when I think of Larysa. Intermittently she quipped that she was "a pensioner," but then she would slip out to see Gunther in skin-tight leather pants no Hell's Angel Mama could imagine wearing: "Come hither, so I can kill you." Living with her was a nightmare; I found myself walled in and regressing into shock over her behavior. The women in my family are not unlike Larysa, women who leave me shuddering and sad.

When in late August, I returned "to university," as they say in Canada, the international studies administrator asked for my photos. She was planning a brochure on summer study in L'viv through the university. I handed over a batch of snapshots and before I knew it, there was the brochure in its shiny plexi-holder on the counter in the Department of Modern Languages and Cultural Studies office. (2.6) Gazing out from its cover, in a yellow rain slicker, thick Cossack braid snaking down her right shoulder, having just bought a fresh batch of worms at *Krakivs'kiy* market was Larysa. Her eyes seemed to beckon students to experience the joys of summer language study in L'viv, Ukraine.

The day of that particular photo, another rainy day in L'viv, Larysa was amused momentarily for I insisted she get away from the worms and stand in front of the cheerful candy bins. My photos of a bosomy caryatid, L'viv's commanding 18th century Dominican Church, and a swatch of ruined Polish manor house also graced the MLCS brochure. I received no photo credit.

I, on the other hand, must give credit to Larysa for both catapulting me like a lobster into a boiling pot straight to my issue of trust with women, and for opening the door to the ancestral village that was its genesis.

---

[1] Quote made by Elon Musk—CEO of TeslaMotors and chief designer at Space X— when a keynote speaker at the South-by-Southwest Conference in Austin, Texas, March, 2013. Musk oversees the development of spacecraft for earth-orbit missions and for missions to other planets.

2.1

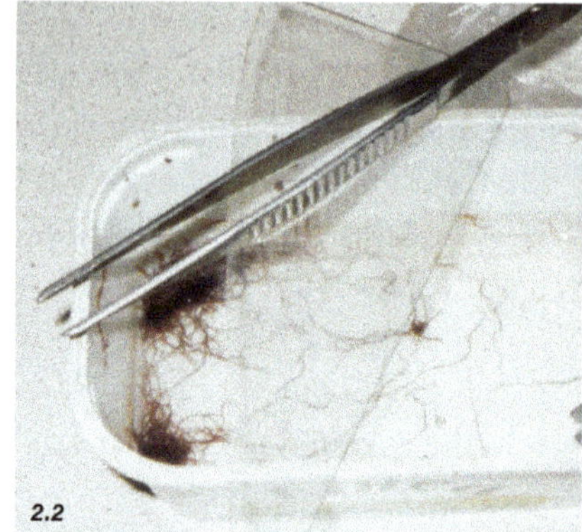
2.2

2.1 *Second from right: Larysa. Sophia, Bulgaria.*

2.2 *Red-brown, hair-like worms waiting to be sliced up and fed to the fish.*

2.3 *Climbing to the Hutsul homestead. Carpathian Mountians. Roman and Larysa.*

2.4 *Makeshift "bedroom" in the Hutsuls'-house-being-build. Single cot. Double cot.*

2.5 *Larysa and Gunther at L'viv restaurant.*

2.6 *Opposite page: MLCS brochure, University of Alberta. An invitation to study in L'viv, Ukraine.*

2.4

2.5

July 15 to August 16, 2002

Department of Modern Languages
and Cultural Studies:
Germanic, Romance, Slavic

2.6

CHAPTER 3

Mother and Her Sisters

"She is always sad like a house on fire. . . ."

—The House on Mango Street[1]

THE second summer I spent in Ukraine, every third woman in L'viv was wearing a basic shift made of a bold flame print. From hemline to neckline large fingers of orange-yellow flame rose against a royal blue background. (Illustration 3.1) When I finally found the fabric store that sold the blazing rayon, I snapped up two meters and made my own red-hot version for the +39C° (99°F) days. It remains my blockbuster-fire dress for Julys and Augusts.

I have a complex relationship with fire. Certainly I love the warmth, the pattern and the color of any cozy fireplace or campfire, but that is not the kind of fire that comes to mind if I were to say "I am drawn to fire." Indeed, one of my more memorable birthdays was spent watching a five-story apartment building in San Francisco gutted in a five-alarm blaze.

Such fire-events are hard-to-admit guilty pleasures, for they invariably come bearing tragedy. I don't enjoy the tragedy part of a big fire. Never that! It is a fire's visual drama that I love; the way flames leap and dance, the way they defy expectation and take on any size and every shade of yellow-orange-red-violet-blue-white. That said, as a child I myself was the victim of a fire, but one of a much more subtle nature than a burning structure.

By the age of five or six, I had become aware that a kind of darkness informed Mother's soul. My first encounter with that darkness involved fire of a sort, and came in the form of an accident with my brother.

Way back during the golden foolish days in Fort Wayne, when my father contrived to buy a new car each year, my brother and I woke one Saturday to find another pristine Buick in the driveway. A new car is a great toy. By afternoon, we kids—Jim, Roseanne our neighborhood buddy, and I—were rolling around, front seat to back seat, in that Buick, taking turns "driving" the vehicle. (3.2) There were new features for us in this particular model, the cigarette lighter foremost among them. For some reason attached to the peculiar logic of children, we were pretending to burn one another with the lighter. We were utterly unschooled in the workings of the mechanism. We assumed, actually trusted, that the lighter would not light.

But it did. In a simple, random stroke, I touched the lighter to the top of my four-year old brother's wrist. It was red hot. He screamed a curdling scream. I remember the white nickel-sized spiral that appeared on his skin. I don't remember Mother running to the car. I don't remember my brother being taken to a doctor. I only remember silence.

A week or two after the incident, Mother took me to see old Dr. Gladstone. His office was downtown in his parents' home, a graceful Victorian, where he'd grown up. The place smelled of camphor. It was cool and quiet. He had a grandfather clock, ticking and gonging in the entrance vestibule. It called to mind the classic tearjerker song Mother sometimes sang to us, "My grandfather's clock was too tall for the shelf, so it stood ninety years on the floor." And famously stopped short, never to go again, when the old man kicked the proverbial bucket. (3.3) The song and that clock has made me pensive around all grandfather clocks.

When Dr. Gladstone called us in, he had me stand near him. We were in his office, where he sat at his ocean liner of a desk, not in the examining room. Mother seated herself some distance away. It was late afternoon and the sun came slanting onto the carpet through down-turned wooden venetian blinds. Quietly, he asked me why I'd done it, why I'd burned my baby brother?

I was dumbfounded by the question. I hadn't burned my brother for any reason. I could have burned Roseanne just as easily, or she me, or Jim her, or so on. But Mother's silence shocked me to the depths of my soul. In an instant, I understood that she was accusing me of something unspeakable. I loved my brother. I was his fiercest defender, charged with his care whenever our parents were absent. Overwhelmed by guilt, I condemned myself by mute silence. I had no words. Dr. Gladstone leaned towards me, cautioned me never to do such a thing again, sent me off with a cherry-flavored sucker—I chose the flavor because I loved its red color— and Mother and I left his office. We never spoke of it. My brother has no memory of the event.

But just like that, I wordlessly understood that if a situation got really bad, Mother would point her finger at me. I was devastated. How could she so miss the mark? For me, everything broke; if she did not trust me, how could I trust her? And more profoundly, how could I trust myself?

Nothing changed. Twenty years later, when I was pressed to have a hysterectomy because of rampant endometriosis, it was my fault. According to Mother, I hadn't taken care of my body. But I had. There were no cherry lollypops. I held my grief close. We never spoke of it.

After that traumatic exposure to Dr. Gladstone, the paradigm of behavior between Mother and me shifted. *Quantum mutatus*! The unwritten rule was that I was not to assert myself. I was to love her, to soothe her, to encourage her and to acquiesce. Should I stray, Mother would make me "unexist."[2] For that matter, if sufficiently threatened, any and all of her sisters—my aunts—would sell me to the circus in an instant. Gradually, it became clear to me that for Mother and all the women in her family, daughters essentially had no value; they were, in fact, a threat. Containing the threat, channeling the threat, was a pathology that pertained to them all. The deal was not a good one, not for Mother, not for her sisters, and definitely not for me. I was caught. No matter which way I turned, I could not crawl out from under the family's female shadow and from being usurped and powerless. This state was my familiar. If I'd had half-a-wit, I'd have run away and joined Barnum & Bailey.

But I did not run away. Not to join the circus or the flower children in San Francisco—the popular option of my generation. Instead, I turned inward and began to muse upon the origin of that vicious cycle. The women on my father's side of the family were not like that, quite the opposite. Once I got to know them, we would enjoy ourselves so much our ribs would ache from laughing. Too bad that during my youth, they lived in faraway Saskatchewan and Alberta. What lay beneath the surface of my mother and her sisters? What made them act the way they did, think the way they did?

And thus my quest began. And I would find out, disinter really, the root of it all. The journey, once started, had to be finished. In Mother's family, women destroyed women, mothers murdered daughters. The knowledge of that, and the responsibility for it, scarred their collective psyche. It scarred mine.

How did it get this way?

The Sisters

I was still a child when Mother asked me why I didn't invite friends over. She wondered whether I was ashamed of our humble house. The house was her issue, not mine. Actually, it had never occurred to me to invite friends over. It was something neither she, nor her sisters ever did. Her "friends" were family members, her sisters. And they were far from being friends. They would visit once or twice a year from their respective cities. If we had guests in our home, the guests were uncles and aunts.

For the most part, Mother and her sisters relied upon—more accurately, clung to—one another. My *outré* mind goes straight to Dr. Seuss's *Bartholomew And The Oobleck*. How I loved that book as a child. In it, a king, bored with the usual weather, asks his wizards to come up with something novel. Fast upon, *Oobleck* —a sticky, greenish goo—begins to ooze down on the kingdom Every person becomes stuck to every other person. Add to this the horses glued to carts, the carts to roads, the trees to rocks, and so forth. Sticky mess.

I've always thought of my aunts as "stuck" in their own form of *Oobleck*. And, it was indeed, a mess— the interlocking relationships that pushed one way and pulled another, all seemingly inseparably combined; the complex chain of attachment, authority and command that ruled the collective and singular worlds of these women. (3.4) Never then, nor now, do I cease to wonder why and how they could have such a hold on each other. For starters, I can say that all of them—save the joyfully and ravagingly aggressive Katherine—shared Mother's *modus operandi* of commanding attention, though in different combinations, weights and measures. But then they were also highly intelligent, energetic, creative, articulate, disciplined—worthy women. They were merely self-serving and destructive.

Through my own subjective lens, I'd like to introduce them. In birth order, it is Nancy, Katherine, Ann, Vera (mother), Alice and Margaret. From childhood on, I thrilled to their rare visits, hung on Mother's stories about them—to her credit, she tried to be evenhanded. I listened carefully when they spoke in my presence. As an adolescent, I became more guarded: I suppose to protect myself. As an adult, I was buffeted by the rancor among these "mentors"—each, seeing me as Mother's agent, which I was not. Alone among them who took me seriously was aunt Katherine, who occasionally regarded me as my own person, and here and there tucked me under her wing, no doubt because she welcomed my focused attention. She reasoned that she deserved it.

Mother looked up to both Nancy and Katherine, her elders by a decade. But as time passed, Katherine came to rule the day. Nancy's outspoken bitterness distanced Mother—and others—from her. Ann, who had a track record of taking sly advantage of her younger sisters, was someone Mother tried to buffer for me.

The fact was, because of the inconvenient early abandonment by their mother Maria, Mother and Alice considered Katherine as a surrogate mother. For her part, Katherine had no problems dominating her sisters. Alice tended to employ Katherine as a shield whenever sisterly feathers began to fly, particularly around Margaret. As an *ensemble*, they formed a sort of cabal of piquing and pecking. Margaret would find ways to antagonize Katherine by striking at Alice. There were years when Margaret and Ann would align themselves with Nancy against Katherine. Mother and Alice would line up behind Katherine. Without resolution old scores just festered. There was no peace; no one felt loved.

They grew up at Soda Lake in Alberta, Canada. (3.5) There is little there now. Never a village, Soda Lake was once a scattering of mostly Ukrainian immigrant farmers, their wives, children, draft animals and buildings—all this on quarter-sections of land. The area took its name from a nearby slough. Today, Soda Lake, the slough, comes and goes depending upon the annual amount of rain and snow. It took me awhile to understand "slough," for there was no such thing in the places I knew.

"Swamp" is not an apt synonym, though a slough can turn into a swamp. In my experience, a slough is a low spot in the wide open of prairie grasses, where snowmelt and rainwater collect to form small-to-large bodies of water that absorb the alkaline minerals of the surrounding soils. Shallow with grassy-thatched bottoms, some sloughs are taken over by trees, whereupon they edge into swamps. For its part, Soda Lake is an out-in-the-open classical slough—large enough that it exists on geological survey maps and on the "Two Hills County of Alberta" map. (3.6) The first time I tried to find it, I repeatedly drove past it. I thought I was misreading the maps or had misplaced cardinal north. When it dawned on me that the thing could be dried up, I immediately saw the huge white ring of soda salts that had been Soda Lake's shoreline. The "lake" was filled with reddish prairie grasses.

KATHERINE. Katherine was the one clear light for me. It was she who guided me to and through Soda Lake—not unlike Dante's Virgil. It was something she chose to do. Then again, she opened Pandora's box. Among her sisters, it was Katherine who considered herself to be—and, for the most part was—the guardian of family fact and fantasy. (3.7) She had a keen memory, an observant eye and was inclined to express herself in well-formed poetic sentences. She enjoyed talking about herself, but best of all, she relished talking about her near-immigrant past. When I was living in Berkeley, this octogenarian aunt lived in the gated community of Rossmoor, just the other side of the coastal range in Walnut Creek. Close.

It was a drive. To visit her in her condo-apartment, I jockeyed those five lanes of I-580 up the hill behind the Claremont Hotel, often in fog; did the stop-and-go merge at the Caldecott Tunnel approach; rolled dutifully through the tunnel; then hurtled down the hill in the sudden sunshine, exhaling in widened-out lanes, widened-out traffic and a higher speed limit. It was a crossing from coastal murk and blasts of cold wind to hot, semi-arid Contra Costa county—in the shadow of Mount Diablo.

Katherine greeted Diablo from her sun-porch and dining room windows with open arms. It was in her nature. She idolized that mountain, the size and wildness of it, the lore that clung to it—center of creation, sightings of phantom black panthers, protection for escaped-from-the-Spanish native Americans, and later, Joaquin Murietta and the Californios themselves. Katherine had passion for the spirits of a place and found them most anywhere she was. This is not to say she was loopy. She was a magical thinker of substance. I believe she got that from her grandmother, Elena. In the 19th century, she would have been called a Pantheist. It was no accident that her houseplants were well cared for: she wanted their souls to thrive. I looked forward to Saturday afternoons with her.

Katherine felt closest to an elusive core that connected to the psychology of "my" women in that village—Chornivka—in Ukraine. She was a powerful, focused female, intuitive, a stealthy predator with a scorching desire to get ahead, ruthless. If I were to name her as a bird, I'd call her a Shrike—tasteful in grays and blacks; conspicuously perching on exposed sites to watch for prey and to advertise her presence to rivals; impaling small birds, mammals and insects on thorns to feed on them.[3] Having safely extricated herself from the hayseed-peasant background of her rural and ethnic Alberta youth, Katherine could talk dry-eyed for hours, marketing her exoticism and triumphs to any eager ears.

So there we would sit in Katherine's Rossmoor condo, with the view of Mount Diablo shimmering in the distance and the tinkle of her sunroom wind-chime murmuring in the hot dry breeze. We were surrounded by her treasures: the oil studies of lemons she had done while in a painting workshop; the plaster portrait bust she executed while studying sculpture; the Mexican folk art—figurines, textiles, big tissue paper flowers— she collected on trips south-of-the-border; the covey of rooster figures she acquired—one of colored glass from the island of Murano near Venice, another, the Picasso rooster reproduction. "I guess I like to crow," she once told me when I asked her why she filled her rooms with roosters. Then there was the sleekly crafted teakwood furniture she made in woodshops—the coffee table, end tables, bookshelves, the credenza, bedroom dressers and probably the frame for her Minimalist couch. (4.3)

Without saying as much, Katherine considered herself to be an artist. She was visually mindful. She used everything: Katherine, the omnivore. As a girl, Katherine, who cared that the color of thread match the color of the garment, quietly and strategically took over her mother's sewing chores, thus giving herself power—"I had a real 'hold' over my younger sisters. If they didn't do what I wanted, I'd have Mother sew them their next dress," she told me.[4] My mother, who tried to be respectful around Katherine, did not have as high an opinion of her sister as an artist. She thought of Katherine as an artful poser. Be that as it may, Katherine's output supported the image she held of herself.

When I was a child, spending two weeks of summer with Katherine in hushed, heavily shaded, four-blocks-from-the-beach, no kids my age, exclusive Glencoe—a northern suburb of Chicago—it was just the two of us. During the day, her husband worked in the Loop. Katherine's daughters, eight and ten years my seniors, were off to college or dropping out of college or traveling in Mexico or with their boyfriends. Katherine would bake Betty Crocker's Wild Blueberry muffins and we would sit outside at the glass-topped table in the dappled sunlight on the stone terrace, and sip orange juice and butter our muffins. For a child whose father worked days, whose mother worked nights, whose little brother needed to be watched rather consistently, a quiet breakfast of juice and muffins on an outdoor patio seemed terribly adult and enchanting.

Dazed, I would wander around her designer home. It was nothing like the tract house of my parents or the inconsiderable homes and apartments of my other uncles and aunts. At Katherine's there were red brick walls, mirror-shiny black linoleum floors, Chlorox-white shag area carpets and floor-to-ceiling windows that faced the oak trees in the backyard. In my parents' backyard, there was a Honeysuckle hedge, a Lilac bush and a dying Apple tree that held my cardboard tree-house-retreat, built as an escape from my little brother.

Katherine's kitchen and dining room had built-in cupboards without handles. You pushed a door and it sprang open.

Needless to say, there was no jumping on a couch or trampoline-ing in any bed at Katherine's. Dinners were difficult to digest; Uncle Adolf would tear flesh when it came to children and proper table manners. It was one of the few areas where Katherine deferred to him—the family scion at the head of the dining room table. These summer visits were lonely. There were no other children with whom to connect. When my brother finally came to join me, he cried through his boredom and loneliness, watched the commuter trains that rolled through Glencoe and collected cigarette butts. With us, Katherine got to delay her "empty nest" syndrome.

It was no secret; she wedded well. "I made a class change when I married," Katherine confided in one of our talks.[5] She was the *escapée*, the sister who married above her station and rose to it. (3.8) Actually, she maneuvered the indecisive Adie to elope, much to the abiding choler of his mother. He'd been intended for better. The son of a savvy German immigrant who achieved considerable economic success in business in Chicago, Adolf, to his father's chagrin, took an academic route—into economics—and parlayed a B.A. into a mid-level government career. He liked Dry Martinis, lunches at Berghoff's in the Loop, and talking about the year he spent in Heidelberg as a student abroad. It was a "those were the days" sort of thing—good beer, *sauerbraten*, skiing and jolly German folk songs at midnight down *Hauptstrasse*. The year was 1919, a uniquely bad year for most Germans and every person of Jewish extraction. Adolph didn't seem to notice. He grew into managing his father's money. Not a bad deal.

But Katherine's deal, which she concealed, particularly from herself, was not so great. Adie was a cold father. Perhaps he was a cold husband. The nannies, nurses and parental absences of his childhood did him no good. At least he carried himself as a patrician and spoke the King's English with verve. She learned to cook his kind of food, things on platters that had to be carved with sharp knives. She kept him busy with projects and travel—Canada, Mexico, Central America, South America, Turkey, New Zealand.

Katherine liked to take me to visit her difficult mother-in-law, the crusty duchess, Mrs. A.H.B, Sr. I "showed" well, for I held my tongue. One had to be careful around the Senior Mrs. B who, like her son, tolerated little in children. The *grande dame* would have her housekeeper make miniature chicken salad sandwiches for me. If I were particularly charming, she would carry her Hummel figurines out of their glass-front *étagère* and place them on the dining room table to be admired. I was terrified of her.

For years Katherine bore her mother-in-law's disdain and in the early days, her raw rage. After all, Katherine had whisked the golden-boy right out from under his mama's nose. But that's not all she had done. On one of our Rossmoor Saturdays, she intimated that she had spoken too loudly against the Senior Mrs. B's second son. The young man wanted to be an artist. His parents would have none of it. There were runnings-away and alcohol abuse. Adie got the money; the artist-brother committed suicide.

Where did Katherine come upon her outspokenness, her indomitable will? She excelled at competition. I was captivated by Katherine. Later, shortly after the death of my mother, when Alice disowned me, Katherine quickly saw that her own daughters would be the benefactors. She sat next to me reading Alice's final note, pulling feathers out of her mouth.

NANCY. Nancy's mantra was "I can never forgive." In every one of my nine separate interviews with her between 1995 and 2001, she uttered that line. In person, across a table, anyone would be struck by Nancy, primarily because of her eyes. Nancy had extraordinarily beautiful teal blue eyes. Unforgettable. Her grandmother—Elena— reputedly had those same arresting blue eyes. Flawless pale white skin, raven black hair, blue blue eyes and you were said to be a Cossack beauty, royalty among Ukrainians, according to their history and lore. In her youth, Nancy had "Cossack coloring."

Her given name was "Anastasia" and as a child, she was called "Sia" for short. In Ukrainian, the pronunciation is An-AH-sta-SEE-ah, with the strongest emphasis on the SEE-syllable, and a secondary emphasis on the AH-syllable. To my ear, "Anastasia" has a gorgeous melodic lilt. When I study her two-year old likeness in the 1910 family portrait, she is utterly at home in her sheltering father's lap. (3.9) She looks out, curiosity leavened with wariness, and clutches the orange used to distract her for a photographic portrait. Later she will tell me that any recollection of being a small child drew a blank in her mind.

The eldest girl in the family, she was married off at nineteen to a promising farmer ten years her senior, a virulent John Birch Society-type, who, my guess is, was smitten by those eyes. Without really knowing the groom, Nancy's mother, Maria, pushed the naïve Nancy into his arms. The farm he was to inherit was sitting on some of the richest soil in the region and Maria reasoned that her daughter would do well. As for additional plusses, the guy had a car and gave Nancy chocolates. They were married on the cusp of the Great Depression, had an unheard of honeymoon at Niagara Falls and then headed into grinding poverty. Nancy had no idea what she was getting herself into in terms of marriage, but in terms of farming and taking care of children, she knew volumes. She was the girl her father cut out of the herd, along with several brothers, to do heavy manual farm work. "I was a beast-of-burden in the family," she fumed.

No family secret, it was a brutally practical deal made by hard-pressed parents. Maria was determined to keep her first-born, a boy, on an educational track and out of the fields. The boy, no fool, took the hint, excelled and moved on away from the farm to the Ukrainian academic institute in Vegreville, Normal school in Camrose and then to DePaul University in Chicago, where, after several years he transferred to the University of Chicago—easy enough to do in those days. He ran with his fine education away from the family. Of him—in an off-handed toss off during one of my visits to her, Katherine declared, "Al was a *shnurl* (шнурл)," —Ukrainian for "shoelace," "he slipped through all the holes." We laughed conspiratorially. Katherine could be devastating.

Plowing the fields, Nancy watched her sisters and brothers excel in their ways at Prut' school and hi-tail it out of the sticks at the first opportunity.[6] Meanwhile, she—the work-horse, the sacrificial daughter—remained. She grew so bitter, and was so taken for granted, that no one among her siblings flung out an inner tube to keep her from going under. It seared her soul. "It was very unfair and that is one thing that I hold against the family. No one spoke up, later even. I was disadvantaged," she grummed. In truth, there was no cohesive family. In truth, she didn't drown.

In 1957, Mother, Dad, my brother and I drove along the dirt roads near Vegreville. It was the summer of showing-off-the-kids to the Canadian relatives in Calgary and the environs of Edmonton. Along those dirt roads, pinned up on the neatly spaced telephone poles, we observed yellow-gold flyers with Nancy's fading image on them. Nancy had run for office and lost, but her campaign flyers still adorned random poles. (3.10) I was thrilled. By my lights, I had a famous, politically ambitious aunt.

My brother and I stayed overnight with Nancy at her farm. (3.11) For breakfast, she stoked her wood-burning range and fixed, just for us, delicate Buckwheat pancakes, tiny, light. We ate them to bursting. Nancy's brothers actually agreed only on this: Nancy was the best and fastest cook in the family. Her hands would simply fly. Threshing crews appreciated her alacrity. The rate at which she broke dishes was remarkable.

Almost forty years later, when I returned to Edmonton, Nancy met me with suspicion and anger. She was wearing a startling black wig with curls all over it, a kind of a restrained Afro that shouted, "Wig!" At least it softened the impact of her indignant, bristling black eyebrows. With and without that wig, she seemed an eighty-seven year-old fury. There was no equivocation. Nancy detested Katherine, reviled Mother. "I blame them all," she roared, "because no one spoke up for me. No one said, 'Nancy, I'm sorry that I didn't speak up for you. It was partially my fault that you suffered so much more than I did.'"

In contrast to her self-proclaimed subordinate role, Nancy had become well-known and respected in Canadian feminist circles. Fearless, she spoke out in favor of liberal and socialist legislation to help the farmer, women, children, the disadvantaged. She had a robust circle of female-politico friends. The failing however of her bold and visible political involvement was the fact that, in reality it was quite personal—just as her mother's had been: she sought to reverse injustice, to point it out and to shame its perpetrators. She was relentless, and, ultimately, wearying.

Nancy kept a notepad to track every word of a perceived opponent in an infinitesimal scrawl. At public hearings, bewigged, she would rise with her notes to say something like the following, "On Friday, the 11th of April at 1:30pm you used the word 'nonpartisan' which directly contradicts your present statement. Are you telling us you are an honest M.P. now?" In a related, but minor key, letters from her to her brothers and sisters were a barrage of questions, detailed questions that if not answered promptly, each in its order, became a battering ram.

Nancy was nothing, if not focused. The August weekend I agreed to spend with her in Calgary turned into one long "intellectual" discussion pressed upon me. Her global statements resounded with the ring of absolute truth—"the average person does not read, does not know the issues; violence in the U.S. is caused by television and the NRA; whereas, in Canada violence is caused by the Asian gangs and the influence of the U.S." Wonderful, passionate, tar-baby entreaties to muck it up with her.

With Nancy, eyes aflame, declaiming, I could only feel depleted and discouraged. Never once did she inquire after my mother with interest or compassion. It would seem that Nancy was a woman who fought for the empowerment of women purely in the abstract and to validate furious resentment about her life. I later came to accept that she, more than all the others, was the one daughter who carried within her her mother's soul. I cut the weekend short and fled back north to Edmonton, relieved to be free of all that damping intensity.

In the avian kingdom, I think of Nancy as a Starling. An iridescent beauty. A social creature, a complex vocalizer, who associates with others of its kind in large flocks. Strong feet. A direct flight pattern. Not purposely a flesh eater, but an opportunistic one if survival requires it.

ANN. Just before I closed the door to Ann's forlorn Cleveland flat, I reminded her that I'd left a $20 bill on her nightstand This was for a phone call I'd made to my husband in Edmonton. It was a crisp, new twenty. I can still see it on the henna colored wood, lit by a diminutive brass lamp. Weeks later, Ann wrote to say that I owed her $20 for my phone call to Canada. I sent her a check.

I could end the profile right there and most of what I want to say would satisfy. It was the last time I saw Ann. She was ninety and living on the 10th floor of a high-rise apartment building on Edgewater Drive in Shaker Heights. She was still proud of her straight back, her trim body in tight blue jeans and her pin-up girl breasts which had more to do with a great foundation bra than anything else. Ninety in that generation of my family is nothing: Al cleared 100, faded at 101; Nancy passed away eighteen days short of 100; Katherine held out to 97; George made it to 100.

I had driven 377 miles from my parents' home in Indiana to draw Ann out, hoping to get to know her as an adult. I found it a shock to sit in her apartment. Ann's nest was the antithesis of Katherine's or Alice's or Mother's. Furniture seemed strangely orphaned, set to no particular purpose. Expiring art prints hung crookedly on walls. The entirety had a chipped, scratched, cracked, faded, stained quality. When we went out for lunch, walking to "Heinen's," the near-by gourmet food emporium, Ann filled her plate with fried chicken, no vegetables or salads, just chicken. She ate ravenously, grease everywhere, gnawing, tearing the meat with her hands. Earthy. Sensual. Disturbing.

I was uncertain how she would view me. In her mind would I simply be a clone of my mother? The answer was "yes." The animosity between Mother and Ann made a relaxed conversation between us nearly impossible: Mother considered Ann to be a liar and a troublemaker. How I longed to hear some recollections from Ann of childhood at Soda Lake, but, as it turned out, she remained markedly uncooperative, sadly a loss for the documentation of family history and identity. The dementia that finally took her was clearly creeping into the edges of her mind: people were stealing sunglasses from her and poisoning her houseplants and staining her carpet.

The more even-tempered George Hill at Soda Lake had occasion to recall Ann as a girl. This is when he and I were talking at his senior care facility in Willingdon. The two were Prut' school classmates and Soda Lake neighbors. George recalled a community hall evening event. He conjured up a guileful Ann. George-the-teenager had decided to ask Ann to dance, when, clever girl, she feigned sleep. He got the point. She got away with fussy-picking her dance partners. "That's what Ann was like," George said. Ann wanted to be popular, but on her terms.

Her image appears in a group photograph of the more-or-less freshmen class at the Ukrainian Institute (Український Інститут, *Ukrains'kiy Institut*), in Edmonton in 1929-30. Her portrait oval is next to that of my father's. Their surnames are indicated in Cyrillic, П. Кіндракевич (*P. Kindrakevych*) and А. Ропчан (*A. Ropchan*). (3.12) Her coffee brown hair, bobbed with flashy spit curls at dimple-level, is parted in the middle and pinned flat—silent movie star style. She wears lipstick, eye make-up and a dark dress with a contrasting light collar that sets off her acute chin line. At seventeen, Ann looks sleek and sharp.

When I was a child and she was with us, always after a large family dinner she would jump up to insist that we walk briskly around the block. We had to walk off all that food and keep our muscles toned. My father thought she was daft. My brother and I thought she was fun. Too bad Ann was already an elder for the aerobics craze of the 1970s. It was tailor-made for her and her cult-of-body.

On one rare occasion, at Mother's prompting, Ann sent me $50, this while I was grinding through grad school, impecunious. I wrote a thank you letter and probably used the welcome check to buy more tins of tuna fish, jars of peanut butter and boxes of strawberry Jello. Months after the fact, Mother wrote, asking whether I'd thanked Ann. It seems that Ann was complaining to the family-network that I was a thankless niece. I had no copy of the original letter. I wrote a second letter to thank her, and this time kept a copy. I'd just been introduced to a side of Ann, I'd not suspected was there.

Ann did have a history of maneuvering others into doing things she needed done or simply didn't want to do. For example, somewhat incredibly she refused to back up her car, say, into a parking space. Any near-by male was entreated to do the chore. She also balked at repairing her vehicle, leaving that to exasperated brothers and brothers-in-law. Mother would sew buttons back on to Ann's winter coats when she was with us. Ann would return to Cleveland, all tidied up by the family. (3.13)

Circling back to her childhood, to her sibling cohorts, it seemed to Ann that her early years were the worst by comparison. To be sure, she got off to a rough start. She must have been about three or four when she drank formaldehyde. It was used to purify the seed grain before planting and looks like water. So there she was, getting into things like a puppy. She was thirsty. She was hungry. She spotted the wheat seeds in the liquid.

By 1914 or 1915, her parents had a telephone. They ran the post office; they needed the phone. Maria grabbed it, called across the quarter-sections to the Boutilliers, knowing that the elder Mrs. Boutillier had been a nurse during the Great War (WWI) and was there at home. "Sour milk! Pour sour milk down her throat until she throws up," nurse-Boutillier exhorted. It worked. The acid probably did burn some of Ann's esophagus-to-stomach lining tissue. She turned into a finicky eater. She cried a lot. When Ann finished growing, she topped out at about 4'10".

Ann's mother may not have wanted more children, but she didn't want to see any of the ones she had, die. It was a narrow escape. The formaldehyde changed the covenant between Ann and her parents: she was shown deference. At some level, Ann probably realized she could play the "sickly child" card, and, according to more than one sibling, she did. What kid wouldn't at least try for it?

Ann was not kept home. In a unique departure, her parents saw her through one year of college; hence, that oval photograph next to the one of *P. Kindrakevych*. After that, with solid teaching credentials, Ann escaped. She joined Katherine, who, for the moment was living in Cleveland. Ann settled in to secretarial work, sun bathing and dating. When Katherine left for Chicago, Ann, relieved to have a city to herself, remained in Cleveland.

The morning of my decampment, as I finished packing in Ann's bedroom, she called to me from the living room, could I do one favor for her? "Sure," I answered. If I could, I would. The "favor" was to trim her toenails. My face burned red for the wrongness of the request. As far as Ann was concerned, I was a cipher merely saving her the $15 a hospital or clinic would charge her for toenail trimming. How to describe such a parting gesture? I carried affectionate childhood memories of Ann and had hoped for a trace of warmth from her. Her toenails were thick, folded back, sharp, difficult to trim. Now I take the point about Ann. All told, she was up $35.

My avian image of Ann is an English House Sparrow. Both pet and pest, the English House Sparrow is an opportunist, associated with human habitations. It is not a creature of lush woodlands, grasslands or desert, but prefers an urban environment. With its grating, insistent chirp, the House Sparrow aggressively takes over Bluebird nesting sites, killing this still-endangered beauty and its hatchlings. Birders—those who carefully weigh the qualities of our feathered fauna—think of the English House Sparrow as common and uncouth.

MOTHER. Mother maintained that as a child she had not been wanted or loved. As a corollary, her five sisters were a totality of snapping, slapping and tearing at each other. Her five brothers were part of the same collective. Mother's unloved self was hurt and angry. She hunkered down like a solitary Bittern in Bloomington, Indiana, but remained fiercely competitive—imagine pushing down on the accelerator and, at the same time, standing on the brake pedal.

Her name was Vera. In Ukrainian, Віра (*Vira*) means "faith." I rather like the fact that Mother was named after a virtue. To my bewilderment, she loudly told those who would listen how much she hated her name, the dissonant caustic sound of it. As for joy, she was happy she had me and four years later, she was happy my brother came along.

When we were children, she would sing to us at bedtime. My brother was uniquely fond of a refrain from one air—"Polished to a high degree, as each froggie ought to be." That melody, about "polished froggies," got sung a lot to him. But when Mother was older and asked to sing about froggies or fairy airships or grandfather clocks, she would often weep. She was back with her childhood cohort at Prut' school—the other little Ukrainian and Romanian native speakers. They were taught these unintelligible songs and every memorized stanza, phrase and word stuck.

As I grew older, I thought that her life on the prairie—at Soda Lake—had not been all that bad, but then, I never lived on the inside of it. I looked out at it. Soda Lake was a place of unspoiled beauty. In the spring there were Prairie Crocuses, Mother's favorite. Later in the season, wild strawberries grew on any south-facing rise. Blueberries could be collected on the north side of the North Saskatchewan River. Then there was the expanse of land—green, gold or white— below a sweep of cloudless cerulean, whether winter or summer. She grew up with lots of space. She got to walk along the edges of fields or ride in a horse-drawn wagon—a sleigh for snow—to school.

Winters, she warned, the snow did not melt, it simply piled up, near-invisible dry flakes, one layer on top of the next. On rare days when there had been a touch of moisture in the air, thick, thick hoarfrost clung to every detail, turning a pared-down landscape into *frou-frou* fancy. I imagined every blade and branch battered with panko, like Tempura Shrimp.

Streams, sloughs, lakes, the big river froze solid. Mother once told me, that as a child, she dreamed of skating on and away into the night on a frozen vein of water. Early pioneers used the rock-hard North Saskatchewan as a highway to Edmonton. I assume it to be the river Joni Mitchell wants to "skate away on" in her *Blue* album. Ms. Mitchell's formative years were spent next to that river. The first time I heard Joni's song of longing and regret, I thought of Mother ice skating in the dark.

For all of her awareness of the beauty and rhythms of nature at Soda Lake, Mother's internal environment was one long exercise in dread and gnawing despair. She would describe her futile graspings—year after year— for scraps of love. Her father smiled when she did a skit on *Little Black Sambo* at Prut' School for a Christmas pageant; that was something. She helped him plant a line of pine seedlings, a future windbreak for the fields; that was something. But as for her mother, my mother refused to be convinced that any love came from her.

There was farm work. At school, there was long division and fractions. Later, it was British literature and trigonometry. There were no proms, but there were theatricals, dances and picnics at the community hall. There were yearly fasts and feasts around Christmas, Epiphany, and Easter. There was the hush of being part of a big, unhappy family.

When Mother journeyed east to Ontario to marry my father who seems to have found the only Depression-era job left for a Ukrainian-Canadian—mining in the Schumacher-Timmons gold mines, she knit herself a dress for the occasion. It was perfection on her sylph body. I study the dark lines of the collar in her engagement photo, knowing I could never knit such a garment. (3.14)

My father had no future in gold mining. When a questionable wall of rock caved in over his cavalier mining partner, a Croatian immigrant working fifteen feet away, my father decided it was time to look for something else. There was Mother, trained to be a teacher, folding sheets in a Toronto laundry. When Mother's brother floated the possibility of my father's working as a salesman for him in Fort Wayne, Indiana, U.S.A.—Sam had found safe harbor there, my parents freshened up their passports and emigrated.

Mother didn't like Fort Wayne, and for good reason. Her living room windows looked out over a hot dog shop, a hotel, and a heavily trafficked street. The shop with its wieners rolling on a grill in the window is now one of the few remaining draws along Main Street. Our former apartment, as well as the stately 1850 Weber house next door, its postage-stamp yard lined with the first flowers I ever caressed and sniffed, have long since been torn down to make way for a black-topped parking lot: Fort Wayne, city of parking lots.

Mother settled in to the Main Street flat, but never sought to teach. She said she had no patience for it, and I believe her. Instead, she had me, then my brother. We moved to Fairfield Avenue and green grass and that brand-new, pre-fabricated Gunnison home. It cost $11,000, much of which was borrowed from Sam. Mother began to work nights at Lincoln Life Insurance Company in the keypunch section. Early computational machines used cards, with holes punched in them to tabulate all sorts of data. This meant that a data-driven insurance company like Lincoln Life used hundreds of thousands of key cards and Mother was busy.

Mother also sewed garments for me. I've not forgotten one of them. Only the "Tic-Tac-Toe" apron for my Kindergarten finger-painting survives—those "O's" and "X's" embroidered across a wide pocket. I found it in the same black steamer trunk in which she had buried her splendid Willingdon Medal. I speculate, or rather dream, that she could not bear to part with it when it was clear that I was not going to have children. It is presently pinned on a quilt she made, "The Drunkard's Path" that hangs in our bedroom. The X's and O's are so perfectly aligned that whomsoever makes the next move wins. Or loses. Enigmatic, and in a perverse way, the indecision embodies both threat and hope: the next move wins. But who has that upper hand?

Mother loved birds. In the avian kingdom of mowed front yards and backyard understory, Mother would be a Brown Thrasher. She thrilled to rare Brown Thrasher sightings in our yard. A lovely, fox-colored bird—buff chest with vertical brown stripe-like markings, the sleek Thrasher stays inconspicuous along woodland edges as it digs through leaf debris. Its leaf-flipping for tasty insects makes a rustling-thrashing sound. When defending its nest, the bird will attack species as large as a human, but it is prone to be driven out of areas where territory is contested. Elusive—its coloration blends perfectly with the dry leaves in which it forages—and evasive—with its low-level flying, the Thrasher towers over others in terms of melody. It has the largest song repertoire—over 1,000 distinct songs—of all the birds. "My Grandfather's clock...."

ALICE. Alice had the worst of all their troubled childhoods. The year of her birth, misfortune and tragedy seemed to come in waves. I remember Alice as a saucy, quick little creature when she would visit. (3.15) She was a tiny woman, even more petite than Mother or Ann. (3.16) If I were to name her as a bird, she would be a Carolina Wren with its flash of yellow feathers or a velvety green Hummingbird, ferociously territorial. She visited for Thanksgiving or Christmas, arriving via rail on the Erie-Lackawanna from Cleveland or the *Pennsy* from Chicago. I would happily abandon my bedroom to her on the condition that I could sort through the bead necklaces and gold charm bracelets in her suitcase, or watch her apply gloriously red lipstick with a lipstick brush. I think she also had an eyelash curler.

Alice was a more precious version of Mother. As a guest and a curiosity, Alice was a free radical, helpful here, helpless there. Mother—sturdy and practical— knew what to do around spills, fevers or crying baby brothers. One Christmas Alice sent me a canary yellow brooch, a cabochon surrounded by rays of tiny yellow beads and clear faceted Austrian crystal beads. It was a grown-up piece of jewelry, beyond me. At ten or eleven, I was thrilled to have it, to think that Alice was suggesting a stylish direction. Alice has forgotten the gift. No matter, I treasure, and cyclically repair it.

Inspired when it came to color, Alice developed an unerring eye for what goes with what through her careful readings of *Vogue* and *Harper's Bazaar*. Her Oakland or Walnut Creek apartments were light-filled, fresh with just the right cluster of red or orange accent pillows along her ochre couch, truculently Scandinavian Design. She favored warm colors for her home and cool colors for herself. In the 1950s Alice would step down from the train car in high heels, a soft wool coat—grey, blue or black—and an expensive box of a leather purse. In her globe-trotting years with Elderhostel or on a Caribbean cruise, she would deck herself out in turquoise, purple and pink and wear her aerobic dance shoes for traction.

For Alice, travel was the welcome distraction: one year, France; the next Russia; and the next, England. Indeed, she looked for excuses to pack her bags. Yet when asked for her impressions of the *Canal du Midi* through Carcassonne or the spires and onion domes of St. Petersburg, she would remark that the food was greasy, and as for her accommodations—the bed was too soft, the floors creaking. She seemed not to retain the fragrance of any of the exotic locales stamped onto her passport. It follows that Alice determinedly took it upon herself to visit family members scattered across the U.S. and Canada. It was her way of chucking her eternal salad diet and of keeping up with what was going on.

If Mother could have had a true friend, it would have been Alice. Three years apart, the two shared confidences and dependencies. Then again, Alice opted for the role of family messenger. Ever the sieve—the acquisition and subsequent dissemination of family information imbued her with a sense of core importance. Her position could be used to share positive news, but also to humiliate and chasten. If you can't be loved for who you are, you can perhaps gain value for what you can provide.

From Soda Lake to Chicago, Alice attached herself to the impervious Katherine and stayed attached to her all the way to San Francisco. Katherine was quick to remind all that Alice had never properly "bonded" with their mother, and thus, could be difficult. This was not helpful, not for Alice, and certainly not for Mother or me.

When I left the Lone Star State for San Francisco, to start fresh in a new city, I reluctantly agreed to stay with Alice at her home in Oakland. It was awkward even before I had the key in the ignition in Texas—Mother and Alice, enmeshed in my transition. Alice insisted on joining me for part of the drive west. It didn't go well. By the time we got to Chaco Canyon—forty miles of ribbed dirt road in a Honda Prelude, every bolt loosening along the way—we'd had an argument. I was edging a migraine headache and Alice retreated into an angry allergic event.

I wanted solitude, to think about my next steps, to untangle myself from the art career that hadn't worked out. Instead, I got boxed into agreeing to this road warrior thing. I was trailing blood and Alice wanted me to facilitate her "let's do Santa Fe" thingy. A month into my temporary Oakland stay-over, I was accused of stealing! A pot or a bowl had lost itself in Alice's pantry. The accusation bore some resemblance to Ann's finessing for twenty-dollar bills and Margaret's unfounded incriminations. Mother, at the other end of the phone, seemed to know where Alice had gone.

At Mother's death, Alice curtly informed me that she never wanted to see me again and that I was expunged from her Will. Walter was the catalyst of the moment; Alice was angry she said, because I'd hurt Walter's feelings. Walter, Mother's and Alice's youngest brother, had the bad manners to try to edit the obituary I'd written. His edits were flippant, inaccurate and personally denigrating. He offered to pay for the obit if I cut it down two-thirds. My brother suggested I use Walter's credit card number for an all-expenses-paid round-trip to *Cabo san Lucas.*

When I think of Alice, that line from the film *The Interpreter* keeps coming to mind, "Vengeance is a lazy form of grief." Three years later, when Katherine passed away, Alice neglected to inform me of the death. Visualize the god Mercury with wings on his ankles and you have Alice—the self-appointed family messenger. Alice dutifully emailed or called kith-and-kin no matter how far-flung. I was not contacted. It was a gesture calculated to hurt. She knew the depth of my feelings for Katherine.

MARGARET. In the pantheon of loving, nurturing aunts who surrounded me, Margaret is in a category entirely of her own. Her ability to foment sisterly discord, while at the same time be a so-called non-entity at the periphery, is remarkable. Of her person, I recall that she has a nasal voice and in her youth, shared my mother's good looks. Indeed, for years, the two were dead-ringers for one another. After Mother was gone, I rather dreaded the moment, if it should come up, of looking into Margaret's face and seeing that of Mother's. But Margaret refused to see me, so I didn't need to worry about that one.

To me, Margaret is a shade. I had so little interaction with her during my life; she exists in my mind mostly through conversations with others. I was a child when she moved to San Francisco, then an eternity away from the Midwest. In the late 1950s, San Francisco was a pastel poem of a small city, its skyline not yet ruined by high-rise corporate black bank buildings or clogged serpentine freeways. Margaret was there by herself, by choice, long before Alice or Katherine arrived. She was not pleased that they relocated to her coastal *sanctum sanctorum.*

Among family narratives, Margaret remains infamous for inviting a niece to fly-in from Toronto, then locking the door of her condo, turning out the lights, pretending not to be home and leaving Katherine and Alice to pick up the pieces. Word was, for Margaret, it was second-nature to accuse a sister or a niece-guest of just about anything and more specifically, of insulting Margaret in some subtle way, and of so churning the waters that truth sank completely, straight to the bottom, or hid under a submerged rock.

My defining adult experience of Margaret occurred on a trip to the Bay Area in the late 1970s. I needed a vacation from grad school. It was probably Spring Break. Alice would have picked me up at the Oakland Airport, whisked me to her apartment and settled me there for several days, ferrying me east to visit with Katherine in Rossmoor for a morning or an afternoon. On the appointed day, Alice would have dropped me off at Margaret's, on the San Francisco side of the bay. But in the interim, my beau sailed into town and convinced me to join him on a visit to friends in L.A. I reasoned naively that I could learn more about him, if I met some of his long-established friends.

If I'd spent three nights with Alice, I spent two nights with Margaret or if it was two nights with Alice, then it was one night with Margaret. However the story gets told, Margaret felt slighted, enraged actually. She blamed Alice for masterminding my cut-short stay. In truth, my itinerary had nothing to do with either Alice or Margaret. It was tied to my then-penchant for clinging to marginal husband material.

Thirty-five years later, Margaret spurned the invitation to be part of my dissertation research—my interest was in Ukrainian-Canadian family ritual celebration, Easter, Christmas, weddings, births, deaths—on the basis of that missed night back in the 1970s. "Why are you calling me?" she demanded. "Oh, *you* want something, so *you're* calling." Talk about kitchen-cleaver enmity. She leapt to outrage the moment she realized I was on the other end of the line. She hardly knew me. "Absurd" would be too mild a word for Margaret's reaction. Three weeks after her death, most everyone in the family—two had fallen off of her list—received a packet from Margaret's lawyers. Most everyone had not heard from Margaret for decades. Via the lawyers, Margaret wrote— here translating the legalese, "I am giving all of my money to these (listed) causes; don't ever think you can get a penny of it." I doubt that anyone was "after" her money. Snarling from her grave. Obdurate alienation. That was Margaret.

How did it get this way? Is it Goya who gives us the image of stump-legged cripples battering away at each other? It was a sisterhood of pain. (3.17) Mother, her sisters, their daughters, me—none of us could trust each other. Why was this the case? Did it begin with their mother, or her mother, or the mother before that? Most said the situation was cut-and-dried: we descended from a bunch of ignorant peasants, brutal creatures who knew no better than to be brutal. So I guess that meant we were brutal too. I didn't like that. Surely the earlier ones had an impact on we later ones, but was there ever a time before mistrust, the absence of love and betrayal?

3.1

3.2

Song: "My Grandfather's Clock"
(Mother's version)

My grandfather's clock
Was too tall for the shelf,
So it stood ninety years on the floor;

It was taller by half
Than the old man himself,
Though it weighed not a pennyweight more.

It was bought on the morn
Of the day that he was born,
It was always his treasure and pride;

But it stopped short
Never to go again,
When the old man died.

(Refrain:)
Ninety years without slumbering,
Tick, tock, tick, tock,
His life seconds numbering,
Tick, tock, tick, tock,
It stopped short
Never to go again,
When the old man died.

3.3

3.4

3.1 *Shopping for fabric in L'viv, 2001: bold flame print.*

3.2 *Fairfield Avenue, Fort Wayne, Indiana. l-r: Roseanne, Jimmy and Monica. 1950s.*

3.3 *Song my mother learned as a child in school.*

3.4 *Our Main Street apartment, Fort Wayne, Indiana. On the occasion of Sam Ropchan's wedding. 1951. l-r: Alice, Vera (mother), Katherine and Ann (Sam's sisters).*

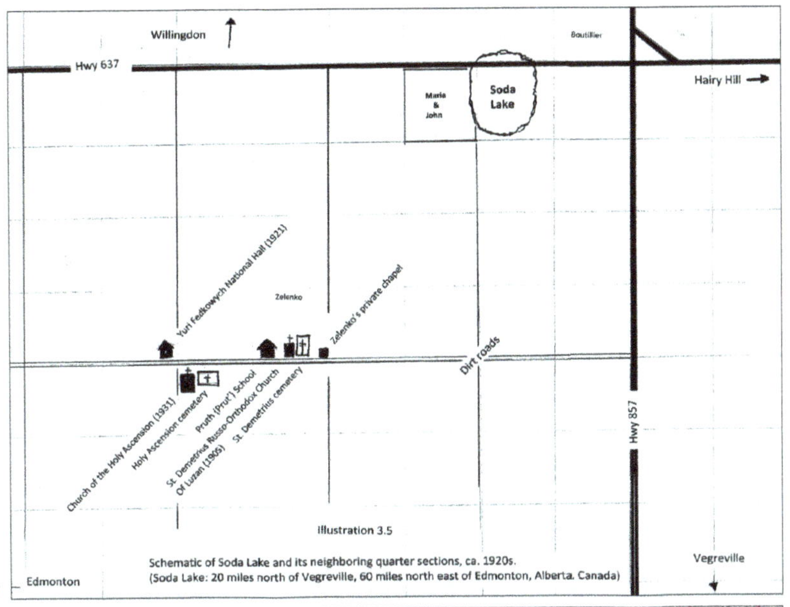

3.5

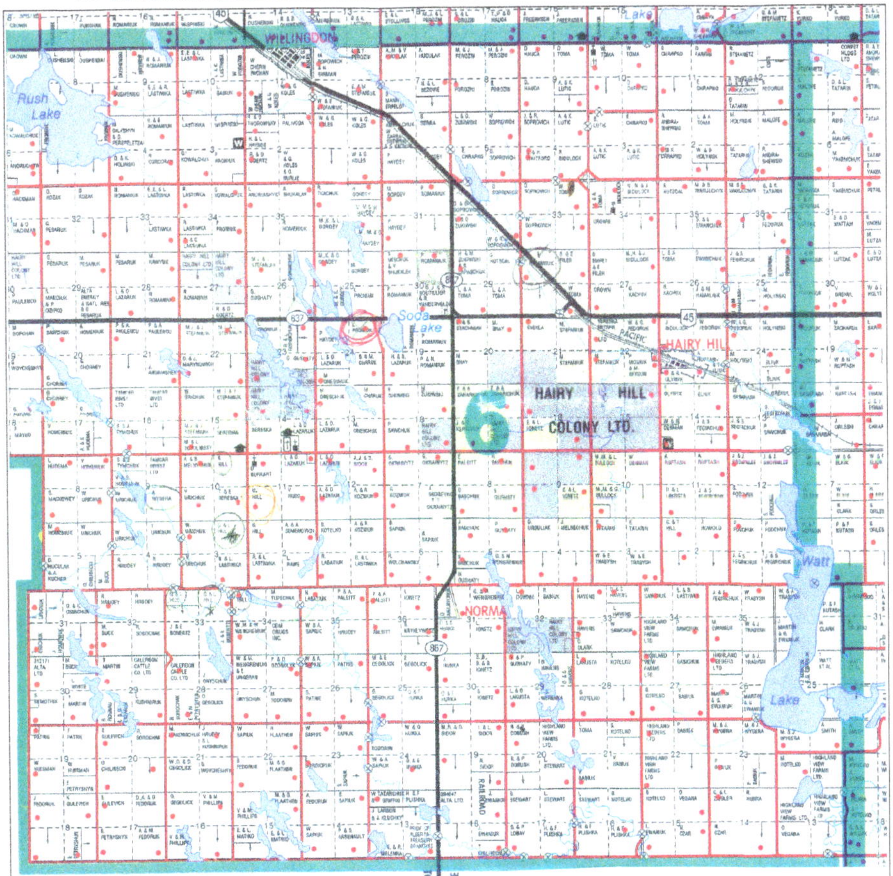

County of Two Hills Map, No. 21, 1994. Alberta, Canada.
Detail showing Soda Lake, quarter section owners.
Each dot represents a building or structure.

3.6

3.5 *Schematic of Soda Lake and its neighboring quarter sections, ca. 1920s. (Soda Lake: 20 miles north of Vegreville, 60 miles northeast of Edmonton, Alberta, Canada).*

3.6 *Soda Lake in Alberta. Near the intersection of Highways 637 and 857.*

3.7 *l-r: Katherine Scraba Ropchan and her uncle, Nick Scraba. Soda Lake, 1920s.*

3.8 *l-r: Adie (Adolph) and Katherine. Newlyweds.*

3.9 *Earliest photo of the John (Ivan) Ropchan family, 1910. l-r: Alex, John Ropchan, Nancy, Bill, Maria Scraba Ropchan, infant Katherine in Maria's lap, Sam. The photo was taken in a Vegreville photo studio, a day's wagon-ride from Soda Lake.*

3.10 *Election flyer for Nancy Ropchan Zaseybida.*

3.11 *Visiting Aunt Nancy's farm near Vegreville, 1958. l-r: (top) Christine (Nancy's daughter), Nancy, Vera (mother); (bottom) Jimmy, Monica.*

3.12 *Professors and class of the Ukrainian Institute in Edmonton, Alberta, 1929-30. Images of P. Kindrakevych (who later married Vera) and Ann Ropchan, Vera's sister.*

3.13 *l-r: Monica, Aunt Ann and Aunt Katherine's foot. On a summer visit to Katherine's home on Hazel Avenue in Glencoe, Illinois, 1950s.*

3.14 *Vera Scraba Ropchan's (mother's) engagement or wedding photo, 1937.*

3.15 *l-r: Monica and Aunt Alice. Summer. Katherine's backyard in Glencoe, Illinois.*

3.16 *Early days—Cleveland, Chicago or Fort Wayne? l-r: Alice, Margaret, Ann, Vera.*

3.17 *Earlier days—Soda Lake farm. l-r: Vera, Ann, Alice, Margaret.*

---

[1] Sandra Cisneros, The House on Mango Street (New York: Vintage Books, A Division of Random House, Inc., 1991), 84.

[2] Gary Shteyngart, Little Failure: A Memoir (New York: Random House, 2014), 126. Shteyngart writes this of his own mother in Little Failure.

[3] The details here about the Shrike and other birds have come from a number of sources. First and foremost, the Golden Press•New York A Guide to Field Identification—Birds of North America by Robbins, Bruun and Zim; secondarily, Wikipedia and various Web sources.

[4] Taped interview with Katherine, Walnut Creek, CA. 19 February 1999.

[5] Taped interview with Katherine, Walnut Creek, CA. 14 March 1997.

[6] The Soda Lake community, not to be confused with Soda Lake slough, was arranged mostly to the north, west and south of the slough. It consisted of farmers and their families on their quarter-sections of land. Many of the Soda Lake settlers—my family included—were from villages along the Prut' River in northern Bukovyna (now Ukraine). The Prut' flows past the city of Chernivtsi, southeasterly into the Danube. As the settlers built their two churches, a school and a community hall, they named these institutions and structures somewhat honorifically, but referred to them more colloquially. Thus, Prut' or Pruth School was officially "Pruth School District #2064," but most called it simply "Pruth School." And "Yuriy Fedkowych Ukrainian Educational Society of Soda Lake" was "the hall," or "the community hall."

CHAPTER 4

Oksana & Katherine

— Getting There —

"If you don't risk anything, you risk even more."

—Erica Jong[1]

I had to start looking for answers. Whimsically, I thought that studying Ukrainian might get me closer to the women in my family—the ancestor ones. This is how I became a Kepler's "regular." It all began with a grand Menlo Park Victorian house near Kepler's Bookstore. The home had been refitted into offices, conference rooms and study rooms. It was there that a bustling young woman with an intractable cold orchestrated meetings between those who wanted to learn a language and those available and credentialed to teach. In all of the extensive Bay Area, where I lived in the 1990s, a Ukrainian language tutor could be found only near Kepler's. The place represented promise.

My first tutor of Ukrainian lasted a week. Chunky, sixtyish and sporting a skin-tight furry black Angora sweater, she was an event. She introduced herself as a fashion designer, actress, filmmaker, motivational instructor, child of Russian nobility and the wife of a rich and famous conductor—repeatedly invited to do this and that in Ukraine and Russia. At our initial and only meeting, I had to remind myself not to stare at her glued-on Tammy Baker black eyelashes. I was relieved that the pancake face powder did not begin to run down her perspiring face. The Russian would teach me how to memorize, as she had learned to do. And I would become fluent. But by mid-week, she called. "The Event" wanted me to take lessons at her apartment. The move was intended to cut "Bustling" out of the pedagogical deal. I respected the work that the language coordinator had already done on my behalf. "No," I said to the Russian. The search for a Ukrainian tutor resumed.

Oksana (Оксана), my second tutor was willowy, fortyish and an actual Ukrainian, the mother of an adolescent daughter and wife of a visiting-to-Stanford Fulbright scholar. Her grandmother and mother had been physicians. A mathematician by training, Oksana worked in Kiev as a translator, Ukrainian-to-English, Russian-to-English and vice versa. She was quiet, pragmatic and quick-witted. I adored the way she swore at her rattletrap

Toyota Tercel—probably purchased to survive for three or four months and unmistakably on its last gasp—the day she drove me to a Slavic bookstore somewhere in Menlo Park. We were on a mission to find me an appropriate Ukrainian dictionary.

Each Wednesday, I would commute to the Victorian, climb the stairs to our meeting-room and sit down to those first days of rudimentary language study, which unsurprisingly began with the Cyrillic alphabet—A, Б, B (*ah, beh, veh*).... Oksana wrote out my lessons, longhand. Next we began to build lists of nouns, of pronouns and to construct simple sentences. Between exercises, Oksana would explain how a certain word or phrase came to be.

I looked forward to her stories about the language. One of them, which I cherish for its lyricism and good sense, is about the months. According to Oksana, a group of scholars are convinced that the Ukrainian language is older than Russian, based on the evidence of the names of the months. Russian names for months follow the Latin system in which the months are numbered. For Rome, September was the 7th (7: septem) month, October was the 8th month (8: octo), November was the 9th (9: novem) and December, the 10th (10: decem). The Ukrainian names for months follow a nature-based, possibly natavistic, system, in other words, a system before the Romans took over and straightened everything out. One simply needs to bring to mind the presiding genie of the month to summon its name—the month when the wind has wolf-like ferocity, the month the Birch trees leaf out, the month of flowers, the month of green grass, the month when the Linden trees bloom, the month when the cherries ripen, the month when the sickle is high in the sky (the great backward "C" in the constellation Leo), the month of golden-yellow leaves, the month when the leaves are falling. (Illustration 4.1)

Only when I was in Ukraine did I understand why a month could be named for when the cherry trees are laden with fruit. Villagers and urban types alike swiftly become pitters and canners of cherries, makers of cherry preserves and, most particularly, distillers of cherry brandy. It is as if everything comes to a stop in order to take advantage of those cherries. Then there is the month of Lindens. When the Linden trees bloom, the very atmosphere is agreeably scented and hums with the exertions of exhausted bees. Seated on a park bench below a majestic Linden, one is enveloped by quadraphonic-sound and all-surround fragrance.

Before I met Oksana, my fantasy of edging towards Ukraine was just that, as insubstantial as a moonbeam. With her, the dream began to take shape. She spoke of Ukrainian villages, towns, cities, rivers and mountains as true places, not abstractions. She told good jokes about bad Ukrainian roads and rightly admired Ukrainian bread. In the months I studied with Oksana, I began to formulate dreams into goals. The immediate result of getting serious was an application to a graduate school where Ukrainian and Ukraine were taught. For those not in the business of applying to graduate school, a "heads-up:" such programs are scarce in North America. In the United States, the general attitude is that Ukrainian is a dialect of Russian: study Russian instead.

And so, I entered an Arcadia where all seemed possible. I now had a plan. I would acquire Ukrainian. From my mother and her ten siblings, I would gather the family stories. When accepted to grad school in Alberta, I would immerse myself in the geography of Soda Lake—that settlement that crossed paths with my group of immigrants. And eventually, I would journey to the village of my grandmother and great-grandmother in Ukraine and find a long-forgotten relative or the foundation of an ancestral cottage (*khata*, хата). What perfection.

Lessons in Ukrainian were in motion. Packets of meticulously filled-out forms were headed north to Edmonton, to a program that broadcast its Ukrainian studies. Katherine, to whom I had easy access, beckoned. Then too suddenly, in August, Oksana and her husband decided the family must return home. It had something to do with his not being able to complete the Fulbright with the mentor-of-choice. I had not expected her to leave so soon. Oksana was a good teacher. I was bereft. The departure plans must have been sudden even for them, for they had yet to be tourists in San Francisco, never mind California. My husband and I hustled them up and down Market Street and out to the Golden Gate Bridge. We fixed them our classic California dinner: salmon grilled with garlic, rice, steamed artichokes and "Sierra Beauty" apple pie. We drank a lot of smooth local Merlot.

"Sparks, Nevada," they said, when we asked what their final stateside plans were. Horror of horrors! All the wonders of California, and they wanted to go to a casino and play the numbers. True, Ihor had completed his PhD in economics, but a smoke-filled casino, spectrally lit, reverberating with the noise of dings and bongs seemed a poor way to exit the United States of America, at least to us. Thus, we resolved to meet Oksana, Ihor and Ol'ha at The Nugget at 8:00am of an August Sunday morning, in order to show them a swath of the Forty-Mile Desert, east of Reno and Sparks.

We wanted our Ukrainian friends to come into contact with an unadulterated piece of America. I also had a secret agenda. Why I thought that Oksana, Ihor and Ol'ha would absorb what I intended, I'll never know. More whimsy, to be sure. As a non-native to the state, having moved there from the Midwest and Texas, I embraced California's history. I read. I studied maps. I ranged through wild flower guides. I instigated long hikes and camping trips to get to know the place—north, south, east. The Forty-Mile Desert—actually in Nevada—came to the fore. It had to do with how people got to California. Books, republished journals and letters, artifacts in museums up and down the state told the stories about California-or-Bust. The Forty-Mile Desert represented a big chapter on hardship and on "or-Bust."

Life's guilty pleasures. My husband and I had become members of an organization of "rut-rats," a buttoned down-to-zany group of overland trail seekers—jeeps, vans and trailers: "get off of the highway and follow history, right here on the ground." We formed small caravans on the desert hardpan, stopping to contemplate the places where wagons, oxen and exhausted travelers staggered or failed. Metaphorically, I began to associate The Forty-Mile Desert with Ukrainian immigrant struggles to get to and to settle Soda Lake. It is this connection that I hoped Oksana, Ihor and Ol'ha might make—how hard it had been for those who left their Ukrainian villages to establish themselves in North America.

The Forty-Mile Desert is an empty place. Thankfully, it offers a commanding view to the west of the Sierra mountain-wall. From the 1830s to the 1850s, emigrants—upon leaving the marsh and natural dike below Humboldt Lake—had no other option but to plunge across alkali hard-pan and sand for forty parched miles, either straight west to the Truckee River, or southwesterly to the Carson River, where a makeshift town of canvas tents called "Ragtown" sprang up. In addition to the "rag" tents, the ground was littered with clothing, scraps to whole cloth. One look at the sublime Sierra and everyone began lightening their load.[2]

Since It took 15-to-24 hours to reach either river, pioneers were counseled to start across the desert at night. The Truckee route was the older of the two and favored for a while because after a level start and a gradual climb past strange volcanic rock formations, you reached water of sorts, a boiling springs, twenty miles out. Now called Brady's Hot Springs and the site of an onion processing plant just off of Interstate 80, its water, when cooled, was drinkable. Children fell into the hot spring's cauldron, thirsty animals jumped in—more than one drover grieved for his dog, lost to the scalding water. Then it was on around the base of a range of low mountains and into a field of sand dunes where unmarked graves—oblong heaps of rocks oriented east-to-west—began to multiply.

Every creature walked, sinking into, pulling away from that sand. Weakened oxen fell and could not be coaxed to rise. At the end of the dune field, was the Truckee which ran through a canyon and had to be forded multiple times—estimates ran from twenty up to thirty zig-zag fordings— in order to reach the widening-out place, "Truckee Meadows," where Reno now stands. In the early 20th century, Fernley, Nevada established itself at the south edge of the sand dune field on the Truckee route. It is now home to the 750,000 square-foot fulfillment center for Amazon.com, unmarked graves from that earlier time nestled all around.

In 1846, the eighty-seven member Donner Party crossed The Forty-Mile Desert along the Truckee route. Having got through it, they waited *one day* too long to confront the Sierra. At the top of the eminence, an October winter storm blew in. Forty-one members of the group did not make it over. The snow fell too fast and was too deep that year. It was a worst-case scenario. Trapped in the Sierra and unable to hunt in snow cover that exceeded twenty-foot depths, the Donner Party resorted to cannibalism. Rescuers could not get to them or if they did, they too were in danger. After the fact, accounts of their ordeal screamed through newspapers of the day. It had the effect of reducing traffic along the Truckee route desert crossing, as did stories of the numerous traverses up Truckee River canyon to the meadow.

Most gold seekers to California and later emigrants took the southwesterly, forty-mile Carson route. It was equally dreadful. These days it can be found running parallel to and slightly west of highway 95. If you are hiking along the visible wagon trail, moving in the direction of Fallon and the river, it is not unusual to be caught off-guard by a "Top Gun" jet streaking overhead, sometimes even tipping its wings in a welcome "Howdy."

Five miles into the Carson route fatigued travelers passed "Double Wells" or "Twin Wells," two square holes cut into the ground offering up briny water that the animals refused to drink. In the dark, the landmark was hard to find and without the sighting one could veer off-course, which some did. Further on loomed Salt Creek. It had to be crossed. The problem there was mucilaginous mud. Oxen, wagon wheels, wagons, anything heavy would get irretrievably stuck in it. Pioneers set large round rocks, stepping-stone like, perpendicular to the water's flow. Perhaps the stones aided in traction or served as a sighting-point for the best place to roll through the shallows. Those who got through the creek then faced a field of sand dunes. At the last, oxen and mules, desperate for water, catching the scent of the Carson River miles out, had to be unhitched to run lest they pull wagons apart in their rush for relief.

The terrible time pioneers had in that desert is there today. Those spherical boulders, uniquely out of character in the flat, chipped landscape, continue to span Salt Creek. They are an eerie reminder that over one hundred and fifty years ago determination and desperation combined. Now, if water conditions are right, a circular ring of red rust is visible in the mud on the south bank of the creek. It is what is left of an iron-rimmed wagon wheel. Almost to California, but catastrophic failure. Bits of metal from wrecked wagons, for example, hand-forged square nails, are easy to turn over in the sand. Tallow stains from the bodies of dead draft animals discolor the desert surface. The stains dapple the ground. Once when I was out there, I played a game of "hop-scotch" from stain-to-stain *for an afternoon.*

We drove out of The Nugget parking lot with Oksana, Ihor and Ol'ha in the backseat of our air-conditioned Jeep Cherokee. Past Sparks, we dropped onto a dirt road that connected to the onion works on the Truckee route and quickly found the trail. We bumped past the "Peculiar Rocks." (4.2) Where the desert has not been compromised, the unmistakable wheel-track depressions or "swales" run on either side of a faint green strip of grasses. A century later and trace-nutrients from animal droppings, fallen between the wheel-tracks, continue to fortify the flora, as does early morning dew or rare precipitation; hence, the green strip of grasses.

Four-wheel drive notwithstanding, we had to return to pavement to get to Salt Creek crossing. The highway bridge on 95 zeros out muck-danger. We stopped the car, walked along the creek, marveled at the round rocks and the clear salty water that flows around them. Our hair tangled on the wind. Our skin dried out. We began to squint. The heat index and the sun climbed. Semi-trucks whined past on the distant I-80 interstate.

The Forty-Mile Desert and Soda Lake are as opposite as red is to green. Yet, for those who encountered them in the 19th century, they shared certain characteristics. They were alien landscapes offering up unexpected pitfalls for even the best prepared. Spaces of elemental danger, they delivered stinging cold and burying snow or sere heat, burying sand and utter desiccation. Silent, immense, these lands seemed to drown human habitation, yet they had to be dealt with. The one flaw in my fine comparison is that immigrants passed through the desert; whereas, they stopped and settled on the less-than-hospitable Northern Great Plains.

As for Oksana, Ihor and Ol'ha, the gift of The Forty-Mile Desert was theirs to take or not. They didn't take it; they were bored. We'd made a valiant attempt to show them the passionate history of westward expansion, the travails of immigrants. They wanted to feel and absorb the extraordinary excess of American indolence, wealth and success. We drove our friends back to The Nugget. Then we retreated west where we pitched a tent just below the Sonora Pass on the east side of the Sierra. Days later, Oksana, Ihor and Ol'ha returned to Ukraine. The good part is that Oksana, a true soul, planted hope in me that I *could* learn Ukrainian and that I *could* go to Ukraine—and be a welcomed guest in her home.

With my plan to learn Ukrainian beginning to unravel, for Oksana was gone, I turned to Katherine. (4.3) It was the year Katherine celebrated her 88th birthday. It seemed logical to shift my attention to her. Katherine—the *ad hoc* family historian, folklorist, fashion designer, artist— was a good choice, because she had access to her parents while they were still relatively young, energetic, optimistic and connected to their original village culture. Katherine was one of the few who genuinely enjoyed talking about Soda Lake. She was one of the few who could speak dispassionately about the place. Soda Lake, like The Forty-Mile Desert, now exists primarily in the written down memories of those who passed through or settled there. She talked; I wrote it down.

Katherine could easily recall that in those early days, one built a *khata* (хата)—a log cabin covered by adobe and roofed with thatch—to face directly south to the sun with the windowless backside to the north and the interior icon corner facing southeast (4.4); one built a huge interior clay oven-furnace-sleeping perch called a "peach" [*peach*, піч] and sometimes painted floral designs on it (4.5); one dug a well; one established a large kitchen garden fenced with tightly clustered willow-stakes; one built an outdoor adobe oven for bread. "After my time, things changed very rapidly," Katherine allowed.[3] To her credit, Katherine had an extraordinary, robust memory.

By way of contrast, Mother spoke reluctantly about her youth. Never could I get her to explain why she so-hated the schoolyard photo of her shaking hands with another student. (4.6) Perhaps, because it was posed and taken by the teacher-of-the-moment whom she feared, and it was totally out of any honest context. At holiday dinners, for example Easter, when a brother or a sister or several together would join us, talk would gravitate to life at Soda Lake. It was something the tribe shared. The stories were usually amusing. No one wanted to weep over the several hundred *perohe* dumplings Mother would pinch together, boil and slather in butter, bacon fat and onions and serve with sour cream for the gathering.

Sam would usually talk about Zelenko, how he plowed his field next to Prut' schoolhouse with an ox and a horse, an unmatched team. Sam-the-daydreamer would gaze out the classroom window, study Zelenko working the third row, look down at his schoolwork for a bit, gaze out again and there was Zelenko, still on the third row. Zelenko was notably old-fashioned; he sent to the Old Country for a mail-order bride. When the woman arrived, she immediately lit out. It was the New World she sought. Then again, it was Zelenko, the consummate naïve folk artist, who put up a tiny onion-domed, private chapel and painted its ceiling sapphire-blue, and added little stars to his ceiling-sky. (4.7)

From Ann, there was the business of walking home from the community hall, officially named the Yuriy Fedkowych Ukrainian Educational Society of Soda Lake, past the cemetery in the dark. It brought on respectful silence, rising terror and a quicker pace, lest a restless soul-spirit float up from the crosses and stones and begin to follow. The family's unofficial historian, Bill remembered that his grandfather's coffin at St. Mary's Russo-Greek Orthodox Church at Shandro contained Wasyl-with-his-pinned-on-medals, proof of his having been in the Russo-Turkish War of 1877-78 on the side of Emperor Franz-Joseph. Up to his own dying day, Bill wanted to have Wasyl dug up so that he might handle those heavy medals and hopefully cash in on them.

But it was Katherine who would ever and always clear the deck. "I remember one time my father hitting Mother with a dipper from the water [bucket]," Katherine purred as we sat with the wind chimes softly toning on her screened-in porch. "With the crack [of the dipper], she started bleeding.... And I screamed...I realized, I had a trump here."[4] A child's screaming might bring unwanted attention to her parents' spat. Katherine, the quick-study.

A farm meadow became Katherine's magic garden. She called it her enchanted spot, her "meadowsweet." When she began to attend the one-room Prut' school—most of the locals had come from villages on one side of the Prut' River in Ukraine or the other, she discovered a children's book about a fairy named Meadow Sweet. In Katherine's mind, the fairy and the meadow were bound together in happy possibility. Left unplowed and un-gardened, the meadow was home to nesting Meadowlarks. "You'd be walking along and be startled out of your wits, because you'd suddenly [hear] '*Frrrrrr...*' and you'd almost stepped on a bird's nest."[5] Fragrant Wolf Willows with silver-grey seeds graced the meadow. In June there might be clumps of Yellow Lady-Slippers. Then, Gimlet-eyed, Katherine would add that the meadow was where her father dumped the dead draft horses. It took too much time to bury them.

The oceanic prairie. The sunset sky. The stars at night. "It was all we had. The colors of nature," Katherine would say. "Winter nights were absolutely clear and unpolluted. The sky, so full of stars, and the stars would be so close."[6] But the colors that I treasured coming from Katherine were of a different nature. She missed little of the social context. Katherine recalled a wedding—her mother corroborated Katherine's recollections and so, Katherine insisted this was no false memory. On October 13th, 1913, George—the brother of Katherine's father, John— married Sanda.

The wedding was a traditional one—more-or-less Bukovynian. (4.8; 4.9) There was no white dress. The bride—a wreath of flowers on her head—wore an intricately cross-stitched linen chemise, a dark woolen wrap-skirt cinched by a colorful woven belt. (4.10) Pinned to the groom's lapel was a small ritual cloth, embroidered expressly for him by his fiancée. The community was invited to celebrate. Women cooked for days. A designated female elder baked the special wedding bread (коровai, *korovai*) (4.9). Someone sprang for a keg of beer. A dance area got mapped out. Musicians were hired—a (hammered) dulcimer player (dulcimer: цумбали, *tsymbaly*), a fiddle player, maybe a flute player (flute: сопілка, *sopilka*). The partying began.

It lasted for nearly three days. Some weddings lasted longer, say, a week. Guests ate in shifts. There was usually too much drinking. The younger men fought each other over *jeunes filles*. The older men got maudlin or fought over their smoldering grudges. Wives, such as Katherine's mother, sat silently—and usually pregnant— keeping an eye on their husbands lest they do something inebriated and regrettable—say, for example, as a distant relative did: whack another guy with a board that had a long rusted nail in it, thereby sparking greater animus, tetanus and death.

That evening found toddler Katherine, running in circles on a bed in the host's *khata*. There were women near-by cooking and trying to keep an eye on the child. Illuminated by kerosene lamps, dancers were heel-toeing and spinning. "I was yelling for my mother and they kept feeding me prunes." My first thought was that this kid must have been constipated. Turns out that, in Katherine's words, "*No*, it was because prunes were a *treat*. And I didn't really want them, but I ate them. And I kept yelling and crying for my mother." Finally and unsurprisingly, she got overlooked and escaped. "I got out of the house and it was pitch-black. And I was still crying and yelling. I heard the noise in the granary where they were dancing...But I also heard the real deep rumble of pigs grunting. I was petrified. I didn't know where the pigs were and where I was going." Farm-savvy, she already understood the danger of an aggressive sow.

In the way that it takes a village to raise a child, someone found Katherine and delivered her to her mother. As for her abiding recollection of the wedding, it was that her mother sat, with a wary eye on her father. They did not share a dance. "We kids were deprived," she noted. "I never saw a sign of affection among adults."

Katherine did get connected to something in the women though, and stayed close to it. From corners and dresser-tops and walls at Rossmoor, Katherine's female mentors began to emerge. The intricately carved wood staff standing in a bouquet of Mexican paper flowers—"Oh, that was mother's distaff," she mentioned offhandedly. The glass bowl in her bedroom, filled with oddly shaped, oddly colored skeins of wool—"My mother carded, spun and dyed this wool using her plant lore—onion skins made yellow. Did you know that?" I certainly did not. On the living room wall, the geometrically patterned wool runner—bitter chocolate brown, hot pink, pine green, coral, canary yellow, iris purple—"Mother hung this on the wall of the icon-room.[7] I think she bought this *kylym* from a neighbor." I was later to find an identical image of the *kylym* in a museum exhibition catalog. (4.11)

The day I brought my collection of family textiles to Katherine—the wide and narrow woven wool belts, girdles really (4.12); the beaded blouse; the beaded sleeves not yet attached to a blouse; the severely shortened hand-spun linen chemise with its smudged red and white embroidery—the result of someone's application of bleach to the garment, she leapt for the narrowest belt. It was the least showy and rather-the-worse-for-wear. "This is what we used to wrap the babies in," she cried out, delighted and caught unawares. I had no idea that the infant of the moment was "wrapped," and could not imagine how the woven belt had a part in it. Katherine-the-engineer showed me.

After tightly binding a baby in a white linen cloth, so that it looked like a silkworm cocoon, the narrow belt would be criss-crossed over the whole, to add sparkle to the bundle. In this way, mothers decorated their babies when they took them to church to be christened. As one of the older girls, Katherine saw her share of baby wrapping and decorating. She probably had a hand in adding sparkle to my mother in her cocoon. I can't help but think that she tied her sisters in knots for the rest of her and their lives.

On that Saturday, encircled by Bukovynian textiles—on the arms of the wingback chair, on the carpet, on the couch—admiring the fine hand of "our" ancestor-women, Katherine casually mentioned she'd received some sort of invitation to a reunion in Canada. She had thrown the invitation away. "What!" I said. I had been interviewing her for several months, asking about family history. I called Mother, who also received the invitation. "It's from some distant cousins of ours," Mother said. "Do you want it?" Mother fed it to me like a doggy treat. That was better than Katherine, who had already denied me the treat. Sheesh!

Without quite intending to or perhaps in spite of herself, Katherine opened a window for me. Andrew, Alberta, July 1994, the Tkachuk family reunion. Katherine's paternal grandmother had been a Tkachuk. Katherine's parents lived with the Tkachuks that first month or two after they'd married. I knew not one Tkachuk. The last time I'd visited Alberta or Edmonton or Andrew, I was eleven years old. I booked a flight north.

	Russian month		**Ukrainian month**		**Possible Derivation**
JAN	Январь	(*Yanvar'*)	Січень	(*Sichen'*)	Snowy month
FEB	февраль	(*Fevral'*)	Лютий	(*Lyutij*)	Furious (лютий) wolf-like month
MAR	Март	(*Mart*)	Березень	(*Berezen'*)	Birch tree (береза) month
APR	Апрель	(*Aprel'*)	Квітень	(*Kviten'*)	Flower (квітка) month
MAY	Май	(*Maij*)	Травень	(*Traven'*)	Grass (трава) month
JUN	Июнь	(*Iyun'*)	Червень	(*Cherven'*)	Cherries (червень) ripen month
JUL	Июль	(*Iyul'*)	Липень	(*Lypen'*)	Linden (липа) month
AUG	Август	(*Avgyst*)	Серпень	(*Serpen'*)	Sickle (серп)/ harvest month
SEP	Сентябрь	(*Sentyabr'*)	Вересень	(*Veresen'*)	Birds'nervous chatter month
OCT	Октябрь	(*Oktyabr'*)	Жовтень	(*Zhovten'*)	Leaves turn yellow (жовтий)
NOV	Ноябрь	(*Noyabr'*)	Листопад	(*Lystopad*)	Leaves (лист) fall (падати)
DEC	Декабрь	(*Dekabr'*)	Грудень	(*Hryden'*)	Lumps of cold earth

4.1

4.1 *The Ukrainian months and their nature-based derivations, some say "shamanistic."* **4.2** *My Ukrainian tutor, Oksana, standing in front of the "Peculiar Rocks" in The Forty Mile Desert, due east of Reno & Sparks, Nevada.* **4.3** *Katherine in her living room, Walnut Creek, California.*

4.2

4.3

4.4

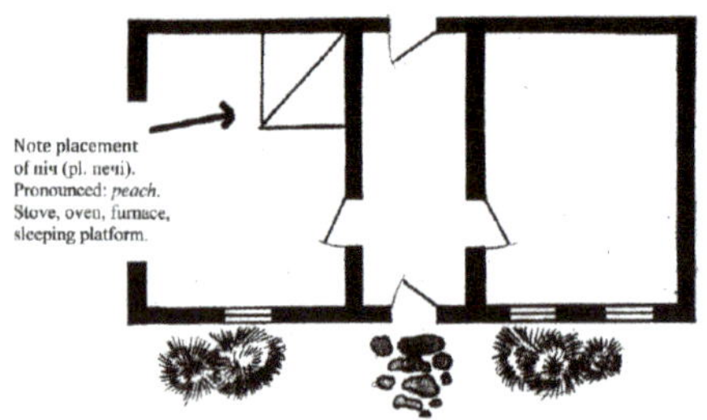

4.5

4.4

4.4. *Examples of Ukrainian folk architecture—the khata (house). Outdoor museum, Kyiv, Ukraine.*

4.5. *Floor plan of traditional Ukrainian khata [Хата] and two drawings of the traditional stove/oven/furnace, called a "peach." [Піч]*

4.6 a *(left) Pruth "School Days" Fair, 1923, Soda Lake, Alberta. Vera stands reluctantly shaking the hand of Johnny Kushneriuk. Photo by Mr. Hutselak, teacher.*

4.6 b *(bottom) l-r: Katherine and her best friend, Kalansha at Pruth "School Days" Fair. 1923. Katherine proudly helped to create the Pruth banner pictured here. The chapel no longer exists, only the entrance stone survives.*

4.7 a *Zelenko's private chapel, Pruth-Soda Lake area. (top) Photo, 1930s. Source: Manoly R. Lupul's (ed) Continuity and Change, pg. 71.*

4.7 b *(right) Sam Ropchan gazing at Zelenko's long-unused chapel, 1970s. The chapel no longer exists, only the entrance stone survives.*

Ukrainian Village Wedding Ritual, 19th century
Has continued into the 20th and 21st centuries in an abbreviated form

Very early on, or sealing the deal
- Inquiries...
- Ceremony of match-making
- Inspection of the groom's assets and the assets of his family
- Finalizing various details concerning the wedding

Preparations for the wedding, or seriously getting organized
- First day of prep or who does what when
- Baking the primary and ritual wedding bread—the *korovai*
- Preparing smaller wedding breads, to be given as gifts
- Inviting the guests—green branches tied to the gateposts
- Ceremony of the *posad*—the betrothed sit together in the corner-of-honor at the bride's parents' home and receive toasts and blessings.
- Ceremony of making the wedding tree, carried by the groom's men.
- Maiden's evening (*Divych vecher*)—commiserating with the bride-to-be
- Wreath-weaving—making the floral crown for the bride
- Couple exchange gifts

Wedding Day
- Preparations—food, gifts, décor—at the bride's home prior to the church service
- Preparations at the groom's home prior to the church service
- Couple's blessing by parents and asking for forgiveness rituals
- Wedding processions—bride's, groom's—to the church
- Church service conducted by a priest
- Groom's wedding procession to the bride's house
- Arrival of the groom and his wedding party at the bride's home
- Bride's mother's greeting
- Unification rite administered by parents
- Ritual sale of the bride
- Distribution of gifts
- Serving the *korovai* to guests
- Incorporation of the bride into the fellowship of married women
- Prior to the couple's departure—hi-jinks, barring the exit, paying ransom
- Arrival at the groom's home
- Wedding night

After the Wedding
- Rituals of purification following the first night
  - Bathing of the newlyweds
  - Performance of lighting the stove and bringing water

4.8

4.8 Abbreviated list of ritual elements/events for a traditional Ukrainian wedding. Source: Sogu Hong.

4.9 a, 4.9 b *Two examples of the Korovai [Коровай], the ritual Ukrainian wedding bread. L'viv. 2001.*

4.10 *Bukovynian bride, 19th c. Tourist postcard reads "Greetings from Ukraine." Painting by Kateryna Biletina.*

4.11

4.11 Detail of the kylym on Katherine's living room wall. An identical kylym, here illustrated, is in the collection of the Provincial Museum of Alberta, Edmonton. Both kylyms are probably by the same Ukrainian-Canadian weaver.

4.12

4.12 Detail of Scraba-Ropchan family textile from the village of Chornivka. Late 19th c., wide woven wool belt/girdle (poias). Usually worn by men.

✣

[1] Julia Cameron, Finding Water. The Art of Perseverance (New York: Jeremy P. Tarcher/Penguin, 2009), 207.

[2] My information about the Forty-Mile Desert and the overland trail crossing comes from myriad sources. Among these are *The California Trail* by George R. Stewart, Ordeal by Hunger: *The Story of the Donner Party* by Stewart, *Fearful Crossing: The Central Overland Trail Through Nevada* by Harold Curran and *Trail of the First Wagons Over the Sierra Nevada (A Guide)* by Charles K. Graydon. *Overland: The California Emigrant Trail of 1841-1870* by Greg MacGregor is a photo/essay of what one sees along the route in 1996. Plate 68 gives a view of Salt Creek Crossing.

[3] Taped interview with Katherine. Walnut Creek, CA. 5 May 1994.

[4] Taped interview with Katherine. Walnut Creek, CA. 23 March 1994.

[5] Taped interview with Katherine. Walnut Creek, CA. 14 May 1994.

[6] Taped interview with Katherine. Walnut Creek, CA. 23 March 1994.

[7] These days we would call it a parlor. In a traditional two-room Ukrainian cottage or khata, you entered through the front door and found yourself standing in a hallway-storage area, a door to your right, a door to your left. (Illustration 4.5) Behind the door on the right was "the great room" (велика хата, velyka khata). It was usually reserved for guests, for important family meals, for ritual meals—weddings, funerals—and for the storage of finery. It might be the site of the icon corner—always on the southeast. The room to the left—"the little room" (мала хата, mala khata), the same size as "the great room," was more pedestrian in nature. It housed the huge adobe stove-oven-furnace-sleeping perch. It was the room where food was prepared, where the family supped, where the family slept.

CHAPTER 5

VERONICA

— Веронiка —

"Even the men was weeping."
—Ruth Tkachuk[1]

"A martyr is not a model to be imitated, but a witness, one who testifies to a new reality."
— Cloister Walk[2]

MY search for the lost ark, the gold ring, the true cross. Me, flitting around North America to find ancestor-women. Air Canada didn't object. I reasoned that if I could locate documents—written, spoken, anything—of the females who had an impact on Mother and her sisters, and by extension, me, then I would be closer to unlocking who the hell we were. At the time of my pilgrimage, some ancestors were merely names, others, less than that.

Veronica was a name. A fine, seemly well-favored name, related to that of my mother's—"Vera." *Veronica.* She is listed as "*Weronia*" in the Soda Lake Register of Births, Marriages and Deaths that her sister-in-law kept. Her name is a variant of the Latin word *veritas,* that is to say, "truth." Latin is the language for saints—incipient Christians standing against the obdurate wall of those pagan gods of Rome—and for the virtues and vices. Thus, Veronica or *Weronia* was thoughtfully named for a Christian virtue—*Truth.* Perhaps when my mother Vera was named for that other Christian virtue, *Faith,* there was a hint of Veronica's name in hers as well—Vera's mother paying respect to her martyred sister-in-law.

Veronica had been Mother's aunt. She lived only three miles—walking distance—from Mother's childhood home at Soda Lake. (Illustration 5.1) Mother and her sisters whispered—among themselves, and to me—that Veronica had been murdered. Is this why her name came up in a nimbus of silence? I wanted to find this mortal; the daughter, sister, mother, aunt who represented what no one in the family wanted to acknowledge. She might be where I could begin.

From San Francisco, I winged over the Sierra and then Salt Lake City—north across

Montana to Calgary and on. In my journal I've written, "A full moon tonight floats above the Wasatch Range." I would come to associate the full moon with Veronica. I already associated the Wasatch Range with the Donner Party—it was where they had to hack out a trail out of no trail. I also note that we "took on extra fuel in Calgary because there was storm turbulence ahead." You bet'cha. Lightning in charcoal grey thunderheads the size of skyscrapers with me in my seat, buckled up, sweaty palms gripping the arm rests, "thumping and bumping along." The merest inconvenience when compared to the adventure of Larysa.

I have many relatives in Edmonton and beyond in Alberta—they were near-strangers then. I'd not been able to reach a one of them. I was so nervous about what I would do after I arrived, that I forgot and left my passport in California. A sleep-deprived, thoroughly irritated customs officer finally let me pass to Canada with only my California driver's license. These days I'd be sent back home. End of discussion.

After a forgettable night in an airport motel, I called my father's brother Jack in Mundare. This time he answered the phone. He had no idea who I was, but, "Sure I can stay" with him and his wife. Relieved, I drove the sixty miles east to Mundare, dazed that it was working. (5.2) I'd actually be attending the Tkachuk Reunion in Andrew. "Why didn't you call Hazel?" Jack asked when I got out of the "Rent-A-Wreck." Hazel, his daughter, my cousin, lives in Edmonton. I didn't know this. Gradually, I got my bearings.

The morning of the reunion, I drove away from Mundare at about 5:30am. I wanted time to find the barn at Soda Lake and then double back west to Andrew and the Tkachuks. I had a photo of the distinctive two-winged brick-red structure. Finding it would situate the homestead quarter-section for me. Geographically speaking, I like to see where things are on the ground, then I understand them better. (5.3)

There I was, up one dirt road, down another. Every field of Canola looked like every other field of Canola. I'd spot a barn, angle to get closer to it and then see it was not "the barn." Four or five barns later, burning up time, gobbling gasoline, I rashly pulled right into a farmer's yard and raced past his tidy wood frame house in order to eye one more possibility. It was around 7:00am and he was up. By the time I'd turned the car around to exit his yard, there he was on his back porch wondering what I was doing on his driveway.

It seemed appropriate to apologize and to explain my fruitless driving-in-circles search. I stopped little black "Rent-A-Wreck" and got out. By then, there were two people standing in wonderment on the porch, the farmer and his wife. I began. Suddenly, the woman burst into tears. "Oh George," she cried, "She looks *just like* Vera!" Vera was my mother. George and Lilly had been her elementary school chums at Prut'. They knew Katherine and Nancy and all of them. I *had* to come in for coffee and rolls. "Never mind the kitchen," Lily offered. It was loaded to the gunnels with Saskatoon berries and rhubarb; she was putting up preserves. Out came the family albums. An hour later, George insisted on personally showing me where the barn, the community hall, the schoolyard, the two churches and the two cemeteries were.

Never a tall man, George was made shorter by three—I repeat, three— failed hip joint replacement surgeries. He moved briskly with the help of two canes. (5.4) In a blink, he was in his low-rider Oldsmobile Holiday Coupe and off. That car, two tons of steel with George behind the wheel, blasted along the township roads in a cumulous cloud of dust. Rent-a-Wreck and I had to scramble to stay with him.

We came to a billowing stop at the intersection of two dirt roads. There was the community hall on the northwest corner and the Holy Ascension Church with its cemetery on the southeast corner. (5.5-5.8) Fields and swarms of mosquitoes stretched to the horizon. Three minutes further east and there was Prut' school—"Pruth School for District #2064," and a minute later, St. Demetrius Ruthenian Greek Orthodox Church of Luzan at the edge of its cemetery. Two miles east and one mile north was the barn. It was all thanks to George and Lilly.

When I walked into the Andrew Community Hall, the organizers knew exactly who I was: the non-native. I was the only person wearing a lumpy t-shirt, wrinkled khakis and hiking boots. (5.9) Up and down the line, the Tkachuks were dressed in heels and hose or suits and neckties. There was nothing to be done for my fashion *faux-pas*, but smile. It gave me some courage to learn that there was no consensus on how the family name should be pronounced—there was option one: CAWchuk and option two: cuhCHUK. There were probably other variants. I liked this mess.

I met a sprinkling of people with my mother's maiden name, her cousins. I had not known of them. For their part, they seemed to regard me as a creature from one of Jupiter's moons. It was awkward to realize that we were related. The cousins wanted to talk about whether Wayne Gretzky would be traded. I wanted to know about their grandparents and great grandparents. For a break, the Hall served a homemade lunch of *borshcht*, dill pickles, egg salad sandwiches and a gelatin dessert. It was instructive to see that there were still places serving solid 1950s cuisine. I'd forgotten all about the joys of Jello.

After the Jello, here's what I found out. Petro, Mychailo, Hryhoriy and "Magdalyna" constituted the four Tkachuk branches. They all immigrated to the Northwest Territories in Canada, but came in two groups. Petro, Mychailo and Hryhoriy and their families came in 1898, landing in Halifax and riding the rails to Edmonton. Sister Magdalyna and her husband, Wasyl Ropchan arrived a year later, passing through New York City instead. My claim to the Tkachuks was the sister. In the afternoon of 1994, those of us derived from Magdalyna and Wasyl sat together in front of a computer-generated family-tree map for a group photograph.

Right away, questions came up. There was no agreement on Magdalyna Tkachuk's name. Was she Magdalyna? Olena? Margarina? Odakia? Edoxia? Margaret?[3] At least we concurred that she once existed. After all, she was the mother of six, all of whom married and had families of their own. But Magdalyna ended up as a case of "the lady vanishes." How long did she live? When did she pass away? Where was she buried? No one knew.

Meanwhile, everyone knew of her husband, Wasyl. A lawsuit he mounted against an employer was one of the first document packets I found at the Provincial Archives of Alberta. At his death, there were photos of the mourners, of his coffin being lowered into the ground, of the very roses on his coffin as it went down. A stone marker was put up for him in the cemetery of St. Mary's Russian Greek Orthodox Church at Shandro; it's still there. (5.10) He was one of the church's founding members.

It was Wasyl who wore three medals in a row. During his funeral, the medals were pinned on by Wasyl's second wife—a thrice-widowed gal, Mrs. Maria Figuerchik Gordey-Ukrainetz-Ropchan. (5.11) There were rumblings from Wasyl's side that "the widow" had never actually married. Vows notwithstanding, one way or another Wasyl and Ms. Figuerchik-Gordey-Ukrainetz were living together in 1907.

More Tkachuks gathered in the Andrew Hall. A program coalesced. There was a head table at which the Tkachuk "elders" sat, facing the rest of the room. There was a master-of-ceremonies microphone area. Seated at long tables arranged in parallel rows, we "youths" faced the elders. We said a prayer. We sang songs in Ukrainian. I did not know one word of anything. We listened to speeches and poetry and watched small children deliver braided wreaths of wheat to the head table honorees. We toasted the room with non-alcoholic, non-Ukrainian, non-Canadian papaya juice. We clapped as older girls in blue tunics, red wooden beads, embroidered skirts, aprons and red leather boots smiled and spun and tapped their busy feet. (5.12)

In the mailed instructions for the Tkachuk Reunion, we were encouraged to bring a modest gift, something that we created, as opposed to purchased. Gift-donations would be raffled at the reunion. Sure enough, the three pair of earrings I designed were all won by highly amused men. The number for the grand prize gift, a white afghan—handmade by one of the reunion organizers—with "The Tkachuk Family Reunion, 23 July 1994" cross-stitched in the center, was, to my amazement, under my plate. I have wondered whether it was "a plant." Learning that I had traveled the furthest for this particular day, the room seemed to agree that I should have the graceful afghan. But I was such a shirt-tail-relative, I felt as if I were stealing the coverlet.

Dinner was memorable for its hundreds of tiny, smallest-finger-sized *holubtsi* (голубці, cabbage rolls) and the *nachynk*a (начунка, corn meal pudding). I ignored the tossed salad, potatoes, dressing, gravy, cranberry sauce, turkey and beef stew for the former. So I supped and visited with my new found second cousins and others, then left before the evening dancing began. I had to drive those twenty miles to Mundare. The reunion's rosy glow stayed with me all the way home to California.

What is it about the everyday reality of one's kitchen that often clarifies thought? Washing some pot or pan, I realized I'd missed my opportunity: it was the head table. The rather shy, dressed-for-Sunday nonagenarians seated up front were the Tkachuks I *should* have been talking to. Why had I clung to my own thin twig on the family tree? By the time I returned to seek them out ten months later, two of the Tkachuk elders had passed away. One had suffered a stroke and could remember nothing. The fourth had left Alberta for British Columbia—somewhere in the mild Okanogan Valley. Only Lena Waselashko, Petro's daughter, was near.

It was May, "an unusually cold one," they all said—snow, sleet, icy gusts of wind, bone-chilling rain. I wore every sweater I'd packed. The "Rent-A-Wreck" people were genuinely warming to me. As Jack suggested earlier, I leaned on Hazel's generosity, and engineered a stay of five weeks. My plan was to visit the Provincial Archives, the little towns, the churches, cemeteries and every relative, friend and former family neighbor on my list.

Typically and optimistically, I skipped the step about learning Edmonton. One is either north of the river on a bluff, or south of the river on a bluff and usually headed uphill or downhill to cross a bridge—High Level Bridge, Low Level Bridge, these are a few of their names. The river in question is the North Saskatchewan River, a respectable north-flowing waterway that can push enough big ice under a bridge in spring to destabilize it—hence, the need for a "high level" bridge. One bad ice-melt-season, late June of 1915, Edmontonians parked a railroad locomotive on Low Level Bridge to keep it from washing away. Fortunately and incredibly, the train and the bridge stayed; the ice proceeded to Hudson Bay.

Even the zippy major thoroughfares of Edmonton can be slippery. Greenhorn driver that I was, afraid of being bullied into driving higher speeds and wrapping my car around a lamp post, a feat even seasoned Edmontonians achieve with alarming regularity, I chose quaint, slower routes to get from Hazel's to any point. In this way, I discovered some of the older corners and the more colorful bridges in the city. I never dared tell anyone I knew how I got from A-to-B. They would have been appalled.

According to plan, I hunkered down at the Provincial Archives. But for all of my hopefulness, my research efforts were an exercise in frustration. Rarely was a professional staff member available for questions: government cut backs. Without knowing precisely how information was systematized, I kept reaching dead ends. A week passed. The length of my coffee recess increased. By chance, during one dejected caffeine break, I met a tea-sipping *emeritus* volunteer possessed with a sixth sense of Provincial Archive holdings. It was my good fortune that she took me on as her project.

"Let's see if anything turns up under legal proceedings," *emeritus* said; this never occurred to me. In quick succession I located the legal brief involving Wasyl; next my grandmother's marriage certificate with her misspelled name; then the Soda Lake register of vital statistics that she kept in her lilting looping script; next the Edmonton family of that thrice-widowed gal, Mrs. Maria Figuerchik Gordey-Ukrainetz, also known as "Wasyl's second wife"—the

Gordey's were current residents of Edmonton; and unbelievably, the death certificate of Wasyl's first wife, the nullity. Here was the illusive Magdalyna, her vital statistics written on a piece of paper, framed by dates. My great-grandmother finally had a name.

My plodding turned into a gallop. In Edmonton and in Andrew, Soda Lake and Vegreville, there were appointments to be set up. I made phone calls by the dozens, then raced off. I met more Deacons of more neat-as-a-pin onion-domed prairie churches than I thought possible. When I parked at Borowich church, I was politely asked to re-park the car. A truck with a crane with a coffin dangling from a cable could not pass through the wrought iron cemetery gate thanks to Rent-A-Wreck. No question that the clock was ticking. I studied crumbling church records in the basements and kitchens of church records-keepers. I heard how documents were lost to nibbling mice and to prairie fires. Wooden crosses, another form of documentation, got incinerated too. I added a cascade of contact phone numbers to my notes. I had no clear idea of what I was searching for. Women who were lost, I guess. Ones like Magdalyna and her daughter Veronica. A part of me, for sure.

All the while, I tried to gain access to Lena Waselashko, Petro's daughter. If Lena had been too young to know Magdalyna, she may have heard stories about her from her own mother or her older sister, Mary. This I reasoned, before I found Magdalyna's death certificate. As it turns out, Lena was born in 1906. Magdalyna died in 1905. But Lena's older sister was twelve when her aunt Magdalyna passed away. Wonder of wonders, she had kept a journal.

Nancy, who knew nothing of Magdalyna, sent me to talk with the ninety-two year old Ruth, who had married into the Mychailo line. Ruth lived in a sun-filled efficiency apartment in a senior center. Her windows faced a stand of soaring fir trees, resplendent in snow. All about her were mementos of her family—photos of daughters, grandchildren, her deceased husband. She wrapped herself in them with great warmth, just as she wrapped herself in a blazing red sweater jacket. (5.13) She was tiny, had sharp wits about her, and, like George of Prut' school, was semi-crippled by questionable hip surgery. She peppered her English with semi-Ukrainian terms. Her creative expressions got the job done.

From Ruth, I learned right away that Mother's mother, Maria, had been a put-down artist. Maria married John, whose parents were Magdalyna and Wasyl. Maria held all Tkachuks in low-esteem, "She wanted to show that she was much better than they," Ruth said.[4] Was this typical of Maria, I wondered? I had been led to believe that in an over-arching way, Maria was a positive force, pro-woman, a nascent Suffragette. Hadn't Maria railed against the Orthodox priests who held women in low esteem? Hadn't Maria taken over Soda Lake Post Office and Public Recorder duties? Hadn't Maria accompanied the county home economist from *khata* to *khata*, hoping to introduce healthful nutritional and child-rearing habits among her cohort? Hadn't Maria gotten herself onto the local school board in order to improve conditions for the children and to show that a woman could do something?

"They don't know enough," Maria had said about the Tkachuks, at least according to Ruth. The word Maria used to label the Tkachuks was "тамний" (*tamniy*, dark). This is a Ukrainian trope, used in the sense of being not-modern, of being superstitious, of being given to doing things in the old Old Country ways. Maria probably considered Zelenko "тамний"—her children certainly did. After Ruth's reconfiguration of Maria, we were off.

Thanks to the Provincial Archives, the *emeritus* volunteer and snippets of family documentation, I discovered that Magdalyna's family, the Tkachuk's, called the village of *Kotul Bainski* home. Somewhere in the appellation "*Kotul Bainski*" is the suggestion—in Romanian—of elbow-curve. Indeed, when one studies maps of the 1870s—I was to find that the University of Alberta has a stellar map collection of 19th century Eastern Europe—there is *Kotul Bainski* on its right-angle curve, spitting distance from Ottoman lands to the east and south. (5.14)

Perhaps mid-19th century, *Kotul Bainski* was just too small for all of its beauties to find suitable suitors. Traditionally, inter-marriage of village youth had been the norm. The boys of *Kotul Bainski* were to marry the girls of *Kotul Bainski*—it was ever a case of the same genes chasing each other around for centuries.[5] Fisticuffs were not uncommon if the lads from one scatter of cottages strayed into another to survey the pool of marriageable maidens.

A larger village, *Molodiia*—original home to the Ropchans, is within walking distance of *Kotul Bainski*. Perhaps there was a territorial truce among the young bucks of *Molodiia* and *Kotul Bainski*—a win-win situation in terms of more available girls. And so, in the way of all fairy tales, the darkly handsome Wasyl of *Molodiia* met the darkly fetching Magdalyna of *Kotul Bainski* and they married in the early 1870s. Their six children were born in two batches: before the Russo-Turkish War of 1877-78 and after the Russo-Turkish War, when Wasyl returned from military duty. The location of the two villages doubtless played a part in Wasyl's getting himself volunteered.

The memorable Russo-Turkish War of 1877-78 unfolded in the following manner: the Russian tsar smelled blood. The Ottoman Turkish Empire was weak. Russia, trying to regain itself after its Crimean debacle in the 1840s and to close in on the Black Sea, saw a new chance to soldier south. Kind'a like Putin and Crimea today. But this would mean that Russia and its other rival, the Austrian-Hapsburg Empire, would sit uneasily side-by-side while sabers were drawn.

Emperor Franz-Joseph decided to smile and to show firmness at the same time. He allowed Russia to use his rail lines to transport troops and supplies towards the Ottomans' Balkan holdings—Romania, Serbia, Montenegro, and he mustered up men from his villages in the east—such as *Molodiia* and *Kotul Bainski*, to stand firm against the Russians should they decide to linger. Wasyl was just the right age to muster. Guarding the borders of Franz-Joseph's empire was not necessarily an honor for a peasant. You got dragooned into service if you had neither the money, nor the connections to avoid it. Conscriptions were punitive in some burgs—upset the mayor or the town constable, then off you went. Unless you had a strong-like-an-ox wife, your farm holdings went to weed and ruin.

If he had been a nice guy before his call-up, Wasyl would have returned to *Molodiia* with a bit of an edge. Military life was brutalizing. Abuse was the norm. Heaven help the common soldier in the emperor's or the tsar's army. As an aristocratic blade, Tolstoy gained traction by writing about his own terrible soldiering experience during the Crimean War. To put the cherry on top, Wasyl would have been traumatized by anything he *saw* during that particularly ghastly skirmish—evisceration, decapitation, drowning in mud. It was certifiably ugly.

Magdalyna's life, while Wasyl was gone, was no Viennese waltz. Peasant soldiers' wives tended to be looked down upon in their communities. They fell into poverty. Some were considered to be no better than whores. True, here and there a lonely wife had an affair or ran off with another man. Who would blame her? Usually most of the village. As a bonus, soldiers' wives had to do the work of two parts of a farm couple. Magdalyna's survival and the survival of her two young children, Margaret and John—respectively and approximately five and three—was a certain victory. In Magdalyna, it showed her mettle. (5.15)

After the twinkling passage of fifteen years during which Wasyl returned from the battlefield; Sovena, Mary, George and Veronica were born; and the opportunity of "free land" in Canada—aggressively advertized in Eastern Europe in the 1890s by the Canadian government—reared its hydra-shaped head; Wasyl and family[6] took the S.S. Patria and steamed to New York City.[7] From there, they rode the rails to Edmonton. A combination of sheer determination and word-of-mouth got them to Magdalyna's brothers—the aforementioned Petro, Mychailo and Hryhoriy—camped out on their quarter sections sixty miles northeast of Edmonton.

It was June when Magdalyna and Wasyl arrived to NE14-57-16.W4M. They found pretty much of nothing there, save virgin northern prairie—intact with grasses and flowers, scrub willows, black and white poplars and sloughs beyond count. Like others of their ilk, they quickly put up a *burdei* (бурдей) to have some protection from the elements, just in case early summer delivered weather like the May I spent at Hazel's. Late season snow is not unheard of at that latitude and longitude.

In Bukovyna, a sheepherder high up in the Carpathians might construct a *burdei* if a bad storm were approaching. It is an architectural entity never intended as a permanent structure—a branches-and-grasses pup tent over a square-cut hole in the *terra firma*. Half above, half below ground, the *burdei* goes up in a day and provides some protection. *Burdeis* in the Shandro-Andrew area later became chicken coops or pigpens before they melted back into the earth. Given the approach of winter and the time it would take to chop down, de-branch, haul and season pine, tamarack or poplar for a tried-and-true *khata*, the *burdei* was a practical short-term solution. (5.16)

But the "solution" was hardly comfortable or healthful. Arid summers, a *burdei* could be cool and dry, but with rain, it would leak like a sieve, and continue to leak after the rain stopped. In a *burdei*, a family of seven, such as Wasyl's, would be a crowd by any standard. Add damp, add standing water, add cold, add the myriad varmints that wandered in—out of curiosity or haplessness, and the mites that rode in with old wood brought from the forest because there was no time to log and season new wood, and a picture of misery, potential illness and stress comes into focus.

A year after the *burdei* went up, "at 3:00 o'clock pm on the 26th day of December," Wasyl was involved in a lawsuit.[8] Wasyl sought to sue a Mr. Lepage who had failed to pay him the agreed-upon $20 for one month of farm labor. On April 2nd, 1901, the Honorable Mr. Justice Scott ruled against Lepage and ordered him to pay the court and the defendant. Wasyl's lawsuit was cheeky. Here was a Ukrainian peasant-farmer, one year off the boat, regarded by Anglo Canadians as the social equivalent of a Cree or Blackfoot Indian; a fellow who could neither read nor write—he signed all court documents with an "X," who could not speak the language of the court—he required a translator, who had no qualms about leaving his wife and five children to run his farm operation for eight days in the throes of an arctic winter, who hardly minded the great distance—sixty miles on foot—from home to court and back. This was a man not to be toyed with.

On one tea-sipping afternoon I was sitting in the Gordeys' living room, surrounded by Gordeys. I asked them about Wasyl's supposedly second "wife," Ms. Maria Fegirchuk-Gordey-Ukrainetz-Ropchan. It was my *emeritus* docent friend at the Provincial Archives who had given me a "heads-up" about the Gordeys. They too were doing due diligence on their own ancestral project, hence my sitting in their living room. The Gordeys didn't think the widow married Wasyl either. They were descendants of John Gordey Jr, issue of the widow's first marriage. Mr. Gordey Sr. died slowly of a lung wound he'd sustained during the Russo-Turkish War. No wonder the widow and Wasyl gravitated to each other. She was a military wife and had the experience of that war.

There were rumors that the widow worked a step-daughter—by way of her Ukrainetz marriage—to death. After Gordey Sr.'s passing, she'd married Kost Ukrainetz—a widower with two daughters. When Kost and Maria immigrated to Canada, one girl opted to stay behind; the second came along. Gradually, the break-up of his family, along with memories of the war and the hardships of pioneer life, began to prey on Kost's mind. He devolved from depression and illness into a delirious state and death.

Meanwhile and relentlessly, the widow pushed her son and step-daughter. She had the girl turning furrows from a walking plow. Unbroken prairie, with its thick net of grass roots, was notoriously difficult to plow—the solution to which made fortune and fame for an enterprising blacksmith named John Deere. For Kost's daughter, the strain "caused something to break." [9] The gravediggers in the Sunland area did well in 1905. Kost gave it up on March 5th, Wasyl's wife Magdalyna died on July 21st, and Kost's sixteen-year old daughter expired around August 9th.[10] The widow may well have first laid eyes on Wasyl—sorted out his particular predicament—at the season's burial extravaganzas.

Wasyl's quarter-section was mostly sloughs. Thus, he turned to raising cattle and pigs, grazing them on the parts of his homestead that were not under water. From 1907 on, the widow helped him in this venture.[11] Although toughened by the circumstances of her life, the widow "met her match in Wasyl," this according to the Gordeys.[12] None of her ferocity kept her from fleeing Wasyl when he had been drinking—"She'd go sleep in the barn so he wouldn't beat her up.... He was a mean drunk; he liked his liquor," the Gordeys said in chorus.[13] Chuckles all around, they warmed to the image of their grandmother hiding among the pigs to camouflage herself. In the end, the widow got the pigs and cattle. She also pinned Wasyl's war medals to his lifeless chest at Shandro. When she died, Wasyl's son George inherited the sloughs at NE14-57-16.W4M.[14]

It stands to reason that Wasyl's youngest child, Veronica, was the daughter of an assertive, at times aggressive, ill-tempered, willful, occasionally dangerous man, and for closers, the veteran of a brutal war. She was also the daughter of a mother who distinguished herself in the one way that mattered. Like Tamsen Donner of the doomed Donner Party, Magdalyna kept her children alive.

The year her family immigrated to that sodden patch of prairie, the six-year old Veronica would have helped in all the ways a child was required by pioneering parents—watching the domestic animal(s), collecting sticks for firewood, fetching water, picking mushrooms, setting snares for rabbits and grouse, weeding the garden, stirring the *kasha*. For tutors, she had two older sisters—Sovena and Mary. There was no school—none had been established yet.

At ten, Veronica would have joined the modest wedding festivities for John, her eldest brother, and his bride, Maria. Her aunt Axenia, Mychailo's wife, was the Matron-of-Honor. Months after the June wedding, when the newlyweds left Wasyl and Magdalyna's home and headed for Soda Lake, more work would have fallen to Veronica and her remaining siblings.

August of 1904, when sister Sovena married and headed for British Columbia, Veronica was eleven. Then in July, 1905, Veronica's mother, the forty-eight year-old Magdalyna died. How to make sense of so much change when you are a mere twelve? In her journal, Lena Waselasko's sister writes that Magdalyna's coffin was carried to the burial ground in an ox-drawn wagon.[15] Veronica must have walked behind it, stunned. The women among the group of mourners who followed, would have been keening. A year later, Veronica's sister Mary married and was gone.[16] Wasyl, George and Veronica were left. That's when Ms. Maria Fegirchuk-Gordey-Ukrainetz appeared.

Veronica, the declared family beauty, was approaching sixteen. Rumor had it that Veronica's aunts and her sister-in-law conspired to spirit the girl away from Wasyl's watery farming venture, out of reach of her father and the widow. From the living room of his Florida ranch house in West Palm Beach, Veronica's nephew Al said, "They hid her in a wagon, the wagon-box, covered her with blankets, this is what we [children] were told. They hauled her away to marry this Sembaliuk." As an afterthought, he added, "They settled on a farm that was maybe three miles from our farm."[17] Bad day at Black Rock—Veronica hitched to Nick Sembaliuk.

"Nauscious," Ruth said; that was Sembaliuk in a nutshell. She found him so foul that she coined a word for him: "nauscious," a conflation of obnoxious and nauseous.[18] According to Ruth, he was "good looking, well-talking, used to acting as if he knew more than others" and "mean to his wife." Lena Waselasko was more direct about Nick Sembaliuk: "He was a charlatan."[19]

For Veronica's dowry, Wasyl gave the couple a cow—no small gift. Think of it as a major household appliance. In order to transport the dowry to their Soda Lake quarter, Veronica drove the wagon, Nick walked behind, the cow tied to the back of the wagon. But the animal began to balk—unused to being roped to a wagon or loath to leave familiar surroundings. Nick beat it. He beat it until bloodied and bruised, the cow collapsed into a ditch along the side of the road. "Its skin was beaten raw," Lena said. Nick untied the creature and left it. Word rippled back to Wasyl, from one quarter section to the next, that the cow was dying at road's edge. "Old man Ropchan [Wasyl] went every day looking after that cow, watering and feeding it," Ruth said, "until he could get it back to his herd."[20] Veronica's husband, the "nauscious" Sembaliuk, secured his reputation.

By nineteen, Veronica was the mother of a son. At twenty, pregnant again, pushed down a root-cellar staircase, thrown against a wall, slammed with a board or a pot, locked outside in the cold, Veronica was dead. "He threw her out in the cold, beat her. She died," Ruth said of Nick. "There was quite a splash of blood there," the Babiiuks—on the quarter immediately to the north— reported to the Gordey's—on the quarter immediately to the east.

Before the police arrived, the Babiiuks cleaned it up.[21] No one wanted to get into trouble. Called to help, the good doctor "Yak"—Yakymshak—drove through the night and momentarily lost his bearings at Soda Lake. Veronica's sister-in-law, Maria dashed from Soda Lake up the snowy roads, really paths, to reach Veronica. She knew the way. The snow-covered ground was lit. As Al remembered, there was a full moon—actually, it was on the waning edge of full—that October 22nd.

At Veronica's funeral, Ruth recalled, "Even the men was weeping." She died nine days after her brother's—George's—wedding. It was the wedding where baby Katherine got stuffed with prunes and escaped past the pigs to her mother. That wedding may have been a contributing factor to Veronica's final moments. In the context of a Ukrainian wedding—notorious for duration and the free-flow of lightning spirits such as moonshine—the pregnant beauty may have sparked some jealousy or rebuke from her cocked-like-a-pistol husband. Regarding lightning spirits, I learned the hard way. At the first Ukrainian wedding I attended in L'viv, I fared rather poorly. By the second wedding, I'd learned to pace myself and give wide berth to certain deceptively clear elixirs.

The marker at Borowich cemetery lies over a plot originally intended for the Sembaliuk line. (5.17) It indicates that Veronica and her unborn son, posthumously named Ivan (John)—the reference is undoubtedly to St. John the Baptist and to Veronica's brother John—were buried together there. Instead of a wood cross, a stone slab was chosen for the grave.[22] Was the greater expense a guilt offering or a gesture to indicate that Veronica was to be remembered for all eternity with a fire-resistant rock?

As for Nick Sembaliuk, he quietly slouched east, towards Lloydminster. According to Lena, the elder Mrs. Sembaliuk, "made a great show of piety in church after Veronica's death and her son nowhere." Lena went on, hissing and spitting out words, "Old Mrs. Sembaliuk attended that church at Shandro like a *dyak* (дуак, deacon) and when she died, she left her money to the priest." There is no question that Lena thought Mrs. Sembaliuk's gesture futile. For a murdering son, her soul was going to be visited by *chorti* (чорти, devils), no matter the gift.

Why did we not discuss Veronica? If the topic of her murder was not entirely taboo among the women in my family, the less said, the better. When I was a child and Veronica was reluctantly mentioned at those family dinners, I fastened upon the drama of her story. Everyone knew it. She was young, beautiful and alone. Her life was unfair. I had anger for Sembaliuk, that "N. Cymbaluk" inscribed onto the northwest corner of Section 34, (NW34-55-15.W4th) Homestead #178709 on the Department of the Interior Topographical Survey map I was later to find. Later still, after I had gotten to know him through research, I had anger for Wasyl.

Who can deny that the girl sustained shock after shock? There was the massive relocation from a familiar village and its culture to rank wilderness. There were the hardships of a primitive pioneer life. With certain finality, there were the departures of mentoring elder siblings. There was the day-to-day dealing with a sometimes menacing father. At twelve, there was the death of her mother. Two years later found her faced with a Cinderella-style evil stepmother, capable of hooking her to a plow to turn over virgin sod. Veronica's final indignity was getting connected to a pathologically abusive husband. Why did she not go raving mad? Then again, perhaps she fought back and it got her dead.

When my mother spoke of Veronica, her "lesson" took a prosaic turn: marry the wrong man and that's what happens to you, be too pretty and helpless and that's what happens to you. It was long ago. The culture was different, chock-a-block with animal brutality. Veronica's death was no big whoop—one peasant offing another, an entitled husband ending the life of his young wife just for defying him. Everyone saw it coming. The whole neighborhood heard of Sembaliuk's nearly destroying a valuable cow, just for being a cow. Right?

Wrong! Underneath it all, Veronica is one collective shudder. What I see is that the family resolved, in unspoken collusion, to turn away and avoid the irreconcilable pain of confrontation with Veronica's death. In the face of unspeakable cruelty, Veronica became the unmentionable; what no one ever wanted to acknowledge. But the fact remains that Veronica's desperate plight and vicious murder continue to reverberate among the women: she was one of us and we looked the other way.

Many in the family today are unaware of the girl's history and the family's reaction to it. A too distant history or history gliding into legend. But like a stone tossed in a pond, the ripple effect continues to lap outward. Reality changed, but no lesson was drawn from it or imparted to Veronica's heirs. It got easier to desert those who struggled. As a consequence of needing to protect oneself, distrust only intensified. All told, Veronica is a dangerous memory of abandonment, of catastrophic, massive failure.

In time, everyone got assimilated, moved on, moved out, moved forward, moved south. But something profound got lost. Veronica means so much more than "this is what happens if you marry the wrong guy." She revealed a gaping hole in family support, in female support and solidarity. The women were the ones who had the inside track on the unfortunate girl. What does it mean if a matriarchy sloughs off the weaker ones?

Yarrow. This aromatic blossoming beauty keeps Veronica's spirit company in mid-summer at Borowich. It is a medicinal plant, known since antiquity for its blood clotting properties—reputedly Achilles carried Yarrow with him to Troy to treat battle wounds, hence the plant's Latin name, *Achillea millefolium*. Veronica certainly knew of the plant's dye properties: the women in her family used Yarrow to produce soft brownish yellow-gold for their wool yarns. It grows in the village she left in Bukovyna and across the quarter-sections she came to know in Canada. By fall, Yarrow is dry and crunches underfoot at Borowich, unless, of course, there is an early snowfall that muffles botanical verbiage and amplifies the sounds of all else.

On my last visit to Veronica's grave, it was October. I'd forgotten—then remembered—that October was the month of her death. It was impossible to ignore the early evening callings of waterfowl in a slough somewhere to the west, not far from the North Saskatchewan. No mistaking it, preparations were a-wing for most to fly south. I wanted a bit of silence, to reflect. But Canada geese, Snow geese, Mallards, Blue-winged teals, Cinnamon teals, Northern Shovellers, Northern Pintails, Coots, Lesser Scaups, Buffelheads, Common-Goldeneyes, Killdeer, Willets, Northern Harriers, Sharp-shinned hawks, Red-tailed hawks, seagulls of every ilk, Red-winged blackbirds, Golden-headed blackbirds were quacking, honking, cawing, chipping, crying to the counter measure of farm dogs on adjacent quarter-sections. Just me, the birds, the dogs and the dried grasses—dusk was an uproar.

Absently, I turned to the east. A cantaloupe orange moon, full, round, as big as eight barns, stood on the ground, confounding belief. How had it risen to the horizon line so quickly and to such enormity? And how had the colossus come up in such silence, as if to set a counter-example to the raucous noise of everything else? I don't think I expected strains of Wagner, Mussorgsky or Berlioz, but I found the muteness of the immense moon eerie.

Instantly, I associated the moon with Veronica. In my heart, even now, I call it "Veronica's Moon." As a person, and it is no doubt a character flaw, I gravitate towards emotive poetical language and imagery—Veronica's wan light, her transcendent beauty, her remoteness in memory, her hovering spirit. Then I decided that the moon carried some sort of message. After all, I was standing near Veronica's marker when the moon caught me unawares. Surely there was meaning in the congruence of the harvest moon, Veronica and me.

By slow degrees, I realized that my lyrical fancy does not obtain. That solemn melon moon—I see it and am haunted by it still—is ever neutral. It is a voiceless aspect of nature. Its enormity and hush are unmistakably akin to the silence that surrounds Veronica's life and death and has pushed the memory of her out of her own family. That gorgeous, velvety cantaloupe, pumpkin, apricot color notwithstanding.

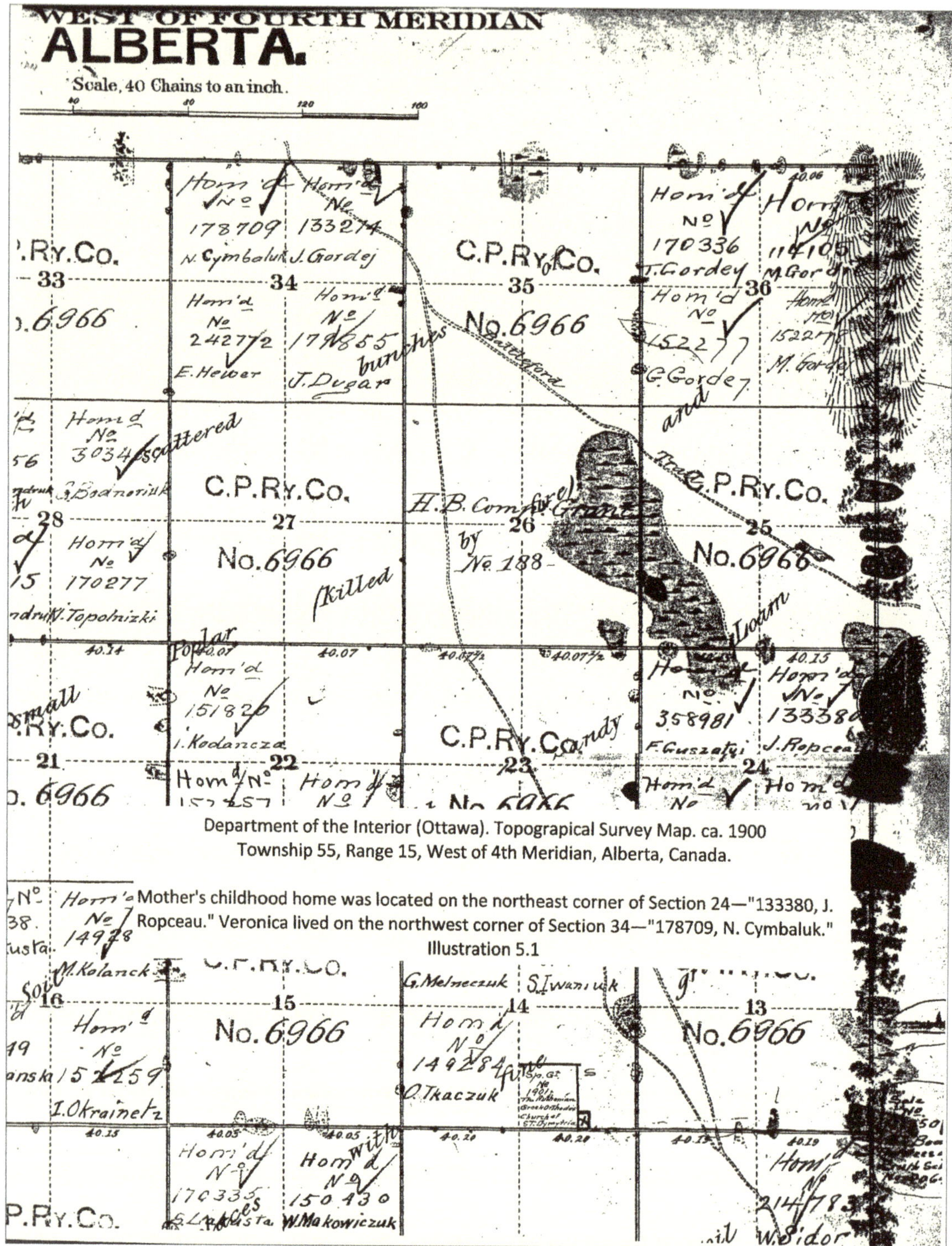

5.1 *Department of the Interior (Ottawa). Topographical Survey Map. ca. 1900. Township 55, range 15, West of 4th Meridian, Alberta, Canada. Mother's childhood home was located on the NE corner of Section 24—133380, J. Ropceau. Veronica lived on the NW corner of Section 34 — 178709, N. Cymbaluk.*

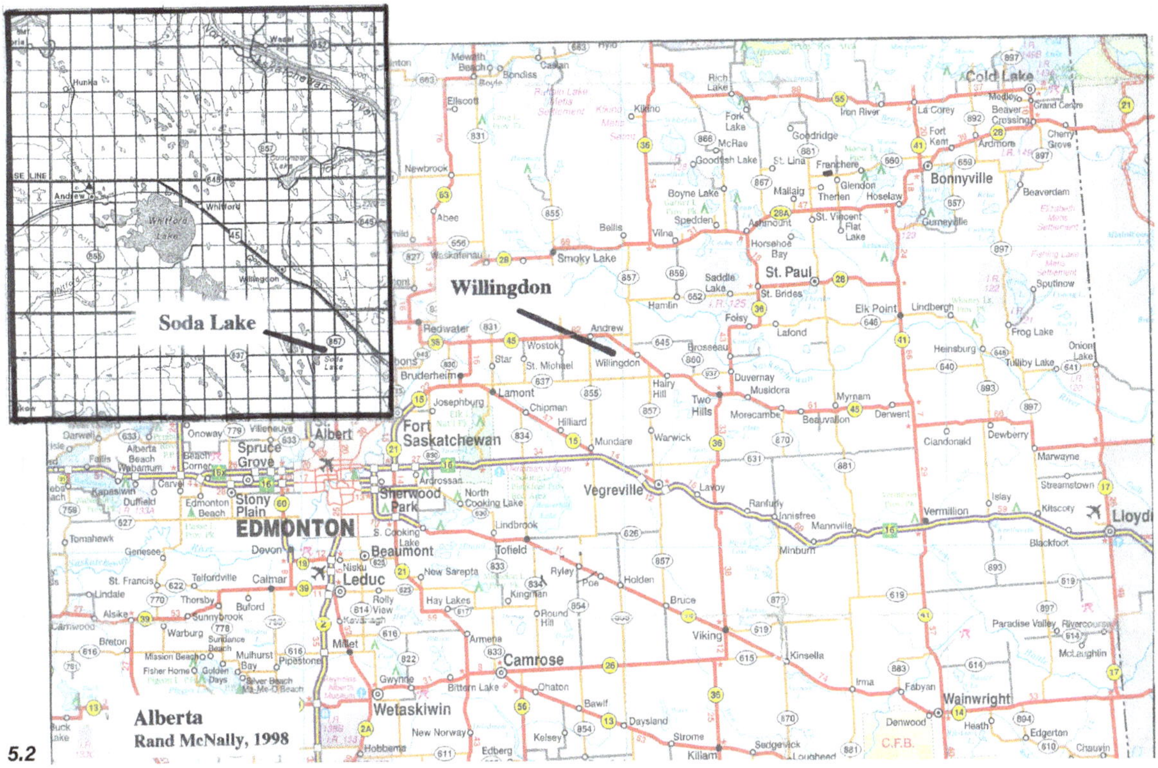

Soda Lake

Willingdon

Alberta
Rand McNally, 1998

5.2

5.2 *Contemporary map of Alberta, Canada (detail). Place names: Edmonton. Andrew. Mundare. Willingdon. Soda Lake.*

5.3a *1920 photo; Ropchan barn at Soda Lake farm. Built by a local craftsman in 1918.*

5.3b *1990s photo;*

5.3c *2004 photo. One wing of the barn has been removed. Standing in front of the barn (l-r) George Ropchan, his wife Vicki, their daughter Glorianne.*

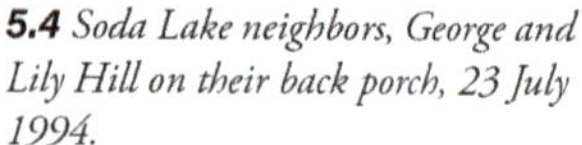

5.4 *Soda Lake neighbors, George and Lily Hill on their back porch, 23 July 1994.*

5.5 *Soda Lake/Pruth Community Hall, completed in 1921. Український Народній Дім імени Юрія Федьковича. Yuri Fedkovych Ukrainian National Home.*

5.6 *Holy Ascension Church, completed in 1932. Soda Lake.*

5.7a, 5.7b *Interior of Holy Ascension Church; during a contemporary service.*

5.8 *(foreground) Holy Ascension cemetery; (background) St. Demetrius cemetery. The two cemeteries face off across the road from each other.*

5.9 *Tkachuk Family Reunion, Saturday, July 23rd, 1994. Andrew, Alberta. Those few of us in attendance for the "Wasyl Ropchan & Magdalyna Tkachuk" line.*

5.10 *(bottom left) Entrance gates, Shandro St. Mary's Russo-Greek Orthodox Church. (bottom right) Wasyl Ropchan's marker at Shandro cemetery. Great-grandson Eugene Scraba Ropchan in attendance.*

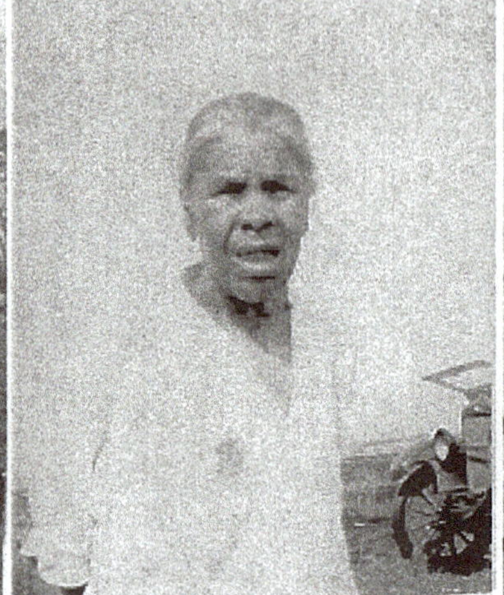

5.11 *Mrs. Maria Fegirchuk-Gordey-Ukrainetz-Ropchan.*

5.12 *Tkachuk Family Reunion, July 23, 1994, Andrew, Alberta. Behind the dancers, seated at the head table, are the Tkachuk elders.*

5.13 *Ruth Tkachuk, 1995. Edmonton, Alberta.*

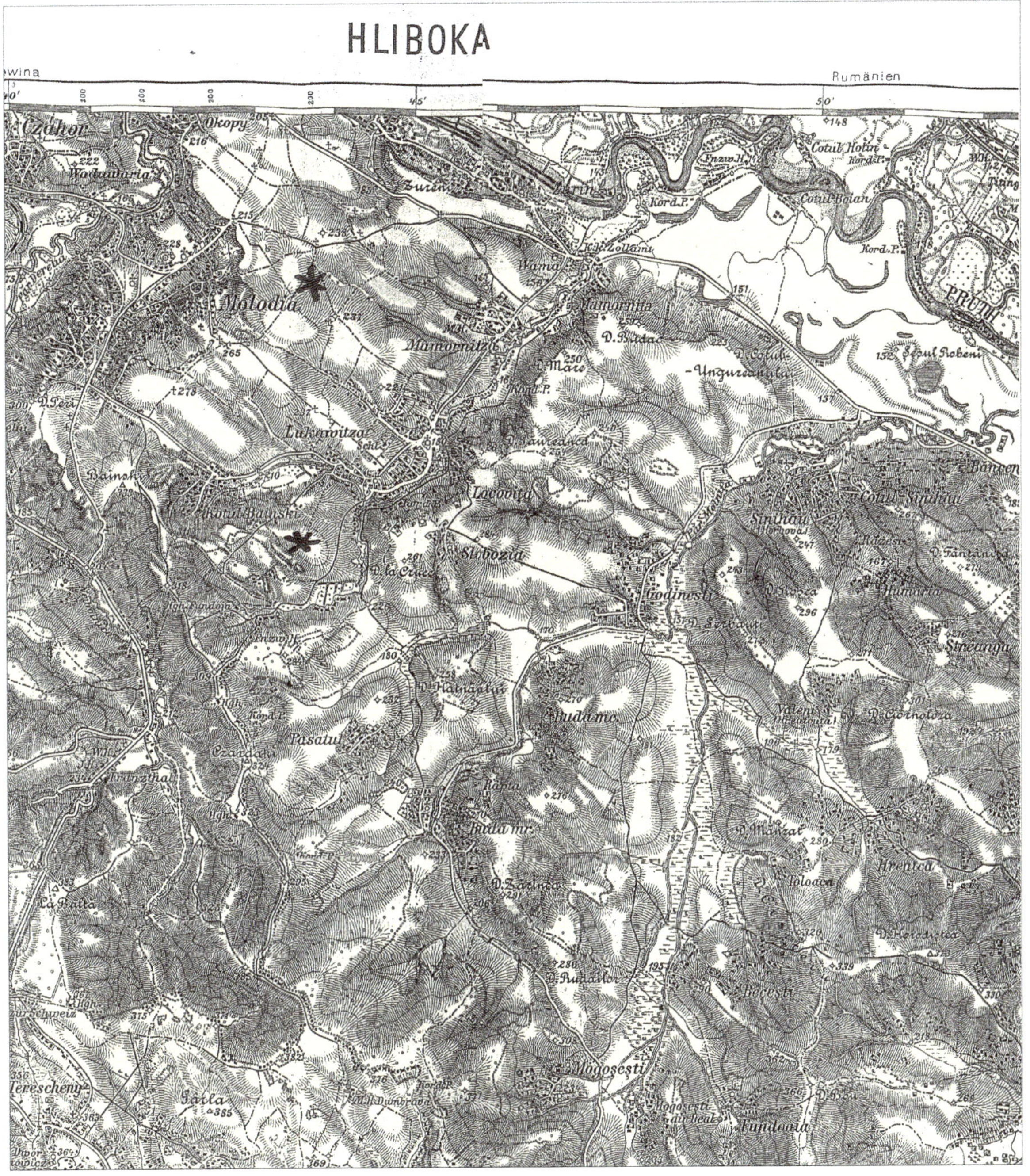

5.14a *Map of Bukovyna in Austria-Hungary (detail), 1894. The Ropchan-Tkachuk villages of Molodiia and Kotul Bainski. The Prut' [Pruth] River is visible to the NE.*

5.14b *Enlarged map detail of Molodiia and Kotul Bainski villages, showing their close proximity. Bukovyna, Austria-Hungary, 1894.*

Magdalyna and Wasyl
(Магдалина і Василь, Madeline and William)

Magdalyna Tkachuk
(Магдалина Ткачук)

Born: ca. 1857, Kotul Bainski
Married: ca. 1873
Immigr.: 1899, 30 April from Hamburg to NYC, 3-5 May, *S.S. Patria*
Died: 21 July 1905, Whitford, AB Canada
Buried: Kysylew "Pioneer" Cem.

Wasyl Ropchan
(Василь Ропчан)

Born: 22 March 1847, Molodiia
Married: ca. 1873
Immigr.: 1899, 30 April from Hamburg to NYC, 3-5 May, *S.S. Patria*
Died: 24 May 1919, Sunland area, AB, Canada
Bur.: Shandro, St. Mary's Russo-Greek

Margaret (?Jean?) (Маргарина)
b. ca. 1874, Molodiia
m. yes
d. in Molodiia area, Ukraine

John (Іван, *Ivan*)
b. 27 August 1875, Molodiia
Immigr. 1899, NYC, *S.S. Patria*
m. 7 June 1903, Wostok, AB, Canada; to Maria Scraba.
d. 13 March 1938, Vegreville, AB, Canada
bur. Vegreville, Riverside Cemetery

Elizaveta—"Sovena" (Єлизавета)
b. 1886, Molodiia
Immigr. 1899, NYC, *S.S. Patria*
m. August 1904 to Fred Kuhnke

Mary (Марія, *Mariia*)
b. 1887, Molodiia
Immigr. 1899, NYC, *S.S. Patria*
m. October 1906 to Dr. John Meyer

George (Григорій, *Hrehorii*)
b. 1889, 18 March, Molodiia
Immigr. 1899, NYC, *S.S. Patria*
m. 13 October 1913, Andrew, AB area to Sanda Zukiwsky
d. 1957
bur. Andrew, AB

Veronica (Веронія, *Veroniia*)
b. 23 March 1893, Molodiia
Immigr. 1899, NYC, *S.S. Patria*
m. ca. 1909-1911 to Nick Sembaliuk
d. 22 October 1913, Soda Lake, AB, Canada
bur. Borowych Church Cemetery, Plot #138.

5.15 *Family Tree of Magdalyna Tkachuk and Wasyl Ropchan.*

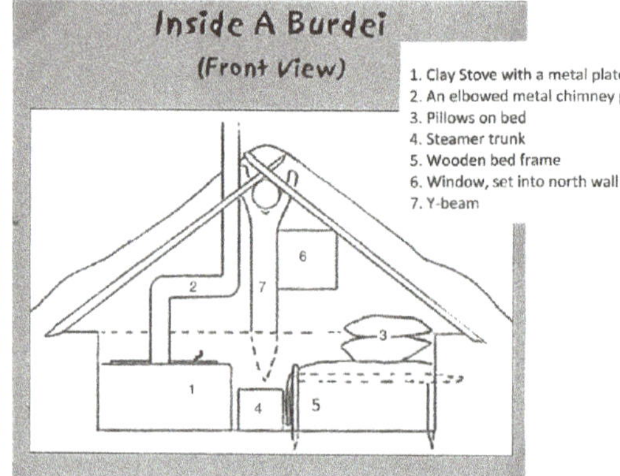

5.16 *(top, left) Photo of a reconstructed бурдей (burdei) at the Ukrainian Cultural Heritage Site, just east of Edmonton, Alberta.*

(top right) Schematic of burdei interior. The two sloping sides of the roof, composed of trimmed branches and grasses, rest upon a large central beam, set into two Y-shaped posts secured into the earth.

5.17 *(right) St. Pokrova Greek Orthodox Church at Borovich.*

(bottom) Borovich cemetery and Veronica Ropchan Sembaliuk's marker.

5.18 *Closer view of Veronica Ropchan Sembaliuk's marker. Her name, in Cyrillic, appears at the base.*

1 Interview with Ruth Tkachuk. Edmonton, Alberta, Canada. 18 July 1997.

2 Kathleen Norris, Cloister Walk (New York: Riverhead Books, 1996), 191.

3 Confusion continues to reign. I have taken the spelling "Magdalyna" because in my notes and files, several of the older interviewees, for example, Bill Ropchan, referred to her and wrote of her as "Magdalyna," and not "Margaret." Margaret appears on the death certificate, but that name would have been an anglicized version of whatever the family called her. In present-day Ukraine, the English equivalent of Magdalyna is Madeline. Quite lovely. My dear friends in Ukraine, Lyuda and Andriy, recently (2015) emailed that their brand new niece, a piece of perfection, has been named "Magdalyna."

4 Interview with Ruth Tkachuk. Edmonton, Alberta, Canada. 18 July 1997.

5 John Kelly, The Great Mortality: An Intimate History of the Black Death, the Most Devastating Plague of All (New York: Harper Collins Publishers, 2005), 190.

6 Magdalyna's and Wasyl's eldest child, daughter Margaret had married. It was incumbent upon her to stay behind with her husband. Thus Magdalyna and Wasyl travelled to the New World with five of their six children.

7 The S.S. Patria steamed across the Atlantic from April 30th to early May of 1899. Departure was from Hamburg, Germany. The S.S. Patria stopped in Boulogne, France and then continued on to New York. My thanks to family members, Alberta Scraba of Edmonton, AB and Eugene Ropchan of Surrey, BC, Canada, for finding this important detail.

8 "Supreme Court of the North-West Territories, No. 2826. Between ROBCZAN, Wasyl of Whitford, Plaintiff And LEPAGE, Louis of Fort Saskatchewan, Defendant." Wasyl sought to sue Mr. Lepage because he did not pay him the agreed-upon $20 for one month of farm labor. Lepage countered that he'd hired Wasyl for three months and planned to pay him at the end of that time, but Wasyl left after only one month of work. This caused Lepage to waste three days looking for a replacement. Then he had to pay the replacement $3 a day, which was more than he would have paid Wasyl under the original agreement. For his part, Wasyl mentioned in his suit that he had to travel 140 miles—70 miles one-way—to get to court in Edmonton, that this necessitated his being absent from home for eight days and that this was a hardship. Furthermore, he had to pay Philipp Mohr $8 for the purpose of interpreting for him.

9 Interview with George Gordey, Esther Gordey Bornec and Sophie Gordey Kowalski, Edmonton, Alberta, Canada. 18 July 1997.

10 The Sunland Area is north of Andrew, Alberta. It is where the Tkachuks and the Wasyl Ropchans first settled. It organized itself into the Bukowina School District No. 1162.

11 Interview with George Gordey, Esther Gordey Borynec and Sophie Gordey Kowalchuk, Edmonton, Alberta, Canada. 18 July 1997.

12 Taped interview with George Gordey, Esther Gordey Borynec and Sophie Gordey Kowalchuk, Edmonton, Alberta, Canada. 21 July 2000.

13 Taped interview with George Gordey, Esther Gordey Borynec and Sophie Gordey Kowalchuk, Edmonton, Alberta, Canada. 21 July 2000.

14 Kysylew Cemetery is Mrs. Maria Fegirchuk-Gordey-Ukrainetz-Ropchan's resting place. She occupies a spot at its southeast corner. Her marker reads "Okrainetz, b. Aug 6, 1853, d. 1932."

15 For the 1905 entry in her "journal," Mary Tkachuk Lichuk wrote "Auntie Margarina Ropchan died in fall. There was no church from which to bury her. Her body was taken to the cemetery by oxen—I rode in the wagon too. The oxen were owned by Mr. Wowk."

16 Married in October of 1906, Mary and her husband also headed for British Columbia.

17 Taped interview with Alex Ropchan, West Palm Beach, Florida. 19 April 1996.

18 Interview with Ruth Tkachuk, Edmonton, Alberta, Canada. 18 July 1997.

19 Interview with Lena Tkachuk Waselasko, her home north of Andrew, Alberta, Canada. 16 May 1995.

20 Interview with Ruth Tkachuk, Edmonton, Alberta, Canada. 17 August 2000.

21 There are no police records of the event. If there once were documents, they did not end up in the Provincial Archives of Alberta. According to Provincial librarians/archivists, Veronica's murder happened before records were kept on the semi-wild prairie lands.

22 The grave marker—standing approximately 3.5 feet or a little over a meter high in the northwest corner of St. Pokrova Greek Orthodox Church at Borovich cemetery— consists of the traditional arched tomb stone topped by a four-square Christian cross (not a cross-barred Orthodox cross). The marker stands on a square stone base inscribed along one edge with Veronica's name, "Verony" [Вероніи]. The marker itself, inscribed in Cyrillic, states the following: "Forever Remembered/ Veronica (Verony)/ Dear Wife of/ Nicolai Sembaliuk/Born 20 March 1893/Died 22 October 1913/God took them to himself." The "them" refers to mother and infant.

CHAPTER 6

MAGDALYNA
Магдалина
–Nul sum–

"You couldn't get your bearings—or, rather, you had no sooner selected them than they went absent without leave."
—Bad Land[1]

For nearly a year after the Tkachuk Reunion, my single raison *d'être* for getting back to Canada was to interview Lena. I thought she could tell me something. I wrote to her daughters in Edmonton. I wrote to my shirttail cousins around Andrew. Letters came back full of vague statements. Lena spoke only Ukrainian. Her home was in a remote place. Her retired farmer son—he'd taken over her farming operation—struggling with lung cancer, a heavy smoker and no favorite among his city-sisters, was living with her. Nothing was posed as a complete impediment to my visiting Lena, but the light was not exactly green either.

July, a year earlier, Lena had been sitting sharp-eyed and silent—peregrine-like— at the head table, watching a hundred-and-fifty or so Tkachuks celebrate their reunion. When she moved about the community hall, I could see that she was tall, slender, sinewy. In spite of her stylish silk sheath, a history of field work was readable in the way she held herself, in her hands. Here was a woman who knew how to hill potatoes, hitch a team of horses to a plow or to drive a tractor. Parts of her face were burned purple by outdoor work in minus-cold. At the time, I was put off by her singular cheerlessness, the severity of her gaze. She was not welcoming.

Only later and far away in California, did I understand who Lena was. Her parents, Petro and Domka, had taken the quarter section immediately south of Magdalyna and Wasyl's. Lena still lived on that quarter—SE14-57-16.W4M. This made her as rare as a robin in winter in Alberta. Few descendants of original homesteaders were on the quarters their elders settled.

Then I received T*he Tkachuk Family* reunion proceedings. In it, there were many photos I'd never seen. There was one of Lena, taken when she was sixteen. (Illustration 6.1) She is standing with her parents in front of their formidable *khata*, the newest family house on SE14-57-16.W4M. She wears a traditional Bukovynian costume—embroidered white linen blouse, dark wool wrap skirt, intricately woven wide belt, a wool jerkin or vest— "Sunday best," and unsmiling, carries her youthful comeliness on an already hardy frame. Lena's older sister, Mary-the-journal-writer, is not in the scene.

No green light? Uncharacteristically, I refused to take polite dithering or "no" for an answer. I simply willed myself to Lena's wee bit of a house above Andrew and Whitford Lake. To her credit, Roberta, the wife of second cousin George who lived in the vicinity of Lena, offered me her home and her copious community connections. I established a research base in Roberta's spotless spare bedroom, and found myself pleasantly surrounded by her porcelain angel collection. After a bit of negotiation, Lena's nearest neighbor—Cindy, a Ukrainian-Canadian—agreed to act as a language intermediary. One evening, 7:00pm the appointed time, I met Cindy at Lena's back porch and together we climbed the steps to her backdoor.

I was so intent on meeting Lena, on setting her at ease so that we might talk, that I failed to notice—standing solid to the west of Lena's present wood-frame tidbit—the formidable *khata*, the one in the photo. (6.1) Built in 1905, the year of Magdalyna's death, it was all sparkling adobe and signal to the hopes and success of Lena's parents. Of it, journal-writer-Mary says, "No livestock was housed here"—a reference to several desperate winters of living in a *burdei*, in uncomfortable proximity to a nevertheless warming cow. As for the rest of Lena's property, I did notice the cluster of sagging sheds inconveniently threatening rusted farm machinery. There were also farm buildings fallen into piles of lumber. There was a field yet-to-be prepared and planted. The line from the film *Dances With Wolves* came to mind, "Not much of a goin' concern."

Just inside Lena's cottage was a mudroom for boots and heavy outerwear. Sensibly, it blocked cold from reaching the kitchen. A door opened into the all-white kitchen where the air—permeated by the aroma of boiled potatoes and sausage—was warm, moist and stale. Crowded and elfin, the kitchen held one cupboard bursting with English bone china and crockery. Large pots covered a small stove. A water bucket with a dipper sat on the adjacent oil cloth-covered table. I took this to be a sign that there was no running water in the house. Fine and prosaic mixed together with ease.

Passing Lena's teacup of a bedroom on the way to the living room, I caught a glimpse of a quilt-covered bed. It gave me hope, for if she were a quilter, peacefully stitching scraps of cotton together into blocks, we had something in common. Once in the living room, I could see it contained an alcove—a booth with built-in seats in a windowed bay, perhaps a breakfast nook, with a superb view of her prairie quarter. I rightly guessed that she appreciated the warming sun in the alcove.

As for the line-of-view landscape from Lena's alcove, undistinguished monotony might begin a description. Surveyors from the 1880s and 1890s wrote, "willow scrub;" "rolling land;" "open prairie with hay marshes;" "scattered bluffs of poplar, willow and scrub;" "sand or clay subsoil;" "willow and poplar killed by fire" on their topographical maps for the Department of the Interior back in Ottawa. A 21st century traveler passing through the area, the far eastern edge of the County of Lamont, will strain to fasten upon landmarks—a lone poplar tree surrounded by field, a solitary boulder at road's edge, a line of pines planted as a windbreak—a reminder that once, nearby was a farm.

Place names such as "Andrew" or "Whitford" are equally undistinguished. (6.2) They give no hint of the color of the country. Early on, it was about the varmints, those furry creatures that thrived among the grasses, among the scrawny poplars, in the sloughs and along the North Saskatchewan River. The players were the Plains Cree, the Blackfoot, the French, the Métis or "half-breeds," and the English. Selling and stealing was the business at hand, more commonly referred to as "The Fur Trade." For example, in 1812, the North-Westers passed through the Whitford Lake area "with 200,000 pounds sterling worth of raw furs which they had stolen from John Jacob Astor at the mouth of the Columbia River."[2]

In the 1870s, the Blackfoot, moving north to escape the ravages of smallpox, encountered a party of Cree camped on the shore of Rush Lake, an arm of Whitford Lake. The Cree men were on an island in Rush Lake "gathering eggs."[3] The Blackfoot stormed the Cree camp, exclusively populated by Cree women and children, who wisely and immediately took refuge in the water, while their enemies secured all the Cree horses. The Cree rallied, but the Blackfoot were able to hold their position. At nightfall the Blackfoot slipped away, horses and all. According to the local source, "as far as is known nobody was hurt in the foray and the horses were recovered some two years after."[4]

In the early 1880s, the Saulteaux Indians established a home on the western shore of Whitford Lake. But they left when, in 1885, the Métis and the Anglos had a falling out. Dubbed the Louis Riel Rebellion, the "rebellion" was a series of Métis battles for independence: the Battle of Duck Lake, the Battle of Fish Creek, the Battle of Cut Knife, the Battle of Loon Lake among them, with the Métis leader, Riel as catalyst.

Phillip and Andrew Whitford were brothers who served as Dominion of Canada guides during the Rebellion. For service to the crown—that is, for helping to vanquish the Métis, the Métis effort to preserve Métis culture, the Métis desire for a place of their own—the Whitfords had bodies of water and hamlets named for them. Large, shallow Whitford Lake, in reality a giant slough, is named in their honor. Andrew Whitford received two quarter-sections—his "military homestead"—of which the southeast quarter became the site for the town of Andrew, the place Lena frequented to buy Stawnichy sausage or Thousand Island salad dressing.

When, in the 1890s, the four Tkachuk families converged on this area of recently gone Blackfoot, Cree, fur traders, French and Métis, they established adjacent homesteads on one complete surveyed section of prairie. (6.3) This is nothing short of extraordinary. That four siblings—they did not arrive concurrently— snapped up four quarters on the same section, as a kind of "Tkachuk neighborhood," hinted at cooperation, diligence, foresight and luck.

Why extraordinary? Every other section was assigned to either government or railroad use, as the northern plains were gridded into ranges, sections and quarter sections. (6.4) What was left over got claimed willy-nilly by the new arrivals—as fast as they could walk the fifty or sixty miles out of Edmonton and pull up a choice marker to indicate that the quarter was "spoken for." There was no guarantee that relatives or former neighbors could live side-by-side, quarter-to-quarter. Theoretically, the Tkachuks' fortuitous proximity meant that, when possible, each could, help the other out. It also meant that between households, everyone knew everyone else's business.

I don't fully remember the introductory pleasantries at Lena's, for I think they were awkward. She sat in a cushiony armchair directly across from me at the nook-edge of her living room. Cindy sat next to me. Lena's son smoked his cigarettes somewhere in the background. The light faded. The room grew darker. I tried to explain to her how we were connected, that we were indeed related. She did not quite believe me, but she enjoyed studying me, observing my efforts to communicate. Did she remember Veronica? Did she remember Wasyl? What about John who had married Maria? Round and round we went, "No, I was too young to remember. That was long ago. I have no recollection," her staccato Ukrainian filling the room. For my part, I refused to believe that she could no longer remember any of them—Magdalyna, Wasyl, John, Sovena, Mary, George, Veronica. (5.15)

Months after my visit with Lena, when I read the relevant parts of her sister's journal, I found it troubling that there were so few references to Magdalyna and Wasyl.[5] When neighbors helped Lena's parents, Mary recorded their names—for example, Ivan Wowk or George and Zahary Melnychuk. The Wowks and the Melnychuks lived several quarters away. Mary also mentioned her uncle and aunt—Mychailo and Axenia—living catty-corner to her parents. (6.3) But Wasyl and Magdalyna, homesteading on the adjacent quarter immediately to the north of Petro and Domka, are never anywhere noted as helping Mary and Lena's parents. Perhaps there was some sort of invisible barrier between Lena's family and that of Magdalyna and Wasyl.

Thanks to Mary and her journal, a picture of the "pioneer" years on Section 14, the NE, SE, NW, and SW quarters, emerged. All those Tkachuks! In mid-July of 1898, there they are, like a flock of Cedar Waxwings landing on a berry-laden Mountain Ash. There is considerable hopping from branch to branch and berry-cluster to berry-cluster, before all are settled. At SE are Petro and thirty-four year old Domka. At NW are Mychailo, twenty-five year old Axenia, a four-year old daughter and a weeks-old baby. At SW, a Tkachuk brother moves out, a cousin moves in. In June 1899, they are joined on NE by Wasyl and Magdalyna, who is the matron among the women at forty-two. Whether SE, SW or NW, they find themselves sitting, walking, sleeping on a 160-acre square of wide-open, un-broken prairie and slough under 180-degrees of summer sky.

Days of endless sunshine grace them. By July and August, the sun sets at midnight and begins to rise at 3:30am. Why sleep? Who can? Every creature, every plant seems to understand that this intense burst of summer and light must not be squandered. Work probably begins immediately. Before fall, everyone has a *burdei*-dugout in some favorable spot—on the backside of a protective rise or at the edge of a stand of poplars.

Mychailo and Axenia begin on an infelicitous note. Their *burdei* leaks "so badly every time it rained that a one-room thatch-roofed log house—[completely above ground]—was built the same summer" to replace it.[6] This would have taken jaw-clenching resolve. For procuring the logs and setting them square; preparing, mixing and applying the adobe; locating, cutting, transporting, binding and orienting the thatch to the roof beams—all this would have been done in a race against time and against exhaustion.

By 1911, this log house must be abandoned, as it "proved to be too close to an existing pond. The muskrats tunneled their way into the cellar, flooding it with water and stealing the winter's supply of potatoes."[7] Another *khata*—covered with a secure shingled roof—is built on yet higher ground. This sturdy structure stands to this day, surrounded in summer by a photo-perfect sea of sulphur-yellow Canola.

Meanwhile, stews and porridges are prepared—campfire style outdoors; gardens are readied; perhaps adobe ovens are built outside to bake bread and to heat casseroles of cabbage and potatoes, or for a refreshing change, of potatoes and cabbage. Anything within reach that might add to comfort is put in place. By September there are hard frosts.

By mid-October, the snow begins to powder down. When no more can be done on the land, the men leave for paying jobs with the railroad or in the coalmines. Work is more or less available around Calgary, Lethbridge, Drumheiller, or Medicine Hat. The men must walk hundreds of miles to get to these places. Their muscle labor does provide the hard cash needed to purchase farm equipment: a steel plow to cut through the tough sod, powerful horses—Belgians, Clydesdales or Percherons—to pull the steel plow. Scrawny runt ponies and wooden plows—Old World necessities—simply can't get the New World job finished.

November. Magdalyna is on her own in the *burdei* with the younger children—Sovena, Mary, George and Veronica. Around them roam moose, deer, black and brown bears, beaver, muskrats, weasels, minks, ermine, badgers, porcupines, red fox, coyotes and an occasional lynx. Far from familiar village life where neighbors are mere meters away, domestic animals are taken for granted and outdoor sounds are reassuring, Magdalyna is probably coping with her solitude. Perhaps she slips into sadness when she remembers her eldest daughter in *Kotul Bainski*. They will never embrace again. Perhaps there are moments when she can visit with the younger Axenia or Domka and they with her, but what with the cold, distance, the demands of children and day-to-day survival, perhaps not.

December. Unlike that of the gentler latitude of Bukovyna, the cold of this new place must be learned; it is drier, deeper, searing. Frozen snow-covered ground extends in every direction for hundreds of miles. No villages interrupt the sweep. Darkness comes early in the afternoon and clings tenaciously to morning. When the sun appears, it rises along a course parallel to the ground, not high into the sky. Some mornings, the air is festive with glitter, sparkling particles of frozen water—microscopic bits— shimmering through the light. On days of preposterous cold, minus forty, the sun, seen through a mist of frozen air, has a rainbow halo around it—a complete circle of sundogs. Children must be watched and constantly accounted for.

Mary tells us that that first winter, her father and a neighbor set out for supplies to Edmonton with two horses. The North Saskatchewan River, a frozen interstate highway, was the easiest route. Along the way, Petro suffered frostbite. Fortunately, what with the volume of traffic—all those other long-distance shoppers walking on the river—someone who could help, encountered him. The Samaritan was able to carry Petro to the edge of Edmonton where he was hospitalized; a "large toe was amputated."[8] This early introduction to the new-style cold, left Petro compromised. The horses did not survive. Gradually, more of the heavy farm work fell onto the shoulders of Mary, Lena and their mother.

Hardship clung to the Tkachuks. Two years in the *burdei*. Mary-the-journalist's August birth coincided with its becoming uninhabitable. Summer rains flooded the *burdei*; Domka was forced to step from bench to bench to stay out of water. Axenia came to Domka's rescue and took mother and child, as well as the family cow, to her drier—on higher ground—shingle-roofed *khata*. With the help of neighbors—neither Magdalyna, nor Wasyl are mentioned—Mary's parents constructed their own first *khata*.

On Wasyl and Magdalyna's slough-pocked quarter, surely similar trials accrued. But there was more adult manpower available to make short work of them. The family quickly graduated from *burdei* misery to a two-room *khata*, which when finished, provided superb protection from the elements, not to mention a modicum of sanity. Their Homestead Application reveals that in four years, Wasyl et al had constructed a temporary *burdei*, a semi-permanent *khata*—14 by 18 feet, a stable for thirteen cattle, a granary, a pig pen for ten pigs; they had located water and dug a well; they had sixteen acres of wheat or rye or barley growing; and Magdalyna was tending a kitchen garden of potatoes, cabbages, carrots, dill, and poppies, neatly and necessarily fenced to keep fur-covered vegetarians out.

Then, like a bolt out of the blue, Magdalyna became an item. Mary tells us, "Auntie

Margaret Ropchan died in fall. There was no church from which to bury her. Her body was taken to the cemetery by oxen—I rode in the wagon too. The oxen were owned by Mr. Wowk." This is the entry in Mary's journal for 1905.[9] A month-shy of her fifth birthday, Mary obviously knows of Magdalyna. She understands their relationship; Magdalyna is "auntie." This is Mary's sole reference to her Tkachuk aunt. In life, Magdalyna must have been a distant figure.

Mary's yearly log is compiled from the vantage point of her adult self, looking back. Its accuracy comes from what her child-mind has retained. For example, riding in the wagon with the coffin in its wagon bed is a big deal for a four-year-old. What child doesn't delight in the experience of bouncing along on the elevated seat of a vehicle, watching the world go by from such a perspective? At the same age, I certainly loved to stand on the front seat of my father's Studebaker and study the trees or the barns hurtling past as he drove from little town to little town on his business calls. Yes, this was in a time before seat belts and car seats for children. And yes, on one occasion my father hit the brakes and I went flying into the dash and cut my lower lip.

Of course, the oxen loom large in child-Mary's memory. They are huge two-ton creatures, great sweet plodding beasts—memorable in their own right— and have impressed her so thoroughly, that she remembers who owned them. It is not her father, but Mr. Wowk. Perhaps, too, adult-Mary writes to signal that "Auntie Margaret's" funeral procession has been facilitated by both family and community—as it should be in her mind.

The singular detail, the one that Mary includes after announcing the death, is that "there was no church from which to bury her." Was Mary struck by this as a child? As an adult, Mary would have found this deficiency unsettling. "No church" meant that Magdalyna's body was buried without the ministrations of a priest. In other words, Magdalyna's grave was not properly "sealed." Magdalyna, who had died before the pioneers had a chance to establish their churches and attendant graveyards, was interred in some sort of burial plot an oxen-plod away from her quarter section—a place of expediency.

As for the inaccuracies in Mary's journal, they are there too. The night I sat at Lena's feet, I had the advantage of only one document: Magdalyna's death certificate. I'd unearthed it at the Provincial Archives. The unadorned certificate—half a standard piece of printer paper—answered some questions, but left many more. The "informant" who filled in the spaces of the slip—the individual who apprised the "Victoria District of the North-West Territories of Canada" of the death—was the very "Reverend M. Skibinsky."[10] "At Wostok this 27th day of July 1905," he wrote.[11] It was six days after the fact. The fourteen miles Wasyl traversed to get to Skibinsky at Wostok, suggests he went to some pains to establish a record for his wife's untimely death.

The full name of the deceased, recorded on the certificate, was "Margaret Robchan" —the first, an Anglicizing attempt; the second an approximation; her date of death, the

"21st day of July 1905;" her age at the time of death, 48 years; the place of her death, "Whitford"—somewhere in the vicinity of the now-gone-hamlet of Whitford or of Whitford Lake. These would have been habitations near her quarter section—official places with names on the 1905 map. The document goes on to note that Magdalyna was born in "Austria"—this, a reference to the Austrian-Hapsburg Empire, that she was "married—wife of a farmer" and of the "Russian Orthodox" faith.[12] She was probably Ukrainian Orthodox, but Skibinsky, an agent of the Russian Orthodox church, no doubt wanted to claim her soul for his flock.

Near the bottom of the certificate is a line: "Name of Physical (if any) attending Fatal Illness." The shorthand would be "Doctor in attendance?" The line is blank on Magdalyna's certificate. Wasyl simply reports to Skibinsky that his wife's cause of death is "Asthma." With no alternative, the priest takes him at his word. Magdalyna has already been buried somewhere close to NE 14-57-16. W4M.

Asthma? There is no grain of family gossip about such a physical infirmity, nor does anyone among us suffer from this specific malady. Is it possible that a forty-eight year old woman, mother of six healthy children—two of whom are on their way to making her a grandmother—a woman who has struggled to hold onto a farm during a war, who has packed up her village home, crossed an ocean and a continent to build a new home in wilderness, would suddenly fall dead from an asthma attack?

When I mentioned that Magdalyna's place of burial remained a mystery to the Gordey siblings, a chorus of "let's go find her" rose from their collective. Mary's journal entry allowed that Magdalyna's "body was taken to the cemetery by oxen," but "that there was no church from which to bury her." A cemetery, but no church. Curious. Was Magdalyna buried in an established cemetery? At the time of her death, the church at Shandro (5.10) was up and running, but a goodly distance from Section 14. I'd checked the Shandro church burial records. No Magdalyna. I had no success locating the Deacon of the Wostok church, and consequently had no access to that church's records. The Kysylew church was closer to Magdalyna's quarter.

A fine August Sunday morning—it happened to be my birthday, the Gordeys and I headed out of Edmonton. With John Jr. Jr.—the son of the first John Jr.—driving his van, we streaked along the dirt roads above Whitford Lake, drowning clouds of mosquitoes in waves of dust. We scoured the cemetery at Kysylew for a marker. No Magdalyna. We checked the framed cemetery chart on a wall in the church vestibule. No Magdalyna. A parishioner, among the last to leave the church after the day's service, helpfully offered that although the Kysylew Church community existed in 1905, neither the present structure nor the cemetery did.

We didn't want to give up. It was a splendid day to be in the country: cloudless sky, golden horizon line, canola, wheat, wild botanicals. We were so close. Magdalyna spent her New World life—those six years—only seven quarters away. On a whim or simply out of a habit of gregariousness, John Jr. Jr. pulled up alongside another parishioner walking to his car. He rolled down the window and hallooed, "Can you think of where we could find someone buried around here in 1905?" [13]

"Have you tried the *pioneer* cemetery?" came the answer. We hit the dirt again, raising more plumes of dust, vanquishing more mosquitoes. We found it. NW14-57-16.W4M., the Kysylew pioneer burial ground lies at the northwest corner of Mychailo and Axenia's former quarter. It is one of the places where early Orthodox inhabitants were buried, before developing communities had the chance to erect their churches and plat their cemeteries.

A discreet square plot, the lumpy ground fenced-in, un-mowed so that the prairie grasses are tall and a wild rose bush grows rampantly, the willy nilly cemetery is remarkable for its green abandon. (6.5) In the center of the tract stands a single granite marker. Substantial. It can be seen from a distance—that is, if one is looking for it. One side of the stone slab reads "In memory of the pioneers and their children now resting in the cemetery. They toiled the land." (6.6)

On the granite's verso side these names are listed:

BABY ANDRIUK
TANASI DANYLUK
ELENA EWANCHUK
EWAN EWANCHUK
KOSHMAN
GAWRYLO ODYNSKY
ALEXA OSTASHEK
HRETSKO OSTASHEK
BASEL PUCHALSKY
SANDA SEMENIUK
OLENA TKACHUK
TSIA TKACHUK
DOMKA WOWK
TODER WOWK

Magdalyna's name is not among them, though it could be hiding behind the designation "Olena Tkachuk." Back at the Tkachuk Reunion in Andrew, no one could remember or agree on what the woman was called—Magdalena? Olena? Margarina? Odakia? Edoxia? Margaret?

It stands to reason that this unkempt burial ground, for those pioneers who died before most church cemeteries existed, might be Magdalyna's final resting place. It was a short distance, one quarter away from her home. It was an easy trip for two oxen pulling a wagon carrying a pine box. It was a direct route along the fence line that delineated the north edge of Wasyl and Magdalyna's quarter, as well as Mychailo and Axenia's.

Driving away from Kysylew's pioneer cemetery, John Gordey, Jr. Jr. extended his arm out of the van's window to point out the barbed-wire fence skirting the field. He grinned wide, "That's why we say 'ghosts walk the fence line'." I knew he was serious. The line runs true and straight to that square on the map, those 160 acres that comprised the brief latter years of Magdalyna's life and death. I can imagine that her restless spirit walks it on occasion.

As I sat with Lena in the dusk, calling out the names of her uncles, aunts and cousins, finally and magically the colloquial diminutive for Elizabeth—Sovena— registered with Lena. "Sovena, Sovena," she uttered the name in an incantatory manner. "There were two girls," she added. "One married a doctor." She was referring to Mary, who married a dentist.

"Did Sovena ever have children?" Lena asked. As events played out, Lena would have lost touch with Sovena after Sovena moved to British Columbia. I explained that Sovena had adopted Veronica's surviving son, Freddie. "I heard a rumor that he had killed her by kneeling on her chest," Lena said. "Veronica?" I prompted. It was counter to all the family stories I had heard about Veronica and Nick Sembaliuk, and I wanted to make sure we were talking about the same woman.

"No," Lena shot back. Again, trying to clarify what I was hearing, I described what I'd been told from multiple sources about Veronica, that her husband had a reputation for cruel and abusive behavior, that he'd pushed her into their root cellar, that her fall was so damaging that she miscarried and died in a pool of blood or that she and her child died from the blow of the fall. "No," Lena said, "the mother."

Again, I pressed her about Veronica and again, Lena pushed back, "With the other woman, it was the knees." There was no equivocation. Lena insisted we were discussing two separate incidents—the one, involving Veronica; the other, involving Magdalyna. The more I suggested she was scrambling Veronica's history, the more adamant Lena became that she was talking about the mother, Wasyl's wife, not his daughter. We went back and forth over the terms "knees" (колінa, kolina) and "cellar" (льох, l'okh). I could hear that Lena was enunciating in Ukrainian precisely and for my benefit, indeed, she was speaking volubly, her Ukrainian tumbling all about. No more uncomfortable silences.

"They had gone to a wedding," she said. "They came home late. He was drinking. In bed, he pummeled her with his knees on her chest. He pushed all the air out of her lungs. She died. It was soon after they got to Canada."[14] That was the story Lena heard and held, that Wasyl asphyxiated his wife. There was no coroner. Wasyl just told the priest what to write.

The story, the rumor might have traveled to Lena's parents, then on to her, from family members in the house at the time—Magdalyna's children: Mary, George and Veronica. To the end, Wasyl's daughter-in-law, Maria, refused to speak to him, to let him into her home, to interact with him in any way on his infrequent visits to her and John's quarter at Soda Lake. Her children were perplexed by this. Wasyl always brought candy for them; they remembered him for it. As for their grandmother, Magdalyna, not one of Maria's eleven children knew anything of her, not even her name. Magdalyna: *nul sum*.

That black night, when I learned the distinction between "cellar" and "knees," I was aghast. I had tried and tried to shake the veracity of Lena's story. She refused to be budged. Her eyes were clear and looking straight into mine. She spoke with ease. Her Ukrainian, my pidgen-Ukrainian, we were communicating effortlessly. Another murder, or the strong possibility of it—it was the last thing I had expected.

That Magdalyna disappeared, that no one wondered after her, that no one spoke her name until it was forgotten—here was a woman who truly got buried. What does it mean or say, to lose track of a woman—just a blank space in the family book—the mother of six children? Surely she possessed a few inspired sparks—when and how to find the most flavorful mushrooms, how to bake a fine batch of bread, or how to execute a tricky cross-stitch pattern at the neck-opening of a chemise; there had to have been sparks.

Magdalyna and Veronica—mother and daughter—those two parts of a fraught whole. My mother's mother knew Magdalyna. She knew Veronica. About them, she remained silent. My mother's father, son and brother to these women, remained silent as well. Was Magdalyna's value so mean to deserve erasure or a kind of deletion from memory? If the future is constructed devoid of the past, then from where have we come? Perhaps I am a subtle variant of a warthog or a fruit bat. What wisdom have we acquired? Might there not be some slight unease at such familial slippage? There is no peace in these thoughts.

It came time to leave. I closed the back door of Lena's house, moved down the wooden steps from the porch and rounded the corner of a wall to get to my car. The horizon—end to end—was on fire. I gazed at it, uncomprehending, shocked. I shook my head. I shook it again. No, the horizon was truly on fire. I could smell it, the smoke of burning grasses. It wasn't just me trying to absorb violent death among the women in my bloodline. I confess that I was still carrying Lena's "fire" over what she knew to be Magdalyna's fate. Instead, the conflagration was the result of a rather clever farmer trying to hide the very illegal act of burning stubble off his fields under darkness of night. Guess he thought no one would spot a horizon on fire.

Not long after Lena passed away, my husband and I drove out to see her quarter. Her son had pre-deceased her, and her daughters in town had sold the quarter to another farmer. I wanted to remember Lena. It was January. White. Still. A minus-cold. When we arrived to the intersection where Lena's former place was, the land was there, but all the buildings were gone—scraped into a heap of big splinters near the intersection. Even the stately *khata*—a historic structure, the familiar backdrop for photos of Petro, Domka and Lena—was gone. Corporate Canola farming: immaculate fields.

Dispirited and sliding along on a snow-ice-gravel surface, we drove towards Wasyl and Magdalyna's quarter. An unusually lofty poplar somehow allowed to remain at road's edge came into view. Near its top was a white shape, out-of-place. We stopped in the middle of the road. There was no traffic, not for several leagues. We gazed up at the bare tree. My husband decided that the baffling shape was a white plastic bag caught high in the poplar's branches. I thought not, but couldn't make out what the thing was.

Then it took wing, gliding like a Stealth Bomber to a lone tree in Wasyl and Magdalyna's former field. Instantly, we realized we were in the presence of an Arctic Snowy Owl, a pure white male. He was two feet tall. Big bird. I couldn't calculate the wingspan, for he quickly moved to a second tree in the distance. From perch-to-perch, the owl was hunting for field mice, voles, rabbits—any small mammal that had the machismo to scurry across a snow-covered field.

For the two of us, seeing the Snowy Owl—well, it might as well have been a unicorn. Winter doldrums rolled away. Of course, bad jokes about white plastic bags went on for some time. On another note, I felt better knowing that that magnificent creature frequented Magdalyna's quarter, off-season.

6.1 (top) l-r: Parents, Petro and Domka Tkachuk, seated to the left of their standing daughter, the 16-year old, Lena Tkachuk [Waselashko].

(bottom) An unidentified neighbor standing with Lena and Domka in front of the new khata, its roof first thatched, then later shingled.

Kysyliw Pioneer "Cemetary" (in reality, a burial ground)

Mychailo Tkachuk & Axenia NW.14.57.16	Wasyl Ropchan & Magdalyna (Tkachuk) Ropchan NE.14.57.16
Konstantyn Tkachuk SW.14.57.16	Petro Tkachuk & Domka SE.14.57.16 (Lena's & Mary's parents)

6.3

6.3 *"Sunland District," north of Andrew, Alberta. Section 14.57.16 around 1900 and ... the Tkachuk's fortuitous proximity.*

6.2 *Alberta map (detail, opposite), showing the lands to the east of Edmonton and to the northwest of Vegreille. Place names around Whitford Lake. Note: "Soda Lake" south of Willingdon.*

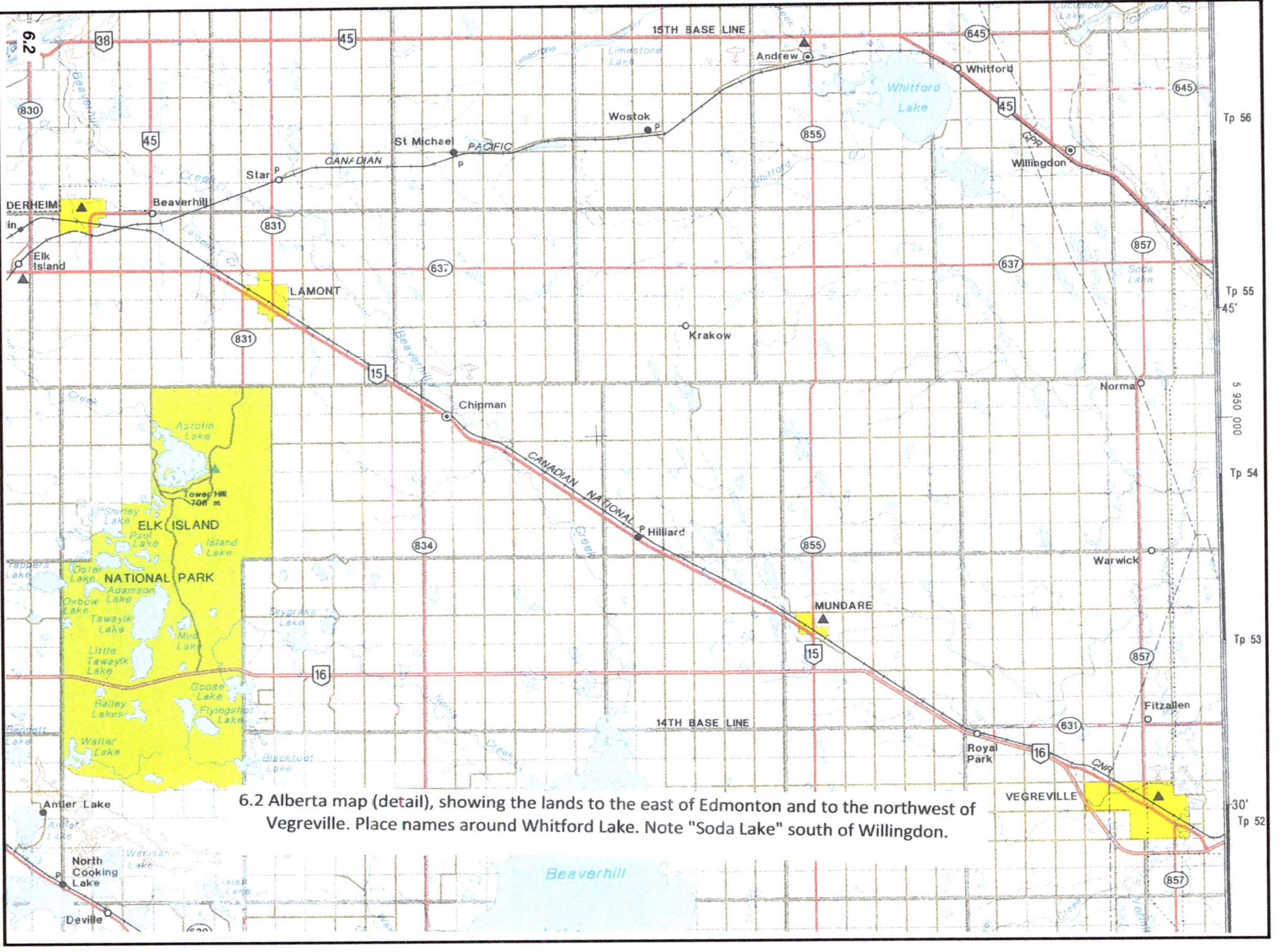

6.2 Alberta map (detail), showing the lands to the east of Edmonton and to the northwest of Vegreville. Place names around Whitford Lake. Note "Soda Lake" south of Willingdon.

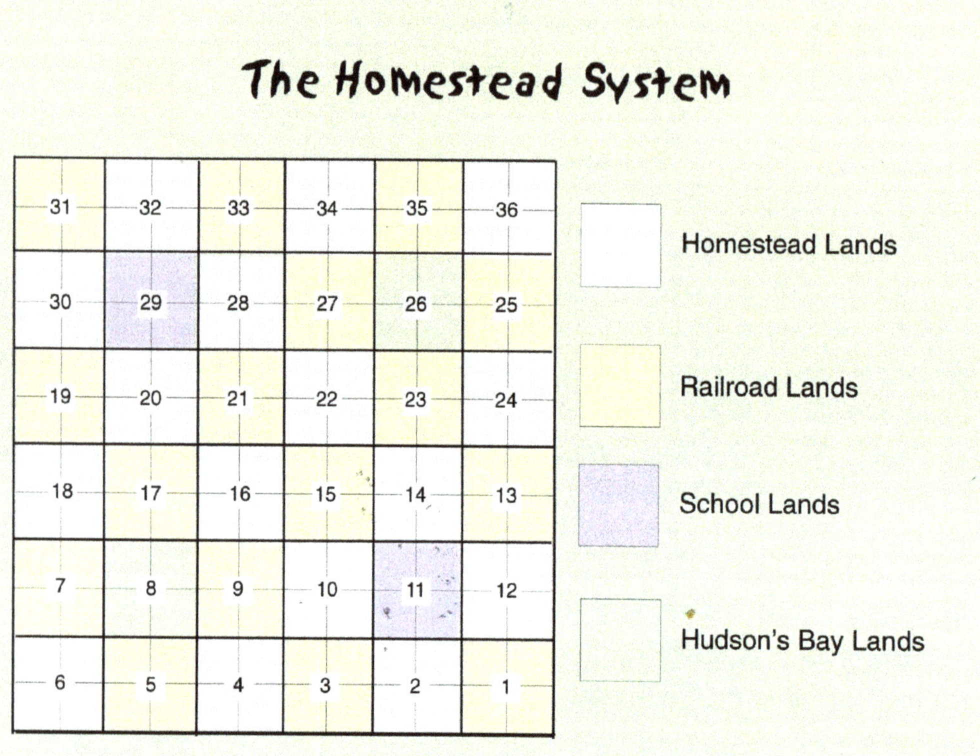

When they arrived in Alberta new settlers had the option of acquiring "free" homestead land from the Canadian government and/or buying additional land from the government, the railways or the Hudson's Bay Company.

Where the land had been surveyed, it was divided into 36 square-mile townships. The townships were subdivided into mile-square sections, which in turn were divided into 160-acre quarter-sections. A little less than one-half the acreage of a township was set aside as "free" homestead land.

The homesteads were scattered throughout the township on even-numbered sections, with the exception of sections eight and 26, which had been allocated to the Hudson's Bay Company. Odd-numbered sections, with the exception of sections 11 and 29, which had been reserved for schools, were the property of the Canadian Pacific Railroad and the other land grant railways.

—Orest T. Martynowych

6.4 *The Homestead System across western Canada.*

The Homestead—Found!

At last, we found ourselves at the edge of a forest which appeared to cover about 60 acres. My father stopped and announced loudly and solemnly: "This forest must be mine—whether it is designated as a homestead or as CPR land. I will not let anyone else have it!" We drove around a bit and, with a watchful eye, I looked for the four holes in the ground, by which we could orient ourselves, or perhaps a straight surveyor's line cut through the bush. Finally, we found what we were looking for; on the edge of the forest I noticed a fallen tree, with a stump about two feet high, felled three or four years ago while the land was being measured by surveyors. Looking toward the trees, I discovered a straight line running north and south. My father and I jumped off the wagon and followed this line cut through the trees until we came to the edge and onto the open prairie. There we saw what we were looking for: the four holes indicating the corners of four sections, with the steel stake in the centre.

—Peter Svarich

Registering a claim did not guarantee receiving a deed. A deed would be granted only after the homestead proved to be a success. And, as decreed by the Homestead Act, success was defined as occupation of the property for at least six months for three consecutive years, with at least 30 acres of wild prairie brought under cultivation, and a habitable house constructed upon it.

Previous homesteaders, mostly British immigrants, argued that 160 acres wasn't enough to make an economic success out of a farm. The government therefore strongly encouraged the settlers to add acreage to their homesteads as quickly as possible. The main way to achieve this was to purchase one of the adjoining 160-acre sections from the railroad. The price offered was $4 per acre, payable in three years, without interest.

Perils

The German [Mennonite at Edna-Star] brought the [team of] horses [that we had bought], and we tried them out and found them completely satisfactory, except for one thing: we were seized with fear because the harness was so complicated that we did not know how to take it off or put it on. We soon learned the trick, although it is true that many a poor immigrant had much difficulty mastering the harnessing procedure.

—Peter Svarich

6.5 *Kysyliw "Pioneer Cemetery." An undistinguished, fenced-off patch of land with a large stone marker at its center. Located at the far northwest corner of NW.14.57.16, Mychailo and Axenia Tkachuk's original quarter. An expedient burial ground for those who passed away before Kysyliw Church & cemetery were formally organized.*

6.6 *Kysyliw Pioneer Cemetery granite marker. Photos of the front and the back of the commemorative marker.*

[1] Jonathan Raban, Bad Land: An American Romance (London: Picador, 1996) 19.
[2] Walter S. Hughson, article that appeared in The Vegreville Observer, 1909 and excerpted by Lillian Semeniuk, editor of Dreams And Destinies: Andrew And District (Andrew, Alberta: Andrew Historical Society, 1980), 2.
[3] Ibid., 3.
[4] Ibid., 3.
[5] Mary Tkachuk Lichuk's journal came up, for the first time, the evening I spent with Lena. Lena also provided me with contact information for Mary's granddaughter—the present keeper of the family manuscript. Generously, the granddaughter mailed me a partial copy of the document a month-or-two after my visit with Lena. Parts of Mary's journal were later published in The Tkachuk Family reunion proceedings from the 1994 Family Reunion in Andrew, Alberta.
[6] The Tkachuk Family. 1994 Family Reunion. Unpublished manuscript. Assembled by Phil Tkachuk and Lillian Semeniuk (Andrew, Alberta, 1996), page 3-5.
[7] The Tkachuk Family. 1994 Family Reunion. Unpublished manuscript. Assembled by Phil Tkachuk and Lillian Semeniuk (Andrew, Alberta, 1996), page 3-5.
[8] Unpublished journal with yearly entries, written by Mary Tkachuk Lichuk, parts of which are in the author's collection, parts of which appear in The Tkachuk Family. 1994 Family Reunion. This information comes from the year 1898.
[9] Mary writes after the fact. Her journal, a year-by-year compilation of the events that she remembers, was requested material via her daughter. So Mary writes as an adult as she recalls her past. There is only slight detail in her narratives. Her yearly entries are descriptive with precise, practical information. For example, she has the correct date for Magdalyna's death year.
[10] Magdalyna's "Registration of Death; Canada/North-West Territories; Record No. 462 of 1905" is in the Provincial Archives of Alberta, ACC. 89.440/2539. I have taken my details from the document. The Reverend Michael Skibinsky [Shebinsky] was a missionary priest, who visited various church communities in the Shandro area, from 1903 on, for the purpose of "sealing graves" and attending to births and marriages. Note that Magdalyna passed away in July and not "in fall" as Mary remembers.
[11] Magdalyna's "Registration of Death; Canada/North-West Territories; Record No. 462 of 1905" is in the Provincial Archives of Alberta, ACC. 89.440/2539. I have taken my details from the document. The Reverend Michael Skibinsky [Shebinsky] was a missionary priest, who visited various church communities in the Shandro area, from 1903 on, for the purpose of "sealing graves" and attending to births and marriages.
[12] Magdalyna's "Registration of Death; Canada/North-West Territories; Record No. 462 of 1905" is in the Provincial Archives of Alberta, ACC. 89.440/2539. I have taken my details from the document. The Reverend Michael Skibinsky [Shebinsky] was a missionary priest, who visited various church communities in the Shandro area, from 1903 on, for the purpose of "sealing graves" and attending to births and marriages.
[13] Field trip and conversations with George Gordey, Sophie Gordey Kowalchuk and Esther Gordey Borynec, area around the "Nativity of the Holy Virgin Church" at Kysylew, a church community in rural Alberta. 13 August 2000.
[14] Interview with Lena Tkachuk Waselasko, her home north of Andrew, Alberta, Canada. 16 May 1995.

CHAPTER 7

"IGNORANT" PEASANTS

Жінка небита, що коса неклепана.

An unbeaten wife is like an unsharpened scythe.
—Ukrainian proverb

SHAKEN as I was by the "discoveries" of Veronica's and Magdalyna's murders, others were more sanguine. As my own mother noted in regard to Veronica's death, one peasant offing another in the bad old days was so common as to be forgettable. Period.

Indeed, violence did ricochet around the heads of the Magdalynas and Veronicas of the world. That said, as much as I would like, I cannot pry open Veronica's life or that of her mother. I cannot "channel" what these women were thinking when… or why exactly they acted as they did. But there is enough adjacent and reliable information available to get closer to the dynamic they inhabited—were schooled in. It was a dynamic they took for granted though not necessarily with relish—those systems and subsystems of abuse, of misogyny, hostility, and violence that adhered to them. Men against women. Women against men. Women against women. They left those Old Country villages hopefully and fearfully behind, but could not seem to shake them from their persons once they'd stepped into the newer place. The habit of violence took new forms, sometimes got subtler, or went underground. Rarely, if ever, did it wholly disappear. As some savant wryly noted, you can take a person out of the village, but you can't take the village out of the person.

From my vantage point here in the 21st century, looking back to the 19th, I had not the smallest inkling of the possibility of Lena's narrative about Magdalyna's death. True, there was circumstance and cause to believe that a case of "simple" domestic violence turned murderous: Wasyl versus Magdalyna. Lena certainly believed so; other women in the family gave Wasyl wide berth. Veronica's fate eight years later, echoing that of her mother's, had since my childhood been alluded to, so there was no surprise in that case of domestic violence morphing to murder.

"A culture that devastates women," This phrase appears in a short and recent news blurb about The Americas.[1] The précis—the country in question is Argentina— is hopeful. Crowds of people gather to demand that "violence against women" stop.[2] "A spate of murders"—the result of domestic violence—has ignited the protests, the crowd rallies. Outrage goes all the way to the top: on her Twitter account, the president of Argentina seems to say it best. It is she who equates domestic violence with utter devastation.[3]

What she leaves unsaid is that violence against women—not just domestic violence—is utter devastation as well. We stalwart news junkies read—nearly every day—of violence directed against females. There is the woman in Italy who has been locked into a room for eighteen years by her mother, sister and brother because of her out-of-wedlock child;[4] the woman in Kabul—a seven-months bride—who has been tortured nearly out of existence by a mother- and sister-in-law because she won't go into prostitution to earn money for the family, while her husband is away, serving in the Afghan Army.[5]

In a village in Russia, a mother and a daughter are boarded-up in their cottage, the structure then set on fire because villagers suspect that the two are witches. They manage to escape; they are not witches, merely victims of invidious gossip. In Donetsk, Ukraine, a woman, trembling in terror, is publically humiliated and physically abused by passers-by—"[they] stop their cars to get out and spit, slap her face and throw tomatoes at her."[6] A pro-Russian militant threatens her with his rifle-thingy—an Uzi or Kalashnikov. She has been accused of aiding the other side, of being pro-Ukraine—until recently, Donetsk was a civilized city in eastern Ukraine. We read that "the captors drove her away to an unknown location."[7] I continue to dread her fate.

Violence against women by men *and* by women—one of humanity's deep-rooted evils—probably goes back to the time just after the dinosaurs, when first there were women and men. Hundreds of thousands of years later, I suspect that my particular sisterhood of pain came by way of violence—the experience of Magdalyna and Veronica and the experience of the others in my line. I think it was serfdom that insinuated violence up and down the family tree. If there were other sources, serfdom was one of the more powerful among them. Serfdom—the institution that took firm hold in 13th century Russia and its neighbors, places like now-Ukraine and Poland. Indeed, with serfdom, violence was so common that no one much bothered with it or quite noticed its effects, not for hundreds of years.

Serfdom in Russia began as a land grab—a stealthy appropriation of peasant farmers' land by decree of a series of tsars to reward and commission their nobles for service. It gravitated into a population grab—by default, a farmer who worked the land became property of the noble on whose land, formerly his own, the rustic found himself. Over time, free peasants became serfs, bound to the land and to their masters.

The deal was cruel. It was economic, centered around performing labor services. Jan Slomka (born in 1841—serfdom ended in Polish and Austrian-Hapsburg lands in 1848—and later to become the mayor of the village of Dzikov), describes what he remembers and what he'd been told of serfdom. His village and its lands belonged to the lords of Dzikov. Slomka wrote that before emancipation, "Every farmer had first to do his dues at the manor house [work began at sunrise and ended at sunset], whether with his team or on foot....If one did not appear as ordered, at once the overseer would come. If he found the wife busy cooking he would throw a pail of water on the fire, or in winter would carry off the windows or the doors. In case that did not work, and men were needed for service, the overseer would come with his foremen and eject the farmer from home and homestead. Another would be put in his place. Nor was there any appeal anywhere, since that was the usage and at bottom the lord of the manor was owner of everything. His was both land and water, yes even the wind; since only he was allowed to build a wind-mill to grind corn."[8]

It was Russia's Catherine II who stripped the serfs in her realm of legal recourse. Never mind the excesses of serfdom, the empress had been receiving too many petitions—pleas for help, for redress. The "nuisance" needed to stop.[9] She decreed that any serf who tried to petition her was to be beaten with the knout—a bundle of leather thongs twisted with wire—and sent to forced labor in Siberia.[10] No kinder, gentler here. Things went from bad to worse.

In time, serf owners held nearly unlimited control over their serfs. They could decide who would marry whom. Uncharacteristically, the less-than-liberal Nicholas I got a law passed decreeing, "parents and unmarried children could not be separated."[11] Peasants of bankrupt nobles were sold at public auctions. At the Moscow serf market, "pretty young serf girls brought good prices."[12] Serfs became military recruit substitutes. Laws to curb traffic in human beings were weak-to-ineffective. Heaven help the poor souls who were tied to sadistic masters—garden variety psychopaths. Callousness, unconscious cruelty and brutality were everywhere. The absence of social disapproval among owner-peers contributed to the misery and serfdom's longevity.

The few serfs who could, ran away to an empty no-man's land in the east—that area of steppes north of the Black Sea or those hard-to-get-to islands in the middle of the big rivers that flowed into the Black Sea, for example the Dnieper. The no-man's land was referred to as "У краі." One was going "to the country"—Y (to) and Kpai (krai, country).[13] Usage of the phrase, "*У к*rai," gradually shaped the word "U-kraine"—first, the name of a region, then a country with Hetman Bohdan Khmel'nyts'kiy at its helm, then a satelite Russian oblast, then a nation fighting to keep its borders intact. The serfs referred to themselves as "Cossacks."

It stands to reason that serfdom was not the same from estate to estate, nor in the larger geography from Russia to Poland to Lithuania to the Austrian-Hapsburg Empire. And, of course, the parameters of it changed over time. Nevertheless, serfdom's constant was its inhumanity—a society where men and women owned their fellow humans.

The ideology that allowed for the East European brand of serfdom—the particular form to which my ancestors were privy—was an ideology of all-encompassing "patriarchy," based on "a social order that extended from God to the tsar to all other fathers."[14] In my family's case, substitute the title "Emperor of the Austrian-Hapsburg Empire" for "Tsar." The structure of this hierarchy served to maintain authority: the subordination of the ruling class to the tsar-emperor; the subordination of peasants to the ruling class; the subordination of women to men.

Misogyny was a major part of the bad deal. Pre-Christians feared women's bodies. Their trepidation—expressed as various taboos around menstruating women—was absorbed into the Old Testament. Ancient Biblical proscriptions influenced and combined with Orthodox paranoia: women were unclean and sexually promiscuous. Staunch Orthodox fathers insisted that females were "capable of fornicating with the devil."[15] Reinforced by Orthodox and Judeo-Christian belief, misogyny was promoted by out-spoken ecclesiastics like St. Basil the Great, who premonished against "the wickedness of women"[16] —his image stands tall in the village church my great-great-grandmothers attended.

On the village street, the perception was that "women's bodies were open and men's sealed."[17] One rustic explained to an interviewer that "a witch's hex laid under a porch was less likely to take effect on a man than a woman because 'he wears pants and therefore it doesn't seize hold [of him].' The peasant was alluding to the fact that because women did not wear underwear, their genitals were exposed to demons released by the spell when they crossed over the porch."[18]

Day-to-day, these beliefs were brought to bear. "Women had to refrain from taking communion while menstruating, and only postmenopausal women could bake communion bread."[19] Upon delivering a child, a woman was considered to be in spiritually dangerous territory and vulnerable. "Ritual purification of mothers forty days after giving birth was a prerequisite for their reentry into the House of God and larger community."[20] In a woman's own household, "the place of honor at the dinner table, located directly under the icons of the so-called holy corner, was reserved for the household head"—a male.[21] Accompanying the rest of the misogynist parcel was the belief "that women were prone to excessive behavior."[22] Only force could contain the excess.

Misogyny aside, in a humble household, a peasant and his wife were an interdependent team—their work divided along gender lines. Marriage was nearly universal and encouraged early. Wives managed the home and its environs—a cottage's interior, the cooking, the children, the garden, the domestic animals. Husbands commandeered the fields, trying to bring unpredictable nature to productivity. At peak times—for example, during the harvest, husband and wife worked in the fields together. Misfortune, familiar to all, was attributed to God's anger or to the knavery of unclean spirits who used humans—some neighbor or acquaintance—to do their bidding.

Centuries rolled past; beliefs and behaviors held fast. A woman's lot did not improve measurably after serf emancipation.[23] The family—full of oppressors and victims in its own right—continued to be core, the main spring of support. It consisted of multiple generations, headed by the eldest male, who—in the best of worlds—kept his eye on the family's common interest. Husband, wife, daughter, son, daughter-in-law—cooperation was achieved by coercion and by muting those with less power.[24] The interests of individual family members were subsumed for the sake of the whole. For example, betrothal agreements were made with regards to the pecuniary success of the extended family—to satisfy labor needs. What's love got to do with it?

For a young woman, marriage was "the greatest point of departure."[25] With it, she joined a new patriarchal household. Because of the implications of this major life event, mothers and community members dedicated themselves to teach young girls the responsibilities that accrued to a wife, mother and daughter-in-law. First and foremost, she learned she must maintain her virginity until marriage. After that, mothers tutored their charges in the very necessary oral culture of songs, prayers and lamentations, as well as "in the arts of preparing flax and hemp, spinning, weaving, embroidery, cooking, baking bread, gardening, animal tending, and threshing, all the chores that would eventually become theirs in married life."[26]

Unfortunately, a peasant girl's virginity was primarily her own responsibility, a fortress every young blade willed himself to conquest. If the innocent slipped, the prevailing attitude, articulated by a Russian peasant male, went something like this, "If she hadn't consented, nothing would have happened, and since she didn't preserve herself until marriage, there is no reason to trust her."[27] The "Catch-22" is that any pretty young thing, or not so pretty young thing, having attained her courtship years—say from fifteen to twenty—was joyfully attending her village's mid-winter evening parties, *vechornytsi*.[28]

The parties were essentially courtship events where dancing, games, songs, talk, flirting, petting and bundling were embraced by the young un-marrieds. Adult supervision was light to non-existent. Let's just say that given a November *vechornytsi* or a fragrant summer's night meadow or some predatory village lad reeking of *horilka*, there were ample opportunities for a virgin to get knocked-up. When the naïf did, Heaven would not help her.

If our maiden deviated from the moral conduct expected of her by family and community, if, say, it became known that she had engaged in premarital sex, or if—in the worst-case scenario— she became pregnant before marriage, public shaming swiftly followed.

She went from one-hundred to zero in one biologically successful encounter. The maid was ostracized from social gatherings—from the all-important winter courting parties. She was rejected out-of-hand as a potential marriage partner—this factor threatened her family's social and economic position in the community. Her sisters' possible wedding matches were put into jeopardy. Community censure took other forms too—her maiden's braid was shorn off, her shirt tarred, the gate posts of her home tarred or covered with dung, windows broken, her skirt tied over her head as she was paraded half-naked through the village. There is a fine example of this in the Ukrainian film *The White Bird with a Black Mark*, directed by Yuri Ilyenko.[29] A group of female elders, who clearly do not approve of a flirty young beauty—an unmarried maiden, shame her by binding her skirt over her arms and head. Cinematic depictions aside, such public humiliation had its effect "in psychologically terrorizing young women."[30]

Obviously, not everyone fit neatly into the box. There were young women who remained unmarried. Theirs was a position even more unenviable than that of their married sisters. In a culture that pressed for universal marriage, these few spinsters were regarded as "potential idlers and parasites."[31] They were derided with pejorative names—"soured," "homely," "homebody"[32]—and condemnatory proverbs—"An old maid is a family ulcer."[33] Even worse, as they aged in solitude, they could be accused of sorcery and witchcraft. Elderly widows, who—in poverty— sometimes kept to themselves, were ever in danger of gossip that insinuated them into the company of supposed "unclean spirits."

Fear and resentment resided in a village where physical violence held sway. This would include most villages in 19th century Eastern Europe. A fear-based culture is a repressive culture. Individuals learned not to cry out when struck. Instead, they expressed their troubles using an effective tool: "blame." By blaming others for what she couldn't explain or for what she wanted to cast off, a villager could lighten her load. If your child fell ill just after a destitute widow came begging at your door, you could blame the widow for the child's illness—this, after you refused to give the widow a crust of bread. Some would call this the projection of guilt, others, the hot potato toss. The hot potato toss, a less-than-charming facet of everyday village life.

Assuming no lapses in moral conduct, a young woman weathered courtship gatherings, betrothal and marriage. But as a freshman wife in her husband's family system, she became "an intruder into established rhythms"—a daughter-in-law tasked with subordinating herself to all of the males, to the elder females of the household and most particularly, to the household's head wife.[34]

Why did women accommodate themselves to this perfidious, degrading arrangement? There had to be compensations. And there were. Men honored them as mothers. Mothers taught their children society's values and helped them find good marriage partners. Husbands protected their wives from false slurs on their reputation. But within the home and the larger community of women, women "carved out their own subsystems of oppression and authority."[35] It was a no-holds-barred power struggle. Every woman vied for the position of female head-of-the- household. "Once a daughter-in-law became a female household head and mother-in-law, she would use her authority exactly as had her mother-in-law to keep her own daughters-in-law in line."[36] It was a case of giving as good as you got.

Maidens on the way to their weddings wept copiously—"A bride-to-be dreaded leaving the security of her parents' home and living with domineering in-laws who were not averse to using physical force against her."[37] To fulfill her responsibilities, the pressures on a young wife were intense. Her success, her social reputation, hinged on "the number of children (especially sons) she bore; her abilities as worker and provider; her submissiveness to male authority; and, until age conferred upon her the status of head-wife, her subordination to older women within the household."[38] Vulnerable to any criticism, a new wife faced anxiety upon anxiety, not to mention a painful lack of privacy—seems that everyone "kept close watch on the frequency and outcomes of pregnancies."[39] Mothers- and sisters-in-law, more often than not, offered little encouragement and less compassion.

The distrust, hostility and lashings-out of a mother-in-law who feared that her authority might be eroded by a daughter-in-law; the power struggles between an adult son—expected to remit his wages— and his father over farming issues, property determinations and the like; a husband's insistence on his wife's complete obedience and her objections to it—tensions and quarrels, both familial and marital, were considered to be a private matter. What was in the family, stayed in the family. Often, tensions were expressed by means of physical force: public and private beatings were quite common. "Violence was recognized as a completely normal and important form of interaction."[40] Outsiders, that is, others in the community, made it their business not to get involved.

Peasant men believed that their practical and psychological success hinged, in part, on total control over both the household and its members. It was a combination of magical thinking and trickle-down patriarchal propaganda. On the propaganda side, the state had a vested interest in supporting patriarchal lucubration as a means of social control.

Thus, any deviation from this system of control—of man to overlord, of woman to man—threatened the collective interest as well as village solidarity. Peasant society cooperated in upholding the ordering of relationships. Flight? There was no place for a woman to run. She belonged at her husband's side, no exceptions—so what if the guy was a vicious woman-beater? Meddling parents—that is, the birth parents of an abused wife— were usually sanctioned. Nearly to a person, unsympathetic judges and elders supported the household head's authority, supported the husband's authority, against recalcitrant family members.

A wife was expected to show absolute obedience to her husband. Husbands eagerly insisted on this point with frequent beatings—if the woman uttered a reproach, if jealously was involved, if he were drunk, if and if. Beatings reinforced a man's authority and were considered a proper way to curb a wife's willful character. Anthropologist and 19th century peasant contemporary, Ms. Olga Semyonova Tian-Shanskaia reported, "They [husbands] beat them [their wives] with sticks, oven prongs, boots, buckets, and whatever else is handy—or just slug or kick them. They drag them by their braids down the front steps so that their heads make a thumpity-thump noise."[41]

Tian-Shanskaia goes on, "A drunken husband sometimes beats his wife when she refused to carry out some order of his, for example, to pull off his boots or put him to bed. She also catches it if she refused to sleep with him. In a word, she is punished for any failure to fulfill her husband's wishes. I knew one peasant man who, when he was drunk, loved to abuse his wife in the following way: 'Down, woman! On your knees! Put your head on the threshold. I am finally going to have my way and kill you!' The woman had to put her head down on the threshold without complaining, while he brandished an ax above her. This usually set the little children to crying and screaming. Then he would say: 'If it were not for the children, you'd be dead by now,' and he would let her go. If she did not obey him, he beat her cruelly, sometimes with a flail about the head. This is called 'to wise up a wife' or 'to heap scorn on a wife.'"[42]

Tian-Shanskaia cited one case in which a drunken husband killed his wife for infidelity: "he rolled her braids around his hand and beat her head on the front steps, on the benches, and on the wall until she lapsed into a coma. She died a day later, never having regained consciousness."[43] When adultery was the issue, community sympathy went exclusively to the husband. He could "punish his wife in any way he wished, short of murder, for sullying her entire family's reputation."[44] As late as the end of the 19th century, wives who strayed could be and were publically humiliated. Husbands "tied them to wagons and led them, tarred and feathered, through the village streets.... All villagers could voice their disapproval of adultery by jeering and throwing garbage at the unfortunate women."[45]

Inspired by their half-Christian, half-pagan beliefs, peasants imbued witches and sorcerers with dangerous powers over the sexual activities of others. This provided fodder for holding community members responsible for the impotence and infertility of humans, animals, and land. For example, "In 1890, a twenty-one-year-old male of the village Sychevka, Karachev district, Orel province, Russia, killed his seventeen-year-old bride on the pretext that she used witchcraft to make him impotent."[46]

The ease with which a woman could be dispatched from the time of serfdom forward is as shocking as it is sobering. In truth, acts of brutality against females were counter-productive and pointless. Why disable, why kill your wife, when she is baking your bread, washing your pantaloons, raising your children, stooking the wheat and putting extra money into your pocket by selling her embroidery? Why condemn your daughter-in-law for the hint of an infraction, when she could be a comfort in your old age?

Children too were beaten as a matter of course or for the slightest infraction. Those who observed village children noted that youngsters were often mistrustful, fearful, abusive and quickly resorted to lying or other stratagems to avoid beatings.

An article that appeared in a Moscow medical newspaper in 1860 enumerated the physical and mental circumstances visited upon peasant women: "poor diets, insufficient sleep, arduous work, cramped and unsanitary living conditions, numerous pregnancies, poor treatment of illness…depressed mental influences, the loss of tranquility [and] hope, the destruction of family happiness, unsuccessful love, and everything else that strikes the human heart."[47] Here were women staggering through their lives. Rare photos of female Russian and Ukrainian peasants in the late 19th century, show women who could chew nails, their faces contorted by the unrelenting cruelty of their lives.

Cruelty and abuse could be had, seemingly from all sides. Pointless brutality—yes, but not without coherence. When my women—Magdalyna and Veronica, among them—arrived to the New World, "wising up a wife" was still taken for granted by the old-guard insiders, the Wasyls of the world. To her credit, Wasyl's widow, Mrs. Maria Fegirchuk-Gordey-Ukrainetz-Ropchan, lit out for the pig shed when she knew that her husband was in a wife-beating mood.

Lest drawing material from the mid-19th century forward seems dated, I disagree. The memory of the kinds of violence, the array of abuse, laid out here, lingered long after the actual fact of it. It hovered at a subcutaneous level in the psyches of my 20th century female predecessors.

So things got better, right? Well, for some, things did get better. Others were too encumbered. How did the brutality of the not-so-distant past affect the survivors? "Elena"—the next chapter—points the way.

[1] "Argentine: Rallies to Protect Women," The Americas, *The New York Times*, 4 June 2015.
[2] Ibid.
[3] Ibid. President Cristina Fernández de Kirchner of Argentina.
[4] "Another Imprisoned Woman Is Found, This Time in Italy," by Elisabetta Povoledo, The New York Times, International Section, 17 June 2008.
[5] "2 Women Held in Torture of Afghan Girl, 15," *The New York Times*, 3 January 2012.
[6] "With Peace Talks Near, Prisoners in Ukraine Are Abused," by Andrew E. Kramer and Andrew Roth, *The New York Times*, International Section, 26 August 2014.
[7] Ibid.
[8] Slomka, Jan, *From Serfdom to Self-Government. Memoirs of a Polish Village Mayor. 1842-1927.* Transl. William John Rose (London: Minerva Publsihing Co., Ltd., 1941) 15.
[9] Blum, Jerome, *Lord and Peasant in Russia From the Ninth to the Nineteenth Century* (Princeton: Princeton University Press, 1961) 440.
[10] Ibid., 440. Catherine II's *ukase* was decreed on 22 August 1767.
[11] Ibid., 428.
[12] Ibid., 426.
[13] Reid, Anna, *Borderland: A Journey Through the History of Ukraine* (London: Phoenix, A Division of Orion Books, Ltd., 2001) 1. Reid translates "Ukraina" as "on the edge" or "borderland."
[14] Worobec, Christine D., *Peasant Russia. Family and Community in the Post-Emancipation Period* (DeKalb: Northern Illinois University Press, 1995) 175.
[15] Ibid., 186.
[16] Ibid., 186.
[17] Worobec, Christine D., *Possessed. Women, Witches, And Demons In Imperial Russia* (DeKalb: Northern Illinois University Press, 2003) 73.
[18] Ibid., 73.
[19] Worobec, Christine D., *Peasant Russia. Family and Community in the Post-Emancipation Period* (DeKalb: Northern Illinois University Press, 1995) 186-187.
[20] Ibid., 186-87.
[21] Ibid., 186.
[22] Ibid., 188.
[23] The serfs were emancipated in the Austrian-Hapsburg Empire in 1848, in the Russian Empire in 1861.
[24] Mironov, Boris N. "Peasant Popular Culture And the Origins of Soviet Authoritarianism," pp. 54-73 in *Cultures in Flux. Lower-Class Values, Practices, and Resistance in Late Imperial Russia*, eds. Stephen P. Frank and Mark D. Steinberg (Princeton: Princeton University Press, 1994) 58.
[25] Worobec, Christine Diane, "Family, Community, And Land In Peasant Russia, 1860-1905," Dissertation (Toronto: University of Toronto, 1984) 267.
[26] Worobec, *Peasant Russia*, 122.
[27] Barbara Alpern Engle, *Between the fields and the city: Women, work, and family in Russia, 1861-1914*, "Patriarchy and its Discontents" (Cambridge: Cambridge University Press, 1994), 9.
[28] *Vechornytsi—vechir*: вечір, means "evening" in Ukrainian.
[29] *The White Bird with a Black Mark* (1970), directed by Yuri Ilyenko, is set in the Carpathian Mountains of Ukraine's Bukovyna region near the Romanian border. The film tells the story of a family of rural wedding musicians torn asunder by World War II. It is one of the few Ukrainian-language feature films produced in the Soviet Union. It won the Grand Prize at the 1971 Moscow Film Festival.
[30] Worobec, *Peasant Russia*, 143.
[31] Ibid., 124.
[32] Ibid., 124.
[33] Ibid., 124.
[34] Worobec, Christine Diane, "Family, Community, And Land In Peasant Russia, 1860-1905," Dissertation (Toronto: University of Toronto, 1984) 267.
[35] Worobec, *Peasant Russia*, 13-14.
[36] Ibid., p. 206.
[37] Ibid., p. 205.
[38] Worobec, Christine D., *Possessed. Women, Witches, And Demons In Imperial Russia* (DeKalb: Northern Illinois University Press, 2003) 204.
[39] Ibid., 204.
[40] Mironov, Boris N. "Peasant Popular Culture And the Origins of Soviet Authoritarianism," pp. 54-73 in *Cultures in Flux. Lower-Class Values, Practices, and Resistance in Late Imperial Russia*, eds. Stephen P. Frank and Mark D. Steinberg (Princeton: Princeton University Press, 1994) 57.
[41] Ransel, David L., ed. *Village Life in Late Tsarist Russia*, by Olga Semyonova Tian-Shanskaia, Transl. David L. Ransel with Michael Levine (Bloomington and Indianapolis: Indiana University Press, 1993) 20.
[42] Ransel and Tian-Shanskaia, 21.
[43] Ibid., 20.
[44] Worobec, *Peasant Russia*, 201.
[45] Ibid., 202.
[46] Worobec, *Possessed*, 99.
[47] Ibid., 128. Source in footnote #58.

CHAPTER 8

ELENA

Єлена

"Someday my prince will come."
— ***Cinderella***

I yearn to know who she was, this emissary of that *terra incognita* from which rare family stories spring. Elena the Silent, in her dotage sitting and gazing out of a window, memories of a lost world circling. Her husband didn't beat her; she was beaten by circumstance. I had and have romantic notions about her. They do not serve.

Mother's maternal grandmother, Elena, the counterpart to the paternal grandmother Magdalyna, had been a beauty. Mother prefaced any mention of Elena by noting her comeliness. Some insisted that she had nicely shaped legs, others that her fair hands never stained while she peeled beets or potatoes. As leader of the chorus, Katherine insisted that Elena was inordinately good looking as a young peasant in Chornivka. For this, Katherine cited the elderly Elena's striking blue eyes, her smooth light skin and her thick white hair as evidence of earlier pulchritude. The hair had once been blackest black. The eyes, hair, skin: Ukrainian Cossack "royalty."

In my endless gawky years, I liked to think that I was related to a *bona fide* beauty. Any story about an attractive ancestor was good, anything to help me. I was also very fond of an anecdote that clung to Elena. It came in various versions. Either she had won a village beauty contest and the aristocratic judge, a prince, invited her to come with him on a trip to the city (Chernivtsi) or she had been singled out for her pleasant looks and invited to join a thespian troupe headed for Chernivtsi. Whatever the case, her beauty implies destiny.

Lest her head be turned, Elena's parents quickly got her married—during the winter courting and marriage season—to a promising peasant, a local—a happy-go-lucky—in line to inherit his family's modest land-holdings. Perhaps, a big perhaps, it was a bullet dodged.

Much later, my uncles would guffaw at the notion that Elena could have been Chernivtsi aristocracy or a Sarah Bernhardt heartthrob, as if they knew how fame or aristocracy worked. No one asked Elena about the truth of these stories, but all of her grandchildren repeated them to one another.

Unlike Magdalyna, Elena's grandchildren knew of her. Most of them had some actual experience of the woman. After all, for brief periods, she lived in a decommissioned *khata* and then in a decommissioned chicken coop on their farm. But few of them—save Al and Katherine—formed any kind of bond with her. My mother only remembered her white, white hair. (8.2)

When Elena was in her sixties and living in St. Paul de Métis—that is, "Saint Paul of the Half-Breed"—ten-year-old Katherine was loaned to her. It was a sweetheart deal. Katherine could help Elena and get taught by the nuns at the local Catholic school; or so Katherine's mother, who had daughters to spare, reasoned. Mostly, Katherine was alarmed by Elena's deeply held beliefs. "That's one of the boys," Elena would say, when a loose-fitting door would creak and swing open in the wind.[1] By then, three of Elena's adult sons were gone. She took for granted that their spirits were come a-home to visit. Of her days with Elena, Katherine recalled, "Whenever I went from a dark room into a light room, I always felt that something was going to catch me and I'd sort of jump in." [2]

Later, Ann was lent to Elena. Ann had a different take on the woman. She thought of her as distant, unloving and cold. Then again, as a sickly child, Ann was catered to at home. Perhaps Elena did not show Ann the deference she expected. Later still, brother George, fleeing Soda Lake, sought out Ivan and Elena. "She was a nasty old lady," George said.[3] However, George liked Ivan.

George's reaction to Elena was worlds away from that of Al, the eldest grandchild who had the earliest experience of her. Elena took Al with her on sun-filled wildflower and herb forays, which she called her "spatseer." [4] In her former village in the Austrian-Hapsburg Empire, Elena must have heard enough German to know that *spazieren*—a German verb meaning *to stroll* or *to walk*—was a pleasant ramble in the country. On her strolls, she tried to introduce Al to the medicinal and magical lore that greeted her in the meadows. Too bad. With him, her lessons went nowhere; whereas, Katherine would have offered a retentive mind. It is possible that even then Elena was collecting herbs to fill her white funerary pillow.

In Edmonton after the interview with Lena, I got it: seek out the oldest persons *first*. I zeroed in on a visit to Julia, the widow of Nick, a son of Elena and Ivan. (8.3) Turns out that after she was widowed, Elena spent her final years living with Nick and Julia and their daughters, essentially as their ward. When Julia invited me to the kitchen to have "tea and a ball"—hot tea and a *Tim Bit* doughnut hole, brainchild of the Tim Horton franchise—I double-timed it.

Once I broached Elena as a topic, I was astonished to find her so-much-present in Julia's life. Among surprises was "Elena's china," this is how Julia referred to it. Graceful green-rimmed, cream-colored china plates crowded the breakfront in Julia's stuffed kitchen. (8.3a) Carefully and piece-by-piece, she showed me bowls and coffee cups. Purchased for Elena's funeral dinner, the porcelain served as a way to honor her. It probably impressed Nick and Julia's guests too.

Out of a closet came a yellow silk shawl, a black wool serge skirt, a boar-bristle brush. They had been Elena's. There were indistinct photos and unflattering photos—in one, Elena looks like a turnip. There was nothing that captured Elena in her days as a beauty. It became obvious to me that Elena-the mother-in-law and Julia-the daughter-in-law spent more of their lives together than either of them planned.

It is to Julia's credit that as Elena's days waned, she listened to Elena's stories. Perhaps even more so considering Julia's attitude about Elena—"Self-centered," "hard to get along with—you couldn't do anything [correctly around her]," "she didn't like kids, didn't like to be disturbed [by them]," she was alone—not that she did anything: she never had hobbies," "she had no friends, she associated with nobody at no time, nobody!" As I drew Julia out about Elena, these were her tart observations.

The pity of the relationship between the two was political, ageist and, finally, typical. Julia's background was Polish and Catholic, anathema to 19th century Orthodox Ukrainians. Elena clung to the religious—and folk—culture she had known as a youth: "Orthodok," Julia would say. Julia was sixteen when she married the thirty-two year old Nick. Elena, at seventy, did not approve of this slip of a girl. The two females eyed each other warily. The upshot of this situation is that the one person in a position to connect with Elena in a way that might communicate her to others, could not and did not do so.

Nevertheless, they talked. Every day Elena told Julia that she, Elena, was supposed to stay behind in Chornivka, that her true destiny had been to remain and marry a prince—"That's all she lived," Julia said. Why would Elena cling to such a fantasy? Was it that the "only way out" of whatever happened to Elena in that village was to fantasize the missed chance at escape and salvation, that is "the prince?"

"He put a spell over me," Elena said of her husband. "He made me turn my head at the moment the prince passed by and I lost the prince." What? Did Ivan make her blush? Giggle? So perhaps there was a bit of sparkle between the two of them, that is, if he had the wherewithal to bewitch her. It was Ivan, who dragged her, unwilling, from one primitive situation to the next, ever a willow-the-wisp, until they had near-nothing.

When in the 18th century the sun shone on the Austrian-Hapsburg Empire, Elena's village, Chornivka (8.1), flickered faintly at its far eastern edge. Surrounded on three sides by forest-covered hills, the village started as a scrap of a feudal outpost. When the Ottoman Turks began flexing their muscles, the village became part of an Ottoman vassal state. It did not volunteer for this. There is a legend that says the hamlet jumped to the other side of Berda Creek in order to hide itself in the overgrowth—unsuccessfully it turns out—from the Turks. Taxes were tough—x number of lads and lasses to be conscripted into slavery per year, plus the usual wheat, draft animals and linens. On a brighter note, village fashion got a boost. The women adopted a shallow version of the Ottoman Fez cap and wore it stylishly on their heads with their shawls draped over the cap, this, on into Elena's time.

Being of an orderly nature, the Austrian-Hapsburg Empire organized its east—namely the land on which Chornivka nestled—into crown provinces. Thus, Bukovyna—so named for its enormous stands of Beech (German: *buk*) trees—is where the village found itself momentarily. But with Romania's 19th century yearnings to become a people and a nation, Chornivka came to reside in Northern Bukovyna, with Southern Bukovyna allied to non-Empire interests, namely those break-away blaggards, the Romanians. During the period of quickening wars that overtook the area in the 20th century, Chornivka was absorbed by Romania, then the Soviet Union, and finally Ukraine. Demonstrably, the village is well-traveled. Elena seems to have taken a page from her village. Chornivka, Limestone Lake, Colville, Soda Lake, Flat Lake, LaFond, St. Paul de Métis, Soda Lake, Condor, Edmonton. That was Elena.

IT must have been wrenching for Elena to leave Chornivka. Regardless of her relations with family and neighbors, Chornivka was all she had known. Its dirt streets—still there— with puddles and gaggles of white geese; the water well where young people would gather of an evening or a Sunday afternoon to sing and flirt and dance; the корчма (*korchma*, pub), *Three Pfennigs*—the name indicating Chornivka's modest Teutonic impress— where Ivan liked to buy rounds for the assembled; the shallow, clear stream that transected the village behind her home; the small frog-filled lake and encircling homespun linen bleaching meadows; Berda Mountain in the distance covered with hardwood trees, the crumbled foundations of the 11th century Turkish fort, and a "who's who" of mushrooms; the small onion-domed church where Elena learned to calculate time by the saints; the two cemeteries, one for the village's Romanian aristocrats—the Hurmuzakis and Petrinos, the much larger one for everyone else; the white storks in their nest, returning each year from Africa to hatch one new brood and to grace the village with harmony and good fortune, at least theoretically; the apple, yellow cherry and plum trees in most yards; and all the legends, the small histories of the villagers, the larger history of the village. Never mind the mud, the drudgery and toil, the gossip, the rivalries.

Elena and Ivan left. As part of my journey, while a student at the University of Alberta, I was introduced to *Memoirs 1877-1904* by Peter Svarich.[5] In page after page of Svarich's book, Elena's and Ivan's "pioneer" experiences come into focus. The truculent Svarich, who—like them—emigrated from Bukovyna (now Ukraine), is somewhat unique among his cohort because he was formally educated, multi-lingual and appropriately proud. With the determination of a back-hoe and a sharp eye for detail, Svarich exercised his ability to write perceptively about his transformative Old World-New World adventure. Reading Svarich, I, like many others, conclude that nobody had a good time, certainly not Elena or Ivan.

Svarich struggled to leave Tulova village—west and up-river (Prut' River) from Chornivka. He writes that at the moment of leaving, grief tightened his chest, copious tears flowed down his cheeks and he wept as "final farewells" were extended.[6] The village's church bells were rung, as if tolling death. Villagers gathered to watch the emigrants as they progressed towards the train station. Svarich confesses, "I was moved by the audible weeping and wailing of the crowd. Some were beside themselves and tore their hair in genuine grief. Some fell on each other's shoulders and kissed passionately like children. Those near our wagon pounded their foreheads against its side...."[7] It was an emotional and—when the train arrived—tumultuous scene. Many believed they were parting forever, and for the most part, they were.

As for Elena through the lens of Svarich, we'll dispense with the sea crossing, characterized by bread, meat, potatoes and coffee; motion sickness; filth and fear. We'll dispense with Halifax or Quebec City, and with clearing health inspection and Canadian immigration where one's name got mangled—Canada was not alone in this type of verbal crosstics. We'll dispense with the interminable train ride west. As a footnote, having only associated bells with village churches, Svarich and his companions were intrigued by the sound of the locomotive's bell. In a sad and warming way, it reminded them of home.

We'll dispense with the growing dismay—as the train rolls on—at seeing only boulders, sheer cliffs, hills, forests and lakes. There is no productive-looking farmland anywhere in sight, certainly not after two days on the rails across eastern Canada. We'll dispense with arrival at Strathcona station on the *south* side of the wide swirling North Saskatchewan, whereas Edmonton, the mercantile center for acquiring goods and, more importantly, a quarter-section, sits on the *north* side of the river. No bridge. No organized way to get across: "Go build your own rafts, you strange people," the locals hissed. Immigrants drowned trying to get the quarter-of-a-mile from Strathcona to Edmonton.

We'll dispense with the wait in Edmonton on the part of the women and children, while the men walked or rode sixty miles north and east into the bush, selected a surveyed quarter-section, walked or rode back into town to register it, bought supplies—basic food stuffs, two horses, a cow, a wagon, a plow, a harrow—and marshaled the supplies and family for the trip back out.

Everyone was brought up short by that unique form of torture— the mosquito. Svarich records his reaction to these nasty biters: "...the voracious insects rose from the swamps in clouds and invaded the city by the thousands, descending on people and beasts and sucking their blood mercilessly....There was only one way to beat back the invaders—to drive them away with smoke. This meant a constant vigil of burning smudges all around the house and filling the yard with acrid black smoke...."[8] All around with forests of Black Spruce, Balsam

Poplar and Tamarack standing in water (muskegs); with lakes more slough than lake; and, finally, with the North Saskatchewan River and the streams that fed into it, everything contributed to a mosquito population, as John McPhee aptly observed, "in numbers a physicist would understand."[9]

No matter. Immigrants like Elena and Ivan or Magdalyna and Wasyl rolled slowly out of Edmonton in their horse-drawn wagons, following Indian trails running parallel to the river. They were lucky if they did not sink into the muck while trying to cross yet another low spot. Having been initiated by a watery trap, Svarich describes this hazard waiting for the uninitiated. The group of immigrants he was traveling with did not heed a warning to lighten its wagons. They were confident that if a wagon became stuck in a "mud hole," they could hitch multiple horse teams to it and free it.[10] Just east of Fort Saskatchewan, the party encountered an expanse of flooded land so broad that there was nothing to be done but line up in tandem—in the hopes of finding good footing somewhere—and proceed on through. Two of three wagons sank simultaneously up to the axles, wheels and horses' legs coated with gluey, tar-like mud.

Horses thrashed backwards and forward in terror and collapsed, laying their heads on wagon shafts to keep from drowning. Men rushed to unhitch them, pry them from the mud and lead them to drier ground. Women and children on the wagon-islands became prime mosquito bait. Soaked and mud-coated volunteers tested the slough's bottom. Only by late afternoon, could wagons be laboriously pushed and pulled—by all but the youngest— towards surer paths. Herculean in scope, the naval engagement was won by means of double- and triple-teams of re-hitched horses. It was a rude and abrupt introduction to the topography.

Like the gold-seeking '49ers traveling across Nevada's Forty Mile Desert fifty years earlier, these former "Austrian" villagers were shadowed by danger. Instead of a desert's threatening aridity and heat, immigrants had to be vigilant around water and cold. Mishap could be found at every dog-leg turn of a barely visible track. And like The Forty Mile Desert, there was risk in the sheer featurelessness of the landscape. Clumps of bushes—Saskatoon, Wolf Willow, Chokecherry, Rose, Buckbrush; tall grasses; distant groves of aspen, paper birch and white spruce were not enough to give any setting definition. There were hundreds of miles of shrub-clumps, of grasses, of groves spread in similar configurations, and, of course, thousands of sloughs.

Svarich recounts how he headed out to find his cows of a Sunday morning. He walked a mile or two in each of the cardinal directions. No cows. No longer morning. He was lost. He had no idea which way "home" lay. After one night in the open in a chilly drizzle that kept dousing his campfire, he straggled into an Indian encampment—a dog barking, a single teepee, a cooking fire and a family group, undoubtedly Plains Cree. He was served roast muskrat—which he soon identified, and to his horror promptly vomited. For Svarich, hospitality had its limits. Regardless, he was given solid directions. He had wandered in circles for two days. The cows made it home much earlier of their own accord.[11]

That featurelessness, in actuality a wildly diverse environment, was unspoiled prairie when Elena and Ivan moved onto it. They were oblivious to the privilege of the ecology. It was not like the land they had known. They had come to domesticate its wildness. That was their job. The land changed them. It destroyed their traditions. Gloriously and sadly, Elena was nothing but tradition-bound. Every moment of her day was tied to a folk belief, a ritual, the magical and spiritual rhythms that had imbued her life in Chornivka.

When Elena, Ivan and their four surviving children—Maria, Gus, Alex and Bill—got to where they determined to go, that quarter along the green bean-shaped Limestone Lake (NE 32-56-17.W.4.M.), they had to work fast. (8.4) But Elena was not a farmhand-type. More than one of her grandchildren commented on the fact that she did not do fieldwork, none of the heavy stuff that their own mother did. It was Katherine who noted that Elena was "doll-like" and kept her person and her interiors "very tidy."[12] I presume that those first days on their parcel, everyone, even the three-year old Bill, pitched-in to get a *burdei* up. They needed protection.

Then, there Elena was—meadow and scrub extending to the horizon for 360°. No women with whom to unwind, with whom to gossip, with whom to share advice or with whom to disagree. No sisters or brothers. No seasoned elders. Nor could she read, write or speak English. "Jam"—which she would have pronounced in her Ukrainian lilt as "*dzhem*," (джем)—was the sole English word she deigned to learn. With this one word, she would walk into a store in Wostok or St. Paul de Métis and walk out with her favorite foodstuff. More than just jam, it was a connection. With its abundant apple, plum and cherry trees, Chornivka produced a hearty crop for jam-making, for fruit-flavored juices and fruit-spirits. In her New World neighborhood, no Anglo farmwoman would stoop to teach Elena how to make Chokecherry jam.

She left three infants, *Zoiitsa*, *Heorhiy* and *Domynika*, buried in the larger of Chornivka's two cemeteries.[13] Eight months after her marriage to Ivan at twenty-one, Elena was pregnant. Her first child, daughter *Zoiitsa*, born on May 1st, christened on May 7th, promptly died. The next child, Maria, who would later become Maria-of-Soda Lake, lived. *Heorhiy*, Elena's third, born on the 30th of a March and christened the 31st, expired. A fifth child, *Domynika*, born on April 26th, christened on the 28th, flickered out.

Village accounts have a midwife or a neighbor sprinting to fetch the priest to baptize a newborn before it passed away. One matron in Chornivka delivered quintuplets and half the village raced for the priest. Everyone knew that five babies would not survive.[14] To be sure, the Chornivka priest christened every one of Elena's infants. She paid him for this service: it was not automatic.[15]

Christening. In addition to its ancient connection to strengthening and purification—

Scythians, Greeks and barbarian-Germans dunked their newborn infants in an ice-cold bath to fortify them; early Christians added the idea of purification to the dunk[16] —christening was a kind of spiritual insurance on the part of the mother. If the child died christened, its soul was taken to be with God as a tiny angel and an innocent. If the child died un-christened, its soul remained in unhappy limbo, unable to reach paradise. The unresolved tiny soul manifested itself as a moth or a butterfly and would beat against the windows of its family's home, trying to find companionship, love, peace and a way into the house. No mother wanted to be haunted by her spirit-infant's frantic, mournful fluttering at a window.

Early infant death was an everyday occurrence in villages across more than one empire. Scholars of 19th century Russia have calculated a fifty per cent die-off for infants under the age of one.[17] Perhaps after *Zoiitsa's* death, Elena became inured to the expectancy of loss. Respiratory illnesses, diarrhea, a mother's lying over a child while nursing in her semi-sleep, poor nourishment, unsanitary conditions, inadequate care, accidents when parents were away, bad treatment of ailments—these factors took many infants.[18] Some would argue that the loss meant little.

For mothers living in extreme poverty in a Brazilian slum in the 20th century and watching infant after infant die, theirs was a stoic acceptance of child death, or at least, so they insisted to anthropologist Nancy Scheper-Hughes. They convinced themselves that certain infants simply had no will to live. Thus, they retreated from these infants, and of course, the babes died. As for grief, the mothers explained that their infants were "without a history… [their] story is not yet made up; it has no shape to it. And so the loss is not a big one; it is not heavy. The death passes over one lightly, and it is soon and easily forgotten."[19] In light of these attitudes, anthropologist Sarah Blaffer Hrdy, reading her colleague Scheper-Hughes, concludes, "When, almost inevitably, death ensues, [Brazilian shanty-town] mothers do not disguise their grief behind a stoic façade—they feel none."[20] Then Hrdy quotes General William Westmoreland, of all people, who of his Vietnam war allies said, "They do not grieve the way we do."[21]

No stoic, Elena seems to have kept close track of her children, counting the living along with the dead. In her kitchen table talks with Julia, Elena would roll through their names. Although she could not read, she kept a leather-bound booklet that was handed to the priest for his annual Blessing of the Dead—*Provody*, forty days after Easter. There, her children are listed—all of them, though in no particular order. It appears that Ivan or Elena had told the priest whom to bless and the priest had written the names in the booklet as fast as he could, occasionally resorting to abbreviations.

The birth and christening dates for Elena's progeny—recorded by the priests of Chornivka—speak volumes about her. (8.9) They give us a sense of how Elena was doing as a mother, that is, how committed she was to her task. Dr. Hrdy's *Mother Nature: Maternal Instincts And How They Shape The Human Species* has led me to consider Elena's role as a mother.

In her exhaustive and eloquent study, Hrdy observes, "Mothers were multifaceted creatures, strategists juggling multiple agendas. As a consequence, their level of commitment to each offspring born was highly contingent on circumstances."[22] What the priests have penned into their registers, what the numbers reveal is that early on, Elena was an ambivalent mother.

I could easily say that as a young mother, Elena was inexperienced, inept, unlucky and facing a wall of potential infection, illness and disease for her infants. This would all be true. More often than not, the first child didn't make it. Then again, Elena had reasons to be distracted. It would be naïve to think that she did not have some say in managing her reproductive effort—Hrdy would put it this way: Elena was "an active strategist."[23] When I came upon the dates for Elena's infants, I was also able to study those of Elena's *mother*—a serf with her own strategic challenges.

Contrary to reason, Elena's mother was more successful, early on, at keeping her own infants alive than was Elena. Some of the mother's good fortune may have been just that: she was able to time her births so that a number of her infants survived expressly because they were born in winter and early spring when she had the wherewithal to breast feed and watch over them. The timing of Elena's births was not as opportune. Yet in terms of birthing knowledge and assistance, Elena had the advantage of the lessons—taught and observed—of three older sisters and her mother. It is signal that she named her children—Anna, Domynika, Maria—after them. One does wonder, with the level of infant mortality Elena suffered, if she used these females as resources or kept her distance from them.

Once Elena was in the wild emptiness of the North West Territories, she was faced with "lethally inadequate rearing conditions" and she faltered.[24] The infant Anna, born sometime after Nick, was approximately three years old when she died of an intestinal blockage. There was nothing to feed her save grain cooked into a thick porridge, which proved indigestible for a toddler. Elena lost track of the year Anna died, nor was she certain of the year she was born. The child's death was surely horrifying for Elena. She simply did not have the wherewithal—certainly physical, possibly psychological—to rear this little girl.

Elena's last child was born with his intestines on the outside of his body. He was neither named nor christened. Julia frequently referred to him as the "Unnamed boy." I assume this is how Elena referred to him. For the pious and tradition-bound Elena, this must have been a thundering, grief stricken omission—no name for an infant. A butterfly of an un-Christened spirit-boy would beat its wings against Elena's windows for eternity. He must have been buried quietly somewhere around the lumber camp in Colville, Washington where Elena, Ivan and the boys were living. There was no priest of any denomination to offer closure. "Unnamed boy," he was a slipping away from anything that still secured Elena's identity. Here was a woman living beyond nightmare.

The nightmare of her New World gypsy life began in June of 1897; Elena and family were homesteading adjacent to Limestone Lake, not far from Wostok. January, on the 7th to be exact, the family was visited by NWMP Inspector P.C.H. Primrose. The North West Mounted Police were sent out to check on the conditions of the immigrants. Primrose tallied Ivan's holdings at two horses, one colt, one cow, one calf and about five acres of land broken. He didn't mention that Elena was trying to keep Nick, Julia's husband-to-be— a month-old infant, alive.

Primrose gave them a piece of pork and half-a-bag of flour. When the Department of the Interior—embarrassed by the reports from the NWMP—sent Commissioner Thomas Bennett out on February 24th, Bennett reported that Ivan had broken his leg via a fall on the ice of the North Saskatchewan. The colt was gone. Six acres of land were open. Ivan had two horses, a cow, a calf, a wagon, plough, harrow and sleigh. The family was living in "a shanty" (*burdei*). Ivan was hauling logs to build a house (*khata*), had spent his money on cattle and implements and had no provisions. Bennett granted relief to the amount of $16.00. Among the approximately thirty-five families who received the NWMP and the Department of Interior "inspections," only the "very poorest," those on the edge of truly going under, received more than $10 of relief funds.

Spring came. Ivan's optimism reasserted itself. He invested in a part-interest in a flourmill in the Wostok area. It failed. The grinding stones being used introduced too much grit to the meal. Next, he invested in a steam-powered threshing machine. That interest went broke too. No one was quite certain how to fix the machine when it bollixed up.

I like to think that Elena took solace in the flora around her. Surely she would have welcomed familiar friends, first seen in the woods, meadows and along stream banks near Chornivka—Celandines, Chamomile, Comfrey, Cow Parsnip, Nettle, Peppermint, Plantain, Sage, Thistle, Yarrow. Her mother and sisters would have taught her where to find them and understood their myriad uses. Blossoms, leaves, stems and roots were good for fortifying teas, decoctions, ointments, cosmetics, purifying smoke and for seasoning food.

In her new and unfamiliar home, Elena would have kept a close eye out in order to fill her medicine chest and her larder. Due diligence. As the former mayor of Dzikov noted, "people used to treat their ailments of old by household remedies, mostly herbs such as lime leaves, lilac blossoms, wormwood, wild thyme, coltsfoot, mustard, etc. All these would be gathered in May and dried to be kept for various ailments. The housewife was ashamed if some need arose and she had no 'herbs' in the house…."[25]

As snow receded, the Prairie Crocus (Pasque Flower) would have been the first to greet her in the alien land. (8.5) With its delicate pale lavender blossoms and soft furry leaves that quiver on the wind, the flower signaled the coming season of Easter, when it usually bloomed. An ethno-botanist writing of the uses of plants by the Indians of the Missouri River watershed said that "When an old Dakota first finds one of these flowers [a Prairie Crocus] in the springtime, it reminds him of his childhood, when he wandered over the prairie hills at play, as free from care and sorrow as the flowers and the birds. He sits down near the flower on the lap of Mother Earth, takes out his pipe and fills it with tobacco. Then he reverently holds the pipe towards the earth, then toward the sky, then toward the north, the east, the south, and the west. After this act of silent invocation, he smokes."[26]

Following the perimeter of a slough or gazing into a low-water area, Elena saw the white flowers of Arum-Leaved Arrowhead (Swamp potato), Water Calla, Water Parsnip and Spotted Water-Hemlock, the most "violently" poisonous plant in North America.[27] With its blotchy "spotted" stems, it thrives at watery edges and in meadows throughout. Its umbrella-shaped clusters of white flowers resemble those of Queen Anne's Lace, carrots, coriander and parsnips. Cases of mistaken identity—leading to several nibbles on the plant's root—result in death. Its toxin merely disrupts the entire central nervous system.[28] Dangerous stuff.

Marsh marigolds must have brought her joy—many-flowered clumps of sunshine-yellow blossoms surrounded by heart-shaped leaves in still water or in a wet meadow. The appellation "marigold" comes from the phrase "Mary's gold."[29] Christians believe that the yellow-gold flower was a favorite of the Virgin Mary. Why should it not be a favorite? Like many a devout Ukrainian mother, Elena named her own daughter "Maria," after the Virgin Mary and, unwittingly, after the tenacious topaz Marigold.

On her "spatseer" forays in the meadows, a Garden-of-Eden lay before her. (8.6) Elena would have accustomed herself to the floral clock. Prairie Crocus was followed by whites such as Prairie Onion, Field Chickweed, Smooth Catchfly, Western Canada Violet, Wild Mint, Northern Bedstraw and into September, the Many-Flowered Aster. For pinks, the Pink-Flowered Onion or Nodding Onion—sought out by bears (a hard-to-miss part of Elena's universe), ground squirrels and marmots—surely piqued her fancy. Perhaps she gathered nosegays of Smooth Fleabane with its tiny pink aster-like flowers. Smoke from bundles of burned Fleabane was thought to repel gnats and fleas, hence the derivation of its common English name "bane of fleas."[30] Elena would have come by this bit of folk-wisdom by some non-English, alternate route.

Patches of dusky dark pink Three-Flowered Avens with their reddish stems and dandelion fluff fruit, were everywhere around her at Limestone Lake, Soda Lake, and LaFond in the summer. Now this flower can be found mostly in cemeteries— Magdalyna's Kysyliw, Veronica's Borowich and Wasyl's Shandro— where bits of prairie soil survive. The enthusiastic Prairie Rose was there too. Showy rose-to-purple Western Wild Bergamot peppered stands of green-to-gold meadow grasses. Its spikey-looking, round cluster of a flower and every other part of the plant were sought out by natives on both sides of the forty-ninth parallel. A veritable pharmacopeia, distillates from Wild Bergamot functioned as eyewashes, stomach soothers, birth control agents, cold-fever-flu-pneumonia remedies, insect repellant, meat preservatives and perfume.[31] Something for every complaint, though this New World specimen was probably not part of Elena's medicine chest.

The blues were discreet and delicate: Blue-Eyed Grass, Early Blue Violet, Harebell, Seneca Root. The yellows were not. Gaillardia (Brown-eyed Susan), Goat's-Beard, Toadflax, Prairie Buttercup, Prairie Coneflower, Prairie Sunflower: they all vied for center-stage. And the grandest of them all, now rare, was the Large Yellow Lady's Slipper. Elena could easily walk among hummocks of these extravagant flowers. How they would have brightened the icon corner of her *khata.*

Al sensed the depth of his grandmother's folk-botanical knowledge, as well as her contemplative side during their strolls. It was then that he was momentarily transformed by her tranquility. Among flowers, Elena intimated that her past was present. "She would stop and examine a flower she had known in the Old Country and tell me about it," Al said. "Then she would walk on in silence as though in deep contemplation."[32]

With spring, Elena had gardening to do; her daughter was off in Bruderheim, working. Reliably Elena said her prayers and honored the saints. The *burdei's* icon corner—a holy place and the focus of Elena's faith—would have given her calm, confidence, and reaffirmation. The icons had magical powers. Tucked into their domestic sanctuary, Elena's icons sheltered the souls of her ancestors and protected her household from evil spirits.[33] In her youth, she learned Bible stories from the icons in Chornivka's church. Like the meadow flowers, the saints in Elena's icon corner were friends and confidants.

During her earliest days in the wild, when she must have yearned for the comfort of her village church, Elena was miles away from any of the few established churches. She probably made a point to see the Orthodox priests who infrequently passed through, christening, marrying and burying. It was one of these fellows who sanctified Magdalyna's death. Later, when Elena's life took on its vagabond quality, her interface with any particular Orthodox church was fleeting. The inimitable Julia quipped, "She never went to church, because there was no church for her to go."[34]

It was a profound loss. What would be today's equivalent? Take away all the books, the public library, the lap top, smart phone, social media like Google, Facebook, Twitter, newspapers, magazines, and most importantly, the calendar—so that one is ignorant of the days for Thanksgiving, Christmas, Valentine's Day, Mardi Gras, Easter, Memorial Day, the First (Canada) or Fourth (USA) of July, Labor Day, Halloween. And add a spiritual dimension to this, so that if one misses any of these events, grace and a touch of holiness go out of one's life. Add to this, the privation of not seeing or hearing others—who is wearing a ribbon, who is pregnant, who has a new child? And in the realm of music, is there anyone still singing the twenty-or-so songs that get you through the day in Chornivka? This was Elena's loss.

If the place in which she lived was now unfamiliar territory, the subtler aspect of telling time, of noting the days, set Elena further apart. The modern numeric calendar was incomprehensible to her. She organized her life around the religious feast days of the Eastern Orthodox church, moving from saint's day to saint's day. (8.7) Elena had been taught this way of reckoning time by Chornivka village, by its priests and her family. Winter, spring, summer and fall all had their cycle of fast and feast, saints and events to be marked with specific services, prayers, foods and activities.

Elena knew as a certainty that on the November 8th commemoration of Saint Demetrius (*Dmytra*), one invited a homeless person or a beggar into one's *khata* for dinner. In this way, the spirit of the saint was venerated. Celebrating Christ's nativity—Christmas Eve—was a major seasonal event for her: preparations were complex and careful. The pre-Christmas forty-day fast—a reference to the forty days Jesus spent in the wilderness—ended.

In the preparatory roll up, at least hemp oil was an allowed foodstuff. After the first star was spotted Christmas Eve night, twelve meatless dishes—for Christ's twelve apostles—were served. Ritually the most important of these was *kutia* (кутя), boiled wheat. Ivan would taste the *kutia*, then invite the family's ancestors and the spirits of nature to join the feast. Honor the wheat; honor the ancestors. Survival depended upon the success of the wheat crop.

Things settled down with Epiphany (Йордан, *Iordan*). For Orthodox faithful like Elena, Jesus was baptized in the Jordan River on this January day. *Iordan's* alternate appellation, *Vodokhreshcha* (Водохреща) or "blessed water," alludes to the priest's blessing of all waters—streams, ponds, rivers, lakes, and even sloughs. For the *Iordan* service near Limestone Lake, an altar and a cross of ice blocks would be set up on a convenient frozen body of water. (8.8) Thus, a priest could bless all water by standing on top of it. In Alberta, the ice was sufficiently thick to accommodate priest and congregation. Devout parishioners, among these Elena, carried "blessed water" home for year-long medicinal use. The more important point, though, is that one counted x-number of days after *Iordan* or before *Dmytra* to prepare the fields, to sow the grain, to begin the harvest.

As much as she could make it so, for the special days, Elena insisted that her home be put to order, that work stop, that a reverential tone prevail. Julia's daughter recalled a Christmas Eve in Elena's "shack." By then, Ivan was gone. Elena had a sheaf of wheat—the *didukh* (дідух) or ancestor-grandfather figure—standing in a corner, fresh straw strewn under the table and sprinkled under an embroidered tablecloth, and some combination of meatless dishes—*kutia*, braided bread, beet soup, cooked wild mushrooms, pickled herring or pike, fish in gelatin, meatless cabbage rolls, dumplings stuffed with mushrooms, potatoes and cheese, sauerkraut, stewed fruit, doughnuts filled with jam. Julia helped with a number of the prescribed dishes. Elena's celebration was consummate. To quote her granddaughter, "She had a flair for arranging whatever she had, nicely."[35] Ritual piety was essential for good fortune, of which Elena had very little.

By 1905-06, with opportunity beckoning, Ivan sold his homestead and business interests at Limestone Lake and packed his wife and four sons to Colville, Washington where work was a-plenty. Maria had moved away to Soda Lake when she married in 1903. The earliest photo I have of Elena is from the Colville days. She stands with "the boys"—Ivan, Gus, Alex, Bill and Nick. They are evenly spaced before a vigorous log cabin. Ivan is at the far left; Elena at the far right. She is fashionably Edwardian in style—a long-sleeved white blouse fastened at the neck and a flowing-to-the-ground black skirt cinched at the waist. Gone is any suggestion of Ukrainian village attire. She holds her hands together in front of her at waist level. She looks down demurely. Her head is uncovered. Her parted hair shines in the summer sun, hollyhocks bloom in the foreground. No one smiles, instead, there is wariness. Ivan looks exhausted, grim. The older boys give us truculence and resignation. Only Nick, nine or ten at the time, stands relaxed grasping the log fence rail in front of him, quizzically regarding the photographer. Still youthful-looking, tightly held within herself, Elena reveals little save uncertainty. (8.10)

In a second Colville photo, probably taken two or three years later, Elena again wears a white blouse and a long black skirt with a wide waistband. This time a dark ribbon with a pendant cross encircles her neck. It is not an Orthodox cross, but it is probably the best she can do in a non-Orthodox setting. There is a modish wide-brimmed straw hat partially shading her face. She has taken care with her ensemble. She stands next to a scrawny fruit tree in bloom—the kind whose fruit will result in *dzhem*. According to a grandchild, the photo was intended to show those back at Soda Lake the verdant quality of the land around Colville where actual fruit trees grow. Meanwhile, a white cat with black markings pauses, arching its back near the tree's toothpick trunk. Ivan pauses behind and on the other side of the tree. (8.11) Here we see Elena's face more clearly. Her eyes and her lips are horizontal lines. Did she once smile? Her gaze is interiorly directed. Although she and Ivan flank the tree, Elena seems alone.

There are other photographs taken during the Colville years, but not of Elena. In one photo we see Gus, Alex and Bill perched wearily on a gargantuan log. Gus sports a bandaged right-hand finger. Alex glares sullenly at the photographer. (8.12) There are also studio photos of the young men, one of which will be used later in a desperate circular. (8.13)

By 1913, the mood had changed in the lower forty-eight. Workers without U.S. citizenship find it harder to keep their jobs, at least in lumbering in the state of Washington. When the family leaves Colville to return to Soda Lake in 1913, Alex remains behind. The sense of it is that he will rejoin them in Alberta. Instead, he disappears. His last post, a playful note to his sister at Soda Lake, is dated January 16th, 1914: *See me. Here I am in a cap.* (8.14) That's it. Elena has lost another child.

At Soda Lake, Maria and John delegate the homeless Elena and Ivan to the *khata* that they have recently abandoned. There Elena watches over her grandchildren. Of her, grandson Sam writes, "her job, besides taking care of the children, helping feed them and keep the crying down, was spinning the wool into yarn." Elena also tries to keep the distance she seems to need—she has her own garden, she sews, she tidies the proffered cottage and wanders in the surrounding prairie meadows. Her surviving sons hire themselves out as farm workers, threshing hands and well diggers. Her husband places futile newspaper ads around the Pacific Northwest and then, to no avail, circles in search of Alex. The family suspects foul-play. Ivan has the priest write "Victim" (Вихтим, *Vikhtim*), instead of "Alex" in the *Provody* booklet. Alex-the-Victim. Elena is silence.

The 1918 Spanish Flu, the notorious influenza pandemic, catches everyone by surprise. Gus, the seasonal worker who travels about, returning to the family enclave when he can, is stricken. No one knows that he is nearing home that October. Without warning, Soda Lake receives a phone call from the hospital in Vegreville, "Come and collect one of yours." Maria's husband hurries the twenty miles to town with the wagon and is pointed to a cloth sack in a hospital corridor. The unceremonious introduction—Gus as just a bag of something—is a shock. There are too many ill, dying and dead.

Gus remains outside at Soda Lake farm, in his pine coffin on the wagon bed.[36] His body lies frozen. By official order, there will be no traditional funerary rituals in the Ukrainian-Canadian community. The danger of infection is too great to bring the deceased into the house. For once, Elena's deficits become assets. She can neither read RCMP edicts, nor understand what the Mounties tell her not to do. Giving herself over to grief, Elena shrieks, howls and chants in the wild and measured language of keening. Her daughter, Maria, places a lit candle in her kitchen window to keep Gus's spirit close for the three days it is believed to be in confused limbo. Maria's eight children are unnerved by the behavior, by the tears and the sounds of mourning. This is their first experience of death and they barely understand what is happening.

But it is Elena who commands the moment. Flouting emergency orders, she invites family and neighbors to gather. She will not be denied inalienable funerary rituals. (8.15) She stands at the head of the wagon, "at the tongue of the wagon," Katherine says. She keens. Loudly she talks directly to the dead Gus and to God, railing against this departure and reminding the mourners that a fine man—the thirty-year old Gus—has been taken from them. Her cry is hair-raising, other-worldly. It is not a stretch to imagine that Elena's declamations are for *Zoiitsa, Heorhiy, Domynika*, Alex, Anna and "Unnamed boy," as well as for Gus. The cardinal memory Katherine has of her grandmother is the occasion of her keening, the moment Elena's sketchy outline seems to solidify.

Just as suddenly, in July of 1920, Elena's son Bill (8.16) dies of a water-borne disease, typhoid perhaps. Ill for several days, he checks himself in to the hospital in Vegreville, but too late. Another pine box. Another candle lit. Bill's body lies in state in the room set aside for guests and for special occasions at Maria's. He is interred next to his brother in the cemetery at St. Demetrius. Someone in the family puts up a picket fence around the two graves. Someone plants two Norway Spruce trees, side-by-side, near the picket fence. The fence falls to disrepair and is taken down. The actual location of the two graves is lost and commemorative markers are put up elsewhere in the cemetery. The two spruce outdistance the cluster of conifers in the graveyard. Even now, from a distance, one can see them soaring above the green mass. Those two trees; Elena's two boys. They keep each other company. No one else in the family—founding members of both church and cemetery—is buried at St. Demetrius.

After Gus and Bill are gone, Elena and Ivan break camp. They move out of their temporary digs at Soda Lake, buy a farm at Flat Lake where their tiny house burns to the ground, give it up and move to LaFond. At LaFond, Ivan and the now-married Nick stitch together two granaries to form a live-in house—Nick and Julia on one side, Ivan and Elena on the other. It doesn't work out. The bank forecloses on LaFond. I can only imagine a catatonic Elena, having turned to stone. "She had a very hard life," Katherine mused. "They had children, children, children and death, death, death."[37] This summation seems about right.

There is a photo of Elena on the steps of a general store in St. Paul de Métis. (8.17) She has foresworn her Edwardian costume and reverted to that of a Ukrainian peasant woman. Covered shoulder to toe in white with a shawl about her head, her hands clasped characteristically in front of her, she angles away from the photographer unsmiling, a reluctant subject. There is a photo of Elena seated outside next to Ivan, the two of them in a garden or field at the edge of a cluster of houses. (8.18) Dressed in her signature white, she is petite on her chair next to him. She slumps, and unlike Ivan, does not engage with the photographer.

Enough is enough. In 1934, Ivan dies. A transient more than ever, Elena follows Nick: St Paul de Métis, Condor, Edmonton. Briefly, she is re-directed to her less-than-welcoming daughter at Soda Lake. The hardy Maria will have little to do with her mother. She keeps distance and a haughty, pitying contempt for Elena between them. Soda Lake doesn't work out. Capitulating, Nick builds his mother "a shack" on his property in Condor, then again in the yard of his 142nd Street home in Edmonton. Here, she spends her last years. On occasion, for human interaction, she walks across the yard to tarry in Julia's kitchen, gaze out of the window and talk about the prince.

In a final photo of Elena, some months before her death, she sits apple-cheeked in a patch of sunlight. (8.19) Her skin has taken on the nearly blinding white color of her long dress. Her eyes disappear, inscrutable almonds of black. There is a pucker-line of worry between and above her eyebrows. She has lost some weight and now fits Katherine's description — "doll-like." If blankness can be attributed to her mien, there is an overlay of sadness in the void. Hers has been a somatic life. Driven deeply inside herself, she has chosen to stay there.

As for her death, Elena was not going to be buried in Canada. She did not want it. Sitting in her chair, looking out of the window in her shack, or seated in Julia's kitchen, Elena would tone that she was supposed to stay behind in Chornivka and marry a prince. When, at the port of Hamburg on the journey to Canada, the nine-year-old Gus wandered off and barely made it back, just before the *S.S. Arcadia* left, Elena attributed his frightening walk-about as a sign that she should go back to her village. Nothing good would come from proceeding to the North West Territories.

Years before she died, Elena had her funeral clothes readied, this too, according to Julia. Her ensemble was all-white, of a satin-like fabric. The blouse and long gathered skirt, she sewed for herself. The stockings, which she purchased somewhere, had white ribbons that one tied just below the knee, to keep them from falling down. "You were supposed to pull them (the ribbons), because there weren't panty hose at that time," Julia tittered. I suppose the fussiness of it amused Julia. I tried to visualize the ribbons somehow attached to the stocking-tops, being pulled through a casing and then tied. Black patent-leather shoes finished the outfit.

For a 19th century Ukrainian funeral, Elena would have been dressed in her best clothes—an ankle-length white linen chemise decorated around the neckline and along the sleeves with fine cross-stitchery, over which was wrapped a dark wool apron skirt and finished by a colorfully woven wool belt. She either had none of these items left or chose not to use them.

Her choice of all-white is curious. Not a color associated with death—not in Ukrainian funerary tradition.[38] White is associated instead with innocence, youth and virginity. As for the satin and the patent-leather shoes, they are elegant symbols of a social strata to which Elena had no ingress. Elena certainly wasn't dressing to meet her husband in the beyond. Her chosen ensemble suggests a final, dream-like fantasy. She would go out virginal, the satin-wearing bride she was meant to be. She would will her fantasy into her soul's reality.

The one genuinely traditional aspect of Elena's death preparation was a pillow—white, and approximately ten-by-twelve inches in size. This, Elena assembled and sewed. The cushion was filled with herbs and flowers she collected, gathered "*for years*," Julia said. The sachet would keep her head resting on something fragrant. The herbage would offer its magical and healing properties and its beauty. Everything Elena knew about individual plants, their lore, would stay with her. The innocent flowers might also be offered to God, who knew of and oversaw the mess of her life.

She was buried in Beechmount Cemetery. The family did not put up a gravestone. I think it had to do with money and with memory—no one remembered who Elena was or had been.

On one of those delicious glowing eighteen-hour summer days in Edmonton, Julia, her daughter and I arranged a visit to Beechmount and Elena's grassy spot. We had a photo shoot. When, back in California, I shared the photos with Katherine, she was indignant: no marker for Elena! In a nonce, Katherine had a marker paid for, made and properly set. "They won that land stump-by-stump and rock-by-rock," Katherine said. "I saw that a stone was put on her grave there."[39] The marble reads, "Arrived in Canada in 1897 with husband John. A pioneer family." I would have written a different inscription, something that had more of Elena in it. Regardless, Katherine did the right thing.

As we sat in Julia's living room, on her mauve velour couch, as Elena unfolded in Julia's vernacular, I asked Julia, "Did Elena ever talk about what she left in the Old Country? Her home in Chornivka?" Julia sat back. "I'll tell you a story that *Boonka* —[Elena]—told me."[40] Julia folded her hands in her lap. "She had an older sister. And this sister got pregnant; she was not married. So, when their mother found out, well, you know, they wore these gathered skirts[41] and for a long time she [the girl] probably didn't even know she was pregnant, didn't pay attention.[42] But when she already was going to give birth, that's when they found out. O.K. So, what are they going to do with her? Her mother went and got a rope. Soaked it in water. And came and beat her to death. Yes."

I could barely stutter, "WHAT!" I was blind-sided by the revelation.

Julia went on, "Yes. She beat her, while she [the girl] was having these contracting pains, giving birth to the baby. She beat her. And, of course, yes, she died....They buried her and the baby is left. So the grandmother has this little baby. She used to take that child to the graveyard every day and beg her daughter to take this child. Now if you don't feed your child, you don't have to beg anybody to take it. You know very well it's going to die, because it's not being fed. So, eventually the baby died."

"What would have happened, if that daughter would have had the baby—if she had had this baby out-of-wedlock? Why was it such a terrible thing?" I asked.

"You know, this is something that I couldn't answer," Julia said. "But this is the story that *Boonka* told me and it stayed with me. This is her *own* mother, who killed her *own* daughter." What more could be said? Julia and I sat silent on the couch among her pink lace-covered throw pillows and silk flowers. Julia had no reason to make-up such a narrative.

Before this visit with Julia, I had not known that Elena had sisters, and certainly never dreamed that there were records of her family, which later I was to find. If such a murder occurred, no wonder Elena wanted a prince to get her out of there! A sixteen-year old would remember a sister's death. Some sixteen-year olds might even be pushed into regression, never mind 19th century peasant culture. Murder was in a class of its own.

If a mother is driven to destroy her adult daughter, this speaks of intense stress and a rage that lays waste to everything around it. It sends shock waves out. Whether Elena's mother killed Elena's sister is moot. The important point is that Elena believed that her mother had beaten her sister to death. She seems to have organized her life around that tragedy—blocking out any guilt she may have had, resorting to the fantasy that a prince should have rescued her from her life.

There are many things that trouble me about my great-grandmother and, no doubt, will continue to trouble me. No one knew her, damaged soul that she was, burdened by grief upon grief. She had every reason to be emotionally detached—from herself, from her husband, from her children, from the rest of the world. At sixteen, Elena could see or sense that her mother was an extreme case of bad mothering. Violence incarnate. How do you hold the knowledge that your mother can kill? How do you protect yourself from the implicit danger?

Perhaps Elena's silence carried terror, as well as guilt. Was she not part of a system of women who looked upon the premature, unfortunate death of a sister and of that sister's child with some measure of impassivity? Yet, *There, but for the grace of God, go I.* The child in question was named "Elena." Little Elena lasted a mere three months. Elena the Silent. Elena the Shade. Elena of Chornivka, Limestone Lake, Colville, Soda Lake, Flat Lake, LaFond, St. Paul de Métis, Condor and Edmonton. She may well have been haunted by the ghost of little Elena. What was left after her sister's death but to retreat? Then she left the village. No, no one knew Elena. No, Elena was simply not there. Elena vacated Elena. At the periphery, granddaughter Katherine, who "got" Elena's grief, may have been the one exception.

When I asked Julia if she had any idea which herbs and flowers Elena might have included in her white pillow-sachet, Julia rasped, "Just wild stuff." And there it was.

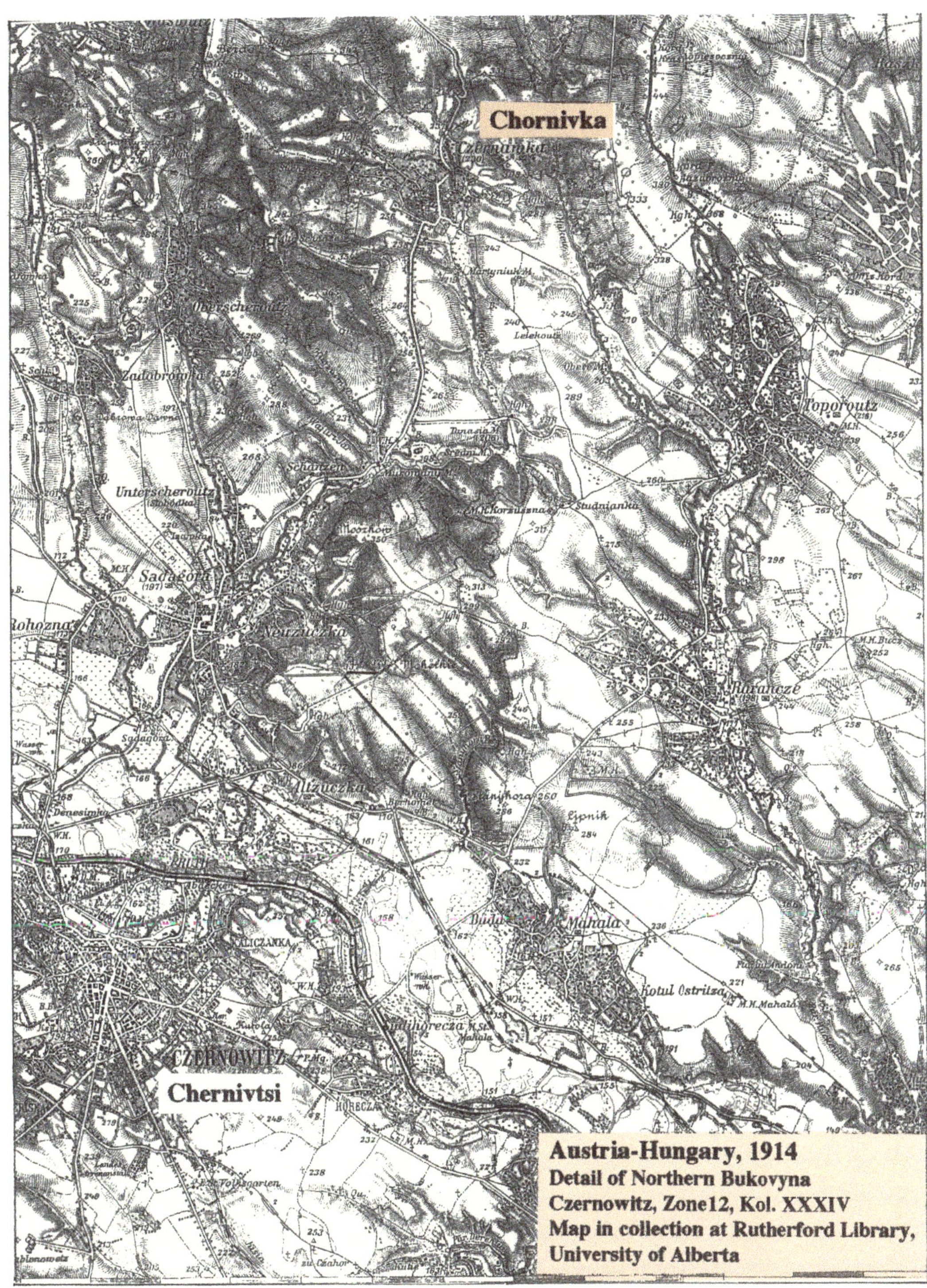

8.1 *Map showing location of Elena's ancestral village, Chornivka. Due north of the present-day city of Chernivtsi in Ukraine and the Prut' (Pruth) River.*

8.2 *Rare photo of Elena with her head uncovered. Her white hair is visible. l-r: Elena's daughter, Maria Scraba Ropchan (head out of frame); Elena's daughter-in-law, Julia (Gadowski) Scraba; Elena (seated); Elena's son, Nick Scraba; Bill Ropchan, Maria's son; Alberta Scraba, Julia and Nick's daughter (child). St. Paul, Alberta.*

8.3 *Julia, Elena's daughter-in-law, seated in her living room with the author. Edmonton, Alberta.*

8.3a *Julia showing "Elena's China." Purchased to host a fitting funerary dinner at Elena's death in 1947. Julia associated the china with Elena.*

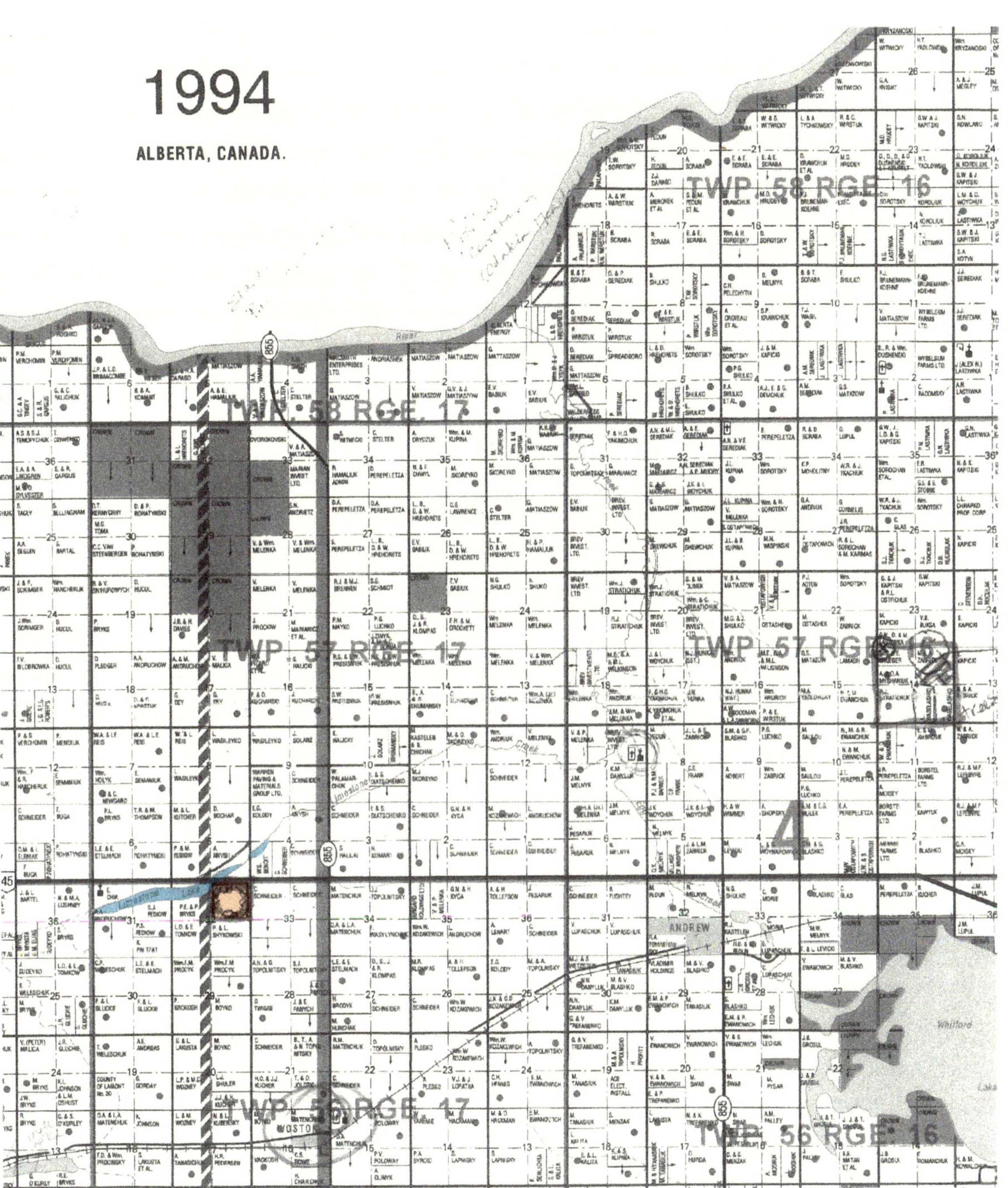

8.4 *Map (detail) of County of Lamont, Alberta, 1994. Location of Limestone Lake, south of the North Saskatchewan River, west of Whitford Lake. Elena and Ivan's original quarter section: NE.32.56.17.W.4.M.*

8.5 *Pasqueflower, Prairie Crocus. Earliest Spring wildflower. A favorite at Soda Lake.*

8.6

Meadow, Slough and Woodland Wildflowers that Elena would have observed

In the Aspen Parklands and Boreal Forest areas of Alberta, Canada, I found them presiding in places associated with Elena.

Whites

Arrow-Leaved Colt's-Foot, *Petasites sagittatus (Pursh) A. Gray*
Arrowhead, *Sagittaria cuneata Sheld.*
Canada Anemone, *Anemone Canadensis L.*
Clustered Oreocarya, *Oreocarya glomerata (Pursh) Greene*
Cow Parsnip (Wild Rhubarb), *Heracleum lanatum Michx.*
Field Chickweed, *Cerastium arvense L.*
Many-Flowered Aster, *Aster pansus (Blake) Cronq.*
Northern Bedstraw, *Galium boreale L.*
Penny Cress, *Thiapsi arvense L.*
Prairie Onion, *Allium textile Nels. and Macbr.*
Smooth Catchfly, *Silene cserei Baumgarten*
Spotted Water Hemlock, *Cicuta maculata L. var. angustifolia Hook.*
Western Canada Violet, *Viola rugulosa Greene*
Wild Lily-of-the-Valley, *Maianthemum canadense*
Wild Mint, *Mentha arvensis L.*
Wild Sarsaparilla (Wild Ginseng), *Aralia nudicaulis L.*
Yarrow, *Achillea millefolium L.*

Blues

Blue-Eyed Grass, *Sisyrinchium montanum Greene*
Early Blue Violet, *Viola adunca J.E. Smith*
Harebell, *Campanula rotundifolia L.*
Prairie Crocus (Pasque Flower), *Anemone patens*
Seneca Root, *Polygala senega L.*
Tall Lungwort, *Mertensia paniculata (Ait.) G. Don.*

Yellows

Agrimony, *Agrimonia striata Michx.*
Brown-eyed Susan (Gaillardia), *Gaillardia aristata Pursh*
Goat's-Beard, *Tragopogon dubius Scop.*
Large Yellow Lady's Slipper, *Cypripedium calceolus L.*
Marsh Marigold, *Caltha palustris L.*
Prairie Buttercup, *Ranunculus cymbalaria Pursh*
Prairie Coneflower, *Ratibida columnifera (Nutt.) Woot. and Standl.*
Prairie Sunflower, *Helianthus petiolaris Nutt.*
Sneezeweed, *Helenium montanum Nutt.*
Toadflax, *Linaria vulgaris P. Mill*
Yellow Avens, *Geum aleppicum Jacq.*
Yellow Pond Lily, *Nuphar variegatum Engelm. ex Durand*
Veiny Meadow Rue, *Thalictrum venulosum Trel.*
Wild Chamomile, *Matricaria chamomilla L.*

Pinks

Common Pink Wintergreen, *Pyrola asarifolia Michx.*
Fireweed, *Epilobium angustifolium L.*
Hedysarum (Sweet Broom), *Hedysarum alpinum L.*
Narrow-leaved Milk Vetch, *Astragalus pectinatus Dougl.*
Pink-flowered Onion (Nodding Onion), *Allium cernuum Roth*
Prairie Rose, *Rosa arkansana Porter*
Red Samphire, *Salicornia rubra A. Nels.*
Smooth Fleabane, *Erigeron glabellus Nutt.*
Three-flowered Avens, *Geum triflorum Pursh*
Western Wild Bergamot, *Monarda fistulosa L.*

Elena's Calendar

Orthodox Calendar of Holy Days, by no means complete

Gregorian (New Style)*	Julian (Old Style)	Feast Day
24 December	06 January	Свят-вечер. *Sviat Vecher*. Christmas Eve.
25 December	07 January	Різдво. *Rizdvo Khrystove*. Christmas.
31 December	13 January	Щедрий вечер. *Shchedryi Vecher*. New Year's Eve, "Generous Eve."
06 January	19 January	Йордан. *Iordan, Vodokhreshcha*. Epiphany. Baptism of Christ by John the Baptist in the River Jordan. Blessing of ALL waters.
02 February	15 February	Стрітення. *Stritennia*. Summer meets winter. Candlemas Day. Christ's presentation at the temple.
March	April	Вербна неділя. *Verbna Nedilia*. Willow Sunday. Palm Sunday. Last Sunday before Easter
26 March	07 April	Благовіщення. *Blahovishchennia*. The Annunciation. Angel Gabriel tells the Virgin Mary she will conceive.
March	April	Великдень. *Velykden'* "Great Day." Easter.
March	April	Проводи. *Provody*. Blessing of the graves. Forty days after Easter.
23 April	06 May	Юрія. *Iuriia*. St. George. Opens the Gates of Heaven to allow spring to descend to earth. Protects domestic animals.
April	May	Зелені свята. *Zeleni Sviata*. Pentecost, Whitsuntide. Fifty days after Easter. Day when the Holy Spirit descended upon the Apostles. Woods & meadow spirits honored (pre-Christian).
07 July		Івана Купала. *Ivana Kupala*. St. John's Eve, Midsummer's Night. Pre-Christian celebration.
29 June	12 July	Петра. *Petra*. Saints Peter & Paul "Wandererers." Special baked rolls called *mandruvaty* [to wander] exchanged.
20 July	02 August	Іллі. *Illi*. St. Elijah. Went to heaven in a whirlwind. Assoc. with dew & summer storms: rain, thunder, lightning, hail.
06 August	19 August	Спас. *Spas*. Christ's Transfiguration. Christ is called "son" by a voice in the sky, is transfigured and becomes radiant. Human nature meets God.
15 August	28 August	Успіння. *Uspinnia*. Dormition. Death of the Virgin Mary. She "falls asleep."
08 September	21 September	Анни. St. Anne. Gives birth to the Virgin.
14 October	27 October	Параскеви. *Paraskevy*. St. Paraskeva. Her name means "preparation," thus preparing for the Sabbath.
26 October	08 November	Дмитра. *Dymytra*. St. Demetrius. Roman military martyr. Honoring ancestors by inviting in beggars, orphans and wanderers.
22 November	04 December	Варвари. *Varvary*. St. Barbara. Protects against sudden death. Her relics reputedly at St. Michael's of the Golden Domes in Kiev.
25 November	07 December	Катерини. *Kateryny*. St. Katherine. Scholar. Patron saint of girls. Rituals to reveal a young woman's future.
06 December	19 December	Миколи. *Mykoly*. St. Nicholas. Generosity.
1 December	13 December	Андрія. *Andriia*. St. Andrew. Patron saint of Ukraine. Visited and blessed the hills of Kiev. Day of young men's games to "show off." (Season of courting)

**Gregorian calendar, introduced by Pope Gregory XIII in 1582. Gregorian date + 13 days = Julian calendar date. The Orthodox church uses Julian calendar.*

8.7 *Elena marked her days by means of this religious and traditional folk calendar.*

Elena and Ivan

(Єлена і Іван, Elena and John)

Elena Koropets'ka + **Ivan Scraba**

Elena Koropets'ka
(Єлена Коропецька)

Born: 29 August 1861 (o.s.), Chornivka
Married: 24 January 1882 (o.s.), Chornivka
Age: 21 years
Immigr.: 2 May 1897 (n.s.), Quebec, *S.S. Arcadia*
Died: 28 November 1947, Edmonton, AB Canada

Ivan Scraba
(Іван Шкраба)

Born: ca. 1859 (o.s.), Chornivka
Married: 24 January 1882 (o.s.)
Age: ca. 24
Immigr.: 2 May 1897 (n.s.)
Died: 15 July 1934, St. Paul, AB, Canada

- Zoiitsa (Зоїца)
  b. 1 May 1883 (o.s.), Chornivka
  christened (X): 7 May
  d. as infant
- Mariia Scraba • (Марія)
  b. 16 August 1884 (o.s.), Chornivka
  X. 18 August 1884
  Immigr. 2 May 1897, Quebec, *S.S. Arcadia*
  m. 7 June 1903 (n.s.), Wostok, AB to John Ropchan
  d. 24 September 1970, Estevan, SK, Canada
- Hrehorii (Григорій)
  b. 30 March 1887 (o.s.), Chornivka
  X. 31 March
  d. as infant
- Konstantyn (Константин, *Kostaki, Gus*) •
  b. 18 February 1888 (o.s.), Chornivka
  X. 19 February
  Immigr. 2 May 1897, Quebec
  d. 31 October 1918 (n.s.), Vegreville, AB Canada
- Domnika (Домніка)
  b. 26 April 1890 (o.s.), Chornivka
  X. 28 April
  d. as infant
- Aleksandr (Александр, *Alex*) •
  b. 2 April 1892 (o.s.), Chornivka
  X. 5 April
  Immigr. 2 May 1897, Quebec
  d. 6 May, 1955, Hermiston, OR
- Wasyl (Василь, *William, Bill*) •
  b. 2 June 1894 (o.s.), Chornivka
  X. 4 June
  Immigr. 2 May 1897, Quebec
  d. 3 July 1920, Vegreville, AB Canada
- Nikolai (Мукола, *Nick*) •
  b. 14 November 1897 (n.s.), Limestone Lake, AB
  m. 25 May 1930, Lake Eliza, AB to Julia G.
  d. 28 August 1961, Edmonton, AB Canada
- Anna (Анна)
  b. ca. 1898-99, Limestone Lake, AB
  d. ca. 1902- 03, Limestone Lake, AB, Canada
- "Unnamed boy"
  b. d. ca. 1907-1912, Coleville, Washington, USA

8.9 *Family Tree: Elena Koropets'ka Scraba and Ivan Scraba.*

8.10 *Photo of Scraba family at logging camp in Colville, Washington, ca. 1907-13. l-r: Ivan, Gus (Konstantyn), Alex, Bill (Wasyl), Nick, Elena.*

8.11 *Ivan and Elena, Colville, Washington, ca. 1907-13*

8.12 *Photo of Elena's sons (l-r) Gus, Alex and Bill. Logging camp, Colville, Washington, ca. 1907-13.*

"Her surviving sons hire themselves out as farm workers, threshing hands and well diggers."

8.13 *Photo of Alex Scraba, possibly used on a flyer or in a newspaper ad to advertise his disappearance. Alex vanished in the Colville area in 1914.*

8.14 *Last family communication. Postcard to Marry Ropchan [sic] from her brother, Alex Scraba, dated 16 January 1914. (recto) photo of Alex and friend; (verso) postcard note.*

8.16 *Studio photo of Bill (Wasyl) Scraba, Elena's son.*

POST CARD

CORRESPONDENCE HERE

Hello sister
I have Received
welcome card and
was glad to hear
from you that is
Me on the picther
I have a cape and
my friend has a hat
Your Brother Alex Scraba

NAME AND ADDRESS

JAN 16 12AM 1914 WASH.

Mrs Marry Rop...
Sodalake
Alta

The family suspects foul-play.

Funeral Ritual and Elena

...a mix of Ukrainian and Romanian practice.

A funeral is a three-day event; burial takes place on the third day.

Mourning is the means by which the living honor the dead. During the funeral, the belief is that the soul watches to see that nothing is omitted. Should this occur, the soul will return and punish the living.

Immediately upon someone's death, female relatives begin to mourn. They speak and chant laments. It's ritually obligatory—it's a sin *not* to lament the dead. Lamenting starts immediately after the ringing of the church bells for the deceased. A particular pattern of bell ringing signals, to the community, that someone has died.

In the home, candles are lit to protect the body from evil spirits and to illuminate the deceased's journey to the other world. Mirrors in the house are covered, so that the deceased's soul is protected from alarming visions. A coffin of *pine* is prepared. Pine: "If the boards had a lot of pitch in them, they were favoured, for the belief was that in such a coffin the corpse would not be reduced so soon to dust." (*From Serfdom to Self-Government*, 133)

The corpse is bathed by someone of the same sex as the deceased, usually by a designated bather-of-the-deceased outside of the family. After the body is cleansed, the bath water is taken from the household and thrown in a remote corner of the property where no one will step in it and lose their life power.

The body is placed on a long wooden bench or table in the "formal" room of the cottage—it is the room usually reserved for special dinners and for entertaining guests, the "great room" of the *khata*. The body is clothed in Sunday attire, or clothing the deceased has made expressly to wear in death.

When the coffin arrives, a mattress and pillow placed in the coffin for the dead are usually filled with shavings from the wood—normally pine—used to make the coffin. Feathers are to be avoided as stuffing—in the world of the dead, the deceased may have to chase after them.

The living wear somber colors—nothing distracting. Female relatives leave their hair unbraided; men remain unshaven; men and boys go bareheaded. These gestures help to prevent obstacles in the path of the deceased.

– Continued next page

8.15 *Ukrainian-Romanian funerary rituals.*

Before the day of burial, food and drink are prepared for the mourners, breads for alms.

The body is never left alone in the "formal" room, but is kept company by a mourner-lamenter throughout the pre-burial period. Early in the 19th century, writers described raucous games played around the body throughout the night in order to keep the deceased's spirit amused and distracted.

Relatives, neighbors and friends come to pay their respects. They view the body in its open coffin. Some add sharp objects—a needle, pins, a small knife—to the body, so that its spirit has weapons to protect itself against evil forces.

The day of the funeral, women approach the coffin and lament. Formulaic and poetic, lamentations recount the particular circumstances of death and the relationship of the deceased to the lamenter and the community; they portray the world of the dead and the process of putrefaction; they extol the virtues of the deceased and how he/she will be missed; they call out to the deceased to return to the world of the living; they ask the deceased to forgive any slights.

The priest arrives, enters the house, blesses the deceased with holy water, extinguishes the candle in his bucket of holy water—this symbolizes the extinction of life. He blesses the house, the courtyard and other structures with holy water and then initiates the removal of the coffin to the burial ground.

The casket must be removed, corpse's feet first, since the deceased is now a traveler to be headed in the direction of his/her journey. Pallbearers transport the coffin over the threshold and out while women lament and keen in passionate, loud cries.

The funeral procession makes its way to the cemetery. Pauses occur at certain locations: a threshold—courtyard gates, the entrance to the cemetery; a crossroad, rivers, streams. At these places, the priest offers prayers, the coffin is raised and lowered three times. These places share the characteristic of ambiguity—between one possibility and another. Prayers assist the dead in maneuvering safely across these obstacles. The priest is paid for each prayer he utters.

In a flood of lamentation, the coffin is placed in its cemetery plot, sprinkled with earth, flowers, holy water. Gravediggers complete the burial. Mourners leave the gravesite to partake of a funeral repast hosted by the family of the deceased.

Nine days after the burial fresh prayers are said. Forty days after the death there is a church service followed by a commemorative meal. One year after the death there is another ritual feast. After that, the deceased is remembered annually, forty days after Easter on *Provody*, with the priest's blessing of the graves and (*Pomona*) baskets of favored foodstuffs left for or gifted in honor of the deceased.

8.17 Photo of Elena on the porch of her son's (Nick's) general store in St. Paul, Alberta, ca. 1920.

"For once, Elena's deficits become assets."

8.18 *Photo of Elena and Ivan Scraba, St. Paul, Alberta, ca. 1932-34.*

8.19 *Photo of Elena, July 1947. She passed away that November.*

[1] Taped interview with Katherine, Walnut Creek, CA. 28 April 1994.
[2] Taped interview with Katherine, Walnut Creek, CA. 28 April 1994.
[3] Taped interview with George, Toronto, Ontario. 13 June 1996.
[4] Ropchan, Alex, "Al's Story: Memoirs of Alexander Ropchan," ed. Stacey Gutierrez, unpublished manuscript, 2002. Author's personal collection.
[5] Peter Svarich, *Peter Svarich Memoirs, 1877 – 1904.* Translated by William Kostash. (Edmonton, Alberta: Ukrainian Pioneers' Association of Alberta, Huculak Chair of Ukrainian Culture and Ethnography, 1999). Bill Kostash was age-equal, here-and-there friend to my uncles and aunts—Elena's grandchildren. Bill's daughter, Myrna, went on to write an excellent angry book about the Ukrainian experience in western Canada—*All of Baba's Children*.
[6] Peter Svarich, *Peter Svarich Memoirs, 1877 – 1904.* Translated by William Kostash. (Edmonton, Alberta: Ukrainian Pioneers' Association of Alberta, Huculak Chair of Ukrainian Culture and Ethnography, 1999) 79.
[7] Ibid., 79-80.
[8] Ibid., 121-122.
[9] John McPhee, *Coming Into the Country* (New York: Farrar, Straus and Giroux, 1976) 286.
Svarich, 124-128.
[10] Ibid., 172-176. Svarich titles this particular vignette "Lost On the Prairies."
[11] Taped interview with Katherine, Walnut Creek, CA. 14 March 1997.
[12] Julia's daughter insists that Elena told Julia that she had had eleven children. In somewhat scrambled family records, there are listings for two Domynikas. However, archival records from the village of Chornivka indicate that before she left for Canada, Elena had seven children, three of whom died in infancy—*Zoiitsa, Heorhiy* and (one) *Domynika*. When she arrived to Canada, Elena had three more children, two of whom died in infancy.
[13] Taped interview with Vera, Bloomington, Indiana. 17 January 2003.
[14] Olga Semyonova Tian-Shanskaia, *Village Life in Late Tsarist Russia*, Editor Davis L. Ransel, translated by David L. Ransel with Michael Levine (Bloomington and Indianapolis: Indiana University Press, 1993), 133. Ms. Tian-Shanskaia lists customary priestly services and accompanying payments. Services include: "Wedding, Baptism, Funeral, Office for the dead, Special mass, Confession, Extreme unction, Prayers requested by the commune for rain, Cleansing ritual against mice." For performing a Baptism, the priest was to receive "fifty kopecks, plus bread."
[15] Sarah Blaffer Hrdy, *Mother Nature: Maternal Instincts And How They Shape The Human Species* (New York: Random House Publishig Group, Ballantine Books, 1999) 464.
[16] Olga Semyonova Tian-Shanskaia, *Village Life in Late Tsarist Russia*, Editor Davis L. Ransel, Translated by David L. Ransel with Michael Levine (Bloomington and Indianapolis: Indiana University Press, 1993) 6.
[17] Tian-Shanskaia, 6.
[18] Nancy Scheper-Hughes, *Death Without Weeping: The Violence of Everyday Life in Brazil* (Berkeley: University of California Press, 1992) 437.
[19] Hrdy, 311.
[20] Ibid., 311.
[21] Ibid., xviii.
[22] Ibid., 21.
[23] Ibid., 519.
[24] *From Serfdom to Self-Government, Memoirs of a Polish Village Mayor, 1842-1927.* [The Memoirs of Jan Slomka] Translated from the Polish by William John Rose, (London: Minerva Publishing Co., Ltd, 1941), 131.
[25] Timothy Coffey, *The History And Folklore of North American Wildflowers* (Boston & New York: Houghton Mifflin Company, 1993) 19. Coffey's reference is taken from Melvin R. Gilmore, *Uses of Plants by the Indians of the Missouri River Region*, 1914. Reprint. (Lincoln, Nebraska: University of Nebraska Press, 1977) 19.
[26] Coffey, 156.
[27] Amy Stewart, *Wicked Plants. The Weed that Killed Lincoln's Mother & Other Botanical Atrocities* (Chapel Hill, NC: Algonquin Books, 2009), 193.
[28] Kathleen Wilkinson, *Wildflowers of Alberta. A Guide to Common Wildflowers and Other Herbaceous Plants.* (Edmonton: The University of Alberta Press and Lone Pine Publishing, 1999) 69.
[29] Wilkinson, 260.
[30] Ibid., 206.
[31] Ropchan, Alex, "Al's Story: Memoirs of Alexander Ropchan," ed. Stacey Gutierrez (Unpublished manuscript, 2002. Author's personal collection.) 10.
[32] Orlando Figes, A People's Tragedy. The Russian Revolution. 1891–1924 (New York: The Penguin Group, 1996) 66.
[33] Taped interview with Julia, Edmonton, Alberta, Canada. 2 May 1995.
[34] Taped interview with Julia, Edmonton, Alberta, Canada. 2 May 1995.
[35] *From Serfdom to Self-Government*, 133. "If the boards had a lot of pitch in them, they were favoured, for the belief was that in such a coffin the corpse would not be reduced so soon to dust."
[36] Taped interview with Katherine, Walnut Creek, CA. 23 March 1994.

[37] In the 19th century village culture of northern Romania, a young girl who died before marriage, was buried in white—she was dressed as a bride for a symbolic wedding ceremony. The belief was that as marriage was crucial to a life fulfilled, to die unmarried was dangerous for the soul. Thus, a ritual marriage took place to placate the soul of the deceased. See Gail Kligman, *The Wedding of the Dead Ritual, Poetics, And Popular Culture In Transylvania* (Berkeley: University of California Press, 1988) 215-248.
[38] Taped interview with Katherine, Walnut Creek, CA. 19 February 1999.
[39] The term "Boonka" that Julia uses is actually "Bunica," an endearing Romanian term for "Auntie."
[40] *From Serfdom to Self-Government*, 24. "With the years, clothing made of bought stuffs became the regular thing; and about 1870 the new fashion caught on....It was also the fashion for the women to wear several skirts, one over the other. The finest, which meant the newest, was put on last. Even with chemises [*sorochkas*] the same thing happened. It was thought an honour to look stout and strong, so that the housewife could scarce get through the door."
[41] Elena's older sister would have known she was pregnant. At twenty-six, she had already given birth to a son. Here, at thirty-two, she finds herself pregnant again.

"What more could be said? Julia and I sat silent on the couch among her pink lace-covered throw pillows and silk flowers."

CHAPTER 9

SODA LAKE AND MARIA

"I had eleven children, and none of them ever went to prison."
— Maria Scraba

IT was our final summer in Canada. My dissertation writing was drawing to an end. Suffering from road-burn, my husband and I were driving west and "home" to Alberta and Edmonton from Saskatchewan and a hugely well-attended family reunion on my father's side—hundreds of Halyks. Bunny—brick-wall solid, short, compact, cheerful—who farmed my dad's parents' original homestead quarter, hosted the reunion. Quietly and additionally, Bunny farmed a further sixteen *sections* of wheat, barley and sunflowers—that is sixty-three quarter sections of land, 160-acres in a quarter, pretty much the entire southeast corner of Saskatchewan.

Understandably, Bunny had a virtual arsenal of gargantuan bright red Case farm machines, concatenations of steel for sowing, tilling, fertilizing and harvesting and metal lodges of equal size in which to store them. (9.1) The reunion programs and meals—for three hundred or so—took place in one of these enclosures. We were near Birmingham, a hamlet that today only exists as a highway sign. Birmingham lay just west of Melville (9.2), a town that continues to cling tenuously to the infinite northern prairie. North of Melville is Yorkton, a more prosperous town, and thanks to the Bronfman brothers, Harry and Sam, original home to the gin and whiskey outfit that became Seagram's. Some of the earlier Halyks got in with the not-always-legal whisky biz; a distant Halyk second-cousin married Al Capone's niece.

Like other irregulars, we asked Bunny about his name; it was official, not a nickname. Seems there were so many small ones in the family that Bunny's father decided he was living in a rabbit hutch and named the next newborn "Bunny." That was that. As for the reunion, it was a dizzying swirl of mostly strangers, but we got to know the tire track back roads; found the family's log-and-adobe *khata*, the wood frame Anglo house, the startlingly substantial barn—the only structure of import left in Birmingham and its environs; and visited the commemorative boulder (9.3)—marking what had once been the one-room school where my father did not learn to read. Then we headed back to Alberta.

Numb from driving five hundred table-flat miles, we decided to drop off of the main highway at Vegreville and amble though the Soda Lake area along highway 637. We expected to see very little, but the place is full of stories that make it interesting to us. Contrary to all expectation, we saw something, a disturbance on the horizon line. Looked like smoke, and as we drew closer, it was. Billowing smoke, right at the corner where the Gorgichuk's place had been. It was a flat-bed trailer, loaded with bales of hay, on fire (9.4)—yellow-orange flames, a booming blaze worthy of rubber-necking and, for a fire-maven, a definite stop.

The cab part of the truck assemblage had been unhitched from the burning flat-bed and parked on the opposite side of the four-way intersection. (9.4) We parked next to the towering cab. The driver stood less-than-thoughtfully near us, smoking his cigarette—*cherchez la femme*, scratching his head. The flat-bed he'd been towing was piled high with gigantic Nabisco shredded wheat-like rolls of drying grasses. It was these that were incinerating, in part, because a stiff prairie wind helped to fan the conflagration. The immediate danger was that airborne embers would spread the fire to the surrounding dry fields and roar along, one farmer's quarter to the next.

We watched the ladies of the Willingdon Volunteer Fire Department—the men were off fighting horrid fires in the Canadian Rockies around Banff— arrive to the scene and spring to action. (9.5) It was an initiation of sorts: we learned that they had yet to use the new uniforms, the new hoses and the new fire truck. They went to work. With force and efficiency, they doused the flat-bed, hoses spraying powerful streams of water that took two or three to hold in line. There were no glitches, but the battle was being lost. The flat-bed's rubber tires melted. The wind controlled the engagement.

A well-muscled farmer rolled in on an equally muscled tractor. He had probably heard of the fire via radio transmissions and saw the smoke. His tractor had a prong-attachment in front, intended to carry similar silage rolls from field to storage. It was agreed that the farmer would try to pull apart the big bales on the flat-bed, to give the firewomen more access to the heart of the flames. So he backed the tractor down the road embankment into an adjacent field, to give himself a running start to the truck for a perpendicular assault. But there in the field, the wheels of the tractor began to sink, noticeably and fast. Turns out, that what was now a field of wheat had once been a slough. The ground underneath was mushy goo.

The intensity of the scrambling intensified. I assume the farmer used the tractor's version of no-holds-barred four-wheel drive; he got very serious about handling the vehicle. Ultimately, the sinking tractor got out of the muck, the bales got pulled apart, the Fireladies delivered a successful soak and the trailer stopped melting. It was a great show.

Mid-near-catastrophe, we were joined by a veteran fire official. He began to talk about the fields and what lay beneath them. A slough was no surprise. Sloughs peppered the land. What farmer didn't dream of filling in a slough in order to plant Canola? Soda Lake, the large slough adjacent to Mother's parent's quarter, had the reputation of disregarding its boundaries and usurping productive farmland in the days when there was more rain and snow. Bad, bad slough.

What I didn't expect was the fire official's additional description of *what lies beneath.* I borrow this phrase from the film title of a chilling murder-mystery. He went on to outline the extensive Devonian shale deposit below—oil and natural gas. On occasion, blue flames dance above ground—natural gas escaping to the surface. Imagine coming upon flickering flames in the dark of a night as you are walking the dirt road those two miles home from the community hall. Eerie does not begin to describe such a picture. Imagine the danger of natural gas flames setting meadow grasses or cultivated fields ablaze. This is the land that became an intimate companion to Elena's daughter, Maria. I think its phosphorescent volatility suited her.

She was on fire. Quick. Smart. Seething to get ahead. She had courage and fortitude. She was proud. She had no patience for ignorance, foolishness or laziness. She would not be cowed by men. Unlike either Elena or Ivan, Maria nurtured her own lambent flame into something scorching.

She comes to me through the narratives of her children, my uncles and aunts, who describe Maria as a rankling figure. I have interviewed and questioned ten of the eleven.[1] In their narratives, Maria comes forward as a force to be reckoned with, confrontational, fierce, divisive, demeaning, insular, resolute, unafraid of taking controversial stands, focused on community issues—the school, the church, the hall.

Injustice brought out the superlative in her. Tough, gruff, scrappy, Maria was all about injustice, that is, injustice in the forms she chose to recognize. This getting back at the disparities and failings of the world was what made her so ardent and so difficult. Of course, she had seen injustice of every sort in Chornivka. What she seems to have learned is that sometimes, fighting has a positive impact.

Her mother was the daughter of a serf. Her grandmother was a serf. It had been going on for centuries. These were not happy, fulfilled women. It stands to reason that what these women didn't know about creating a healthy environment for their offspring was deep in their bones. Soda Lake is where—for my family of women—the ruination in the New World began. I see Maria as the gateway to my mother's miserable, depressive childhood. Nancy, Ann, Alice and Margaret had their own struggles with Maria.

How to understand this Maria? There are so many distinct periods in her life that had a powerful impact on the lives of her children. Of which Maria am I speaking? As a child in Chornivka, she was somewhat privileged—the only surviving daughter in a family of boys; a girl who had the advantage of school in a male-centric culture;[2] the product of a middle-class peasant family that owned its own home; and for a time—with a father who was known for his generosity and garrulousness—perhaps the apple of his eye.

As a girl in the village, Maria had the examples of three aunts and a strong grandmother to fortify her. But with her mother, Elena, there was distance between them. Much later, at Soda Lake, Maria confided to one of her daughters, "My mother didn't like me because my eyes were brown. She never liked me."[3] Maria came to the New World with attitude and with pride—ferociously enabled.

BUT let's not get ahead of the story. To begin, the atypical Maria was a typical 19th century peasant-immigrant from Eastern Europe who, with her parents, resettled in Canada. She was from one of those places where villagers were full of suspicion, envy, mutual mistrust, unwilling to work cooperatively with anyone outside of their own family. It had to do with an unspoken belief on the part of every one in every village across empires: there was only so much "good" to go around.[4] For Maria, her mother and her grandmother, their struggle for scraps never ended. Maria learned to be combative.

Maria spent her semi-feral childhood, tussling with other urchins, playing in the verdant meadows around Chornivka, collecting mushrooms in the surrounding woods, tending the family cow, herding ducks and sliding on her bum into Berda Creek after rains turned its banks muddy.[5] All too quickly, though, Maria was drawn into the adult world of watching babies, stirring the porridge and listening to the complaints of her elders.

At the village school, Maria learned the rudiments of reading, writing and arithmetic in German, the semi-official language of the Austrian-Hapsburg Empire. Battles were fierce between Vienna and the Romanian aristocracy over what language would be the *lingua franca* in the villages at the eastern edge of empire. The Hurmuzakis, who owned Chornivka probably militated for Romanian, but German—the language of administration, the academy and the judiciary—won out. The unforeseen advantage of Maria's third or fourth grade education enabled her to work out non-Cyrillic text when the family arrived on the east coast of English-speaking Canada—*station, track #2, east, west, women, men, Halifax, Winnipeg, Saskatoon, Strathcona* —these were words she could decipher. It was immensely helpful. Her parents and brothers followed her. She was smart. She "got" things fast and early on.

When Elena and Ivan emigrated, the thirteen year-old Maria was done with her village. She rarely looked back. Nothing sublime about Chornivka, but unwittingly she brought it with her—its misanthropic tendencies. True, she missed the ease with which once upon a time she could gather with other young people near the village's central well to gossip, laugh, sing, dance, and cavort. But now, instead of singing songs with her Chornivka clique on Sunday afternoons, Maria-of-Canada's-North-West was sent out, on her own. Desperate for cash, Ivan arranged for Maria's employment with a Bruderheim *hausfrau*.

The primitive conditions on the family's quarter at Limestone Lake, the too-sudden privation, may have had a leavening effect on Maria. Her being sent away to work as a servant in another woman's home, to bring in money for her parents, must also have given her pause. She was fourteen.

The girl helped with gardening, laundry, cooking, dishes and probably the chickens and the pigs. She learned how to sew an Anglo-style man's shirt and how to iron it. For this, she was paid some small sum each month and each month, Ivan would walk twenty miles west from Limestone Lake to collect her earnings. This went on until the *hausfrau* refused to allow Ivan to take Maria's money—"She is dressed in rags. She needs money for herself." The hausfrau is said to have minced no words with Ivan. There are no records of how long Maria stayed in the Bruderheim situation.

On the day of her wedding—John was twenty-eight, she nineteen—one of John's aunts, Axenia Tkachuk, who, as Matron-of-Honor, had come to fetch the bride for the trip to the church, was shocked to see the bareness of Elena's home at Limestone Lake. Axenia later told Ruth, her daughter-in-law, "I never seen a house so empty. Nothing was in."[6] Among peasant-equals in Canada, Elena's straitened circumstances—and by extension, Maria's—were notable and probably painful.

How did Maria meet John, or he meet her? Bachelor John must have sized up Maria at some church service in Shandro or Wostok. Or perhaps the couple eyed each other at a "neighborhood" wedding—that is the neighborhood delimited by Whitford Lake, Limestone Lake, the North Saskatchewan River, Wostok and Bruderheim. Thirty square miles. Usually, everyone was invited to a wedding.

Maria's decision to marry John was a good one. It shows her self-determination. She would not have been her parents' pawn in the matter of matrimony. They would have sensed some interest on her part and encouraged the match. Be that as it may, John was connected to her aspiration. She wanted better for herself. Hadn't she come to the New World to be new? John would help her get to "better."

He was serious, handsome, focused and ready. She had dark eyes, a sharp mind and knew how to roll her sleeves up and work. The two probably agreed on the driving quality of their collective ambition: a thriving, productive farm. Ivan gave John his permission. The couple was married in June by the circuit riding Reverend M. Skibinsky at St. Nickolas Russo-Greek Orthodox Church at Wostok. Most of the "steps" of a traditional Ukrainian wedding were omitted. (4.8) Few had the time or the wherewithal to follow each of the familiar ritual wedding proscriptions. The priest misspelled Maria's name, turning her into "Marry" on her wedding day.[7] Two years later, Skibinsky would sanctify the burial of John's mother, Magdalyna.

As a young wife, Maria went to live on the quarter of her in-laws, Magdalyna and Wasyl, but that didn't last. She would not be the dutiful daughter-in-law, answering to Magdalyna, if, indeed Magdalyna assumed the role of a matriarch. After two months of marriage, the pregnant Maria and John were building their own *burdei*—that raw, barely livable, form of "independent" housing—on their Soda Lake property. John had secured the quarter at Soda Lake the year before wedded bliss. (9.8)

It was a solitary life. Occasionally Wasyl, John's father, would ride in. As far as Maria was concerned, the entirety of John's side of the family held no interest. Those Tkachuks were "dumb;" they "didn't know enough."[8] At least, that's what the exuberantly pejorative Maria communicated to them. She probably thought them to be overly superstitious and rankly unlettered.

In his memoir, Maria's first-born son, Al, made a kind of running list of his mother's prejudices. The list is a startling admission from one who knew his mother well enough to want to hide her darker aspect. But Maria's dynamic was entirely too powerful for a son to suppress.

According to him, Maria was equal-opportunity: no one could be trusted. She disliked Russians and Poles for subjugating the Ukraine; Jews for cheating people and 'living by their wits'; Catholics for their atrocities during the Spanish Inquisition—Maria had a surprisingly long memory; Romanians, probably for running the Chornivka estate; Ukrainians of Galician origin for not being Bukovynian; inhabitants of villages other than Chornivka because they were not from Chornivka; and naturally, Anglo-Saxons in Canada for their arrogance and inferior farming methods.[8] As for New World Gypsies, the Cree, the Blackfoot and persons of African descent, these last would complete the list of Maria's ethnic animosities, but of them, Al, in his account, falls silent.

When it came to her child-rearing philosophy, Maria was subconsciously in keeping with the Old World culture she consciously rejected. She was also in keeping with the childrearing climate around her. Children were a God-given gift, there to work and to bolster the family's economic situation. Your job was to keep them alive and healthy, and to focus them towards work. (9.11) Encouragement, empathy and love were out of the picture. In the initial push for survival, Maria barely had time to have her babies.

In contrast to Elena's abandonment of her own motherhood, Maria—initially, at least—adopted an "I'm here and I'm going to take charge" attitude. Where Elena had been plagued by infant deaths, Maria was graced with life. The March after her June marriage, she had Al; a year later in September, she had Sam; and two years after that, Bill. Three boys in a row, just for starters, but there was no longer a village around her to approve and to congratulate her. John would have been pleased with his trio of sons.

The striking difference in infant mortality between Elena and Maria certainly speaks to the external conditions borne by each woman—Elena's nomadic life versus Maria's rootedness at Soda Lake. Both were distracted mothers, but it would seem that in her early years with John, Maria accepted her procreative responsibilities in marriage. Maria's resourceful, no-nonsense cast of mind, surely contributed to the sturdiness of her infants. (9.12) Ultimately Maria's flock of children divide into two groups—the first five, who recall their mother's energy and benign neglect—she was neither loving nor undercutting, merely too busy for them; and the final six, who bore the brunt of Maria's attacks and her less-than-benign neglect.

In the earliest photo that exists of the family, the 1910 photo, the light has gone out of Maria's eyes. (3.9) At twenty-six, she still has a pretty oval face, a delicate nose. Her figure has thickened beyond that of young woman. Her tanned hands show her brawn. Seated next to John, with their five children arranged around them—the infant of the moment, Katherine, is cradled in her arms—Maria looks solemn, sad, a bit sullen.

John, by way of contrast, glows with pride. He exudes spirited warmth. After all, he is a solid landowner, a successful farmer and unquestionably the paterfamilias. He leans protectively over Nancy, holding her gently, firmly, as she grasps an orange—the fruit intended to fascinate and distract her. His three small boys, Al, Sam and Bill—not yet potty-trained, Bill wears a dress—stand tentatively before him. They gaze pensively and warily at the photographer, as does their mother.

As the roster of little ones lengthened, Maria despaired. Her focus had ever been on the economic success of the farm and on her broad ideals. In an overarching way, she was in good company. According to Dr. Hrdy in *Mother Nature*, "Wherever women have both control over their reproductive opportunities and a chance to better themselves, women opt for well-being and economic security over having more children."[9] Maria wanted things for herself. She was enough of a strategist to use breast-feeding to pace her family production—an infant every two years, but beyond that, she could not refuse John. It was the agreement she'd made when she accepted his hand. She did not have the wherewithal to reject well-ingrained cultural norms.

Nevertheless, with John, she fought back. By the time her family had grown to seven or eight youngsters, Maria's children were observing her choler. Neither a compromiser nor a facilitator, Maria willfully by-passed behavior that might have had a calming effect on everyday tensions. Her sense of timing was unfortunate and impeccable: when the fire was reaching out-of-control, she tossed kerosene on it. Al noted that "her hypercritical remarks would get under Father's skin, occasionally with an explosion of violence on his part." She would start a *mêlée* when her husband was already angry or frustrated, "humiliating him in front of his children."[10]

Katherine deftly captured the end of a set-to.

"I remember my father hitting my mother. But as we grew older, he stopped, because without saying anything, we were so censorious. One time he hit my mother, with a dipper from the water [bucket]. And she was sitting there mending, and he hit her. And with the crack [of the dipper], she started bleeding. And I was a little girl, and I started to scream hysterically. And I ran out of the house, and again it was winter, and I screamed at the top of my voice. I screamed and I screamed. And he came out to try to stop me and I said, 'You had no business hitting her.' And I screamed. And the thing is, in that quiet air, you could hear sleigh bells seven miles away. So that after a while, I realized, I had a trump here. I would keep screaming insanely, as long as I could."[11]

A child in distress would send the neighbors running. The child could be anyone's. On another occasion, Al describes how

"Mother was exasperated by Father's asking me to adjust our hay loading equipment—at some risk to myself—and accused him angrily for the fact that it was not functioning properly. Father, already upset, grabbed a two-by-four plank and angrily began swinging it at her legs. She screamed and sent one of the children to our neighbor."[12]

The *tête-à-têtes* Maria had with John translated into serious tension. Savvy and self-protective, Katherine confided to me that, "If there was too much trouble in the house, I ran away and hid."[13] And here is my mother with a vignette full of the unhappiness of her childhood days, of Maria's having set John off in some unknown way and John's lashing out, his behavior unanticipated and directed at the wrong target.

"At Soda Lake, I can remember the time, because we still lived in that un-insulated house. Our dining room table was a long table, because there were many of us, and the hired men—two of them. And along the wall, us kids sat on a bench. And the adults sat around on chairs. It was Alice, Margaret, George, and I [Vera]. I think Walter was in a high chair then. But we were sitting around there, innocently eating, and like kids, I suppose, no matter how scared you are, you make a lot of noise. And Father was on the *warpath.* He was looking for a clasp cutter, which is a tool about fifteen inches long. And he was *mad.* I don't know where he saw it or found it, but he just shoved it in Alice's mouth! For no reason! Like, 'You're the one who's to blame for this!'

[He didn't cut her mouth,] But it was just like taking a pencil and sticking it in somebody's mouth. Who knows who lost it, or who put that where it was. You know how kids pick things up. I don't remember when Alice says that he hit her or he switched her, but I remember that incident. He was really cruel. That's why I say that I was deathly afraid of him. I was scared to death, because I had seen him argue. I had only seen him hit Mother, once. But, I don't know why, I was just so afraid of him."[14]

It is a picture of a couple at war, with their frightened children as victims. John's outbursts sparked by Maria's anger. Maria, with her anger coming from every direction—angry at every injustice, from within and without; angry at her own mother's "floating," dreamy disconnectedness; angry with the continuing children she no longer wanted. The vernacular at Soda Lake did not include laughter.

Of all the tensions building between Maria and John, gradually the fact of too many children came into focus. Seventy years later and in Walnut Creek, Katherine was still insisting that after the first five, her mother was done. "I'm sure that I was the last that was welcome. That's why this picture (1910 photo) was taken. The complete family."[15] I suppose everyone in the family has their version—most not as grand as Katherine's— of what the 1910 photo means. But Maria had no way to keep infants from coming. She plumbed the doctors. She had heard there were methods to rid one of a pregnancy.

Here is my mother, Vera, tearfully recounting a recurring family theme: "No more babies."

"I'm sure I told you about Father. I guess Mother got pregnant [again] and Father said, 'Why don't we go to Vegreville and ask that young doctor to [perform an abortion].' [My mother could not bring herself to say the word.] There was this young doctor and then there was Dr. Reed, who had been there [for some time]. I guess, in desperation, Mother went with Father to the young doctor, and she said that he gave her Hell. The [young] doctor said to her, 'Your husband is trying to kill you!' He wasn't at all sympathetic. He told her to just forget it.

I don't know whether she screwed up her courage or Father took her to Dr. Reed, but she went to Dr. Reed. Dr. Reed was very kind. He told her it was a very dangerous procedure. It was better to have one more than to orphan all of the family. And she had another baby.... *It could have been me.* I don't know. I know that Sam says that when they found out that she was pregnant with me, the older children were grumbling and complaining: 'No more babies! You promised no more babies!' When I was born, because I was born at home, Mother said, 'Well, do you want to keep her? Or should I get rid of her?' They looked at the little baby; it was cute. That's the way it went."[16]

And then my mother wept: Vera, the un-aborted, the un-wanted, the accident, full of unworthiness, fear, sadness and her own unique Furies.

The message that an infant desperately seeks—"You are wanted and will not be set aside"—key to an infant's sense of security, is not the message that Maria's children heard.[17] Moreover, a secure attachment to "mother" early in life has a long-lasting effect on one's degree of empathy for others.[18] Maria knew none of this. From her point of view, she saw her children as *the* problem—she told them so in subtle and not-so-subtle ways. They trapped her; they were her ball and chain. It was a negative pattern, played out one child after the next.

Alice was born during the worst *annus magnus*. Maria was pregnant with her when her brother—the deceased Gus—got carted home from the Vegreville hospital. After his burial, Maria remained demonstrably depressed. She was thirty-five and about to have number nine—Alice. Close upon the child's May birth, Maria developed a gall bladder problem. Things did not get better at the farm. In July, quick as anything, Maria's brother

Bill died of typhoid. (8.16) August, a killing frost ruined John's wheat crop. Thankfully, Dr. Reed collected her and checked her into the Vegreville hospital for a month-long stay. If the good doctor had not removed Maria from her home, perhaps she would have begun to drown her children in Soda Lake. Even she had her limits.

Alice was handed off to the neighbor to the south, who was nursing her own ninth or tenth. Over the course of time, cute-as-a-bug-Alice was rejected by Maria, simply for being there. She was given abusive epithets. Maria would push the needy little girl away, saying "Go to the devil!"[19] The same kind of outright rejection was George's lot. (9.13) He'd had the misfortune to enter the world after three boys and three girls. A superfluous seventh child. Probably even before George, Maria had abandoned the fundamental precept of nurturing—instead of attachment, she distanced herself both physically and emotionally from her young ones. They were left to fend for themselves. They were left to observe the mistreatment of their siblings.

The Alexandria Quartet of Maria's daughters and sons spoke to their home situation. "My parents were so absorbed in the desperate struggle to run the farm and to provide food and necessities for their brood that they took no time to play with us or to show us love and affection. We never knew the pleasures children derive from parental hugs and kisses," Sam wrote.[20] More than once, Katherine commented on her mother's absence of warmth or sensitivity. "I heard my mother make cruel comparisons [between my sister and me], but I liked it. I preened. I didn't see I was taking advantage of her [my sister]," she said.[21] "You know, there is always that sibling tension and wise parents know how to deal with it. My mother never did. She was just as likely to join in the battle as not."[22] It was, to use Katherine's phrase, "very poisonous" for all of the children.[23]

Who could blame Maria for the difficult situation in which she found herself? The problem was, she could *only* see herself, what was happening to her. In *Mother Nature*, Hrdy and her colleagues speak directly to the situation in Maria's home: "Meeting children's emotional and social demands in a supportive responsive manner fosters a social orientation that values mutually beneficial interactions and relationships, whereas patterns of rearing that are negative, inconsiderate and coercive lead children to behave in ways that are self-centered."[24] As a result, such a child "rather than rely on those around him, [chooses] the most advantageous course open [which is] to become self-reliant and to avoid developing empathetic feeling for others around him."[25] Maria's parenting style was probably an inbred form of self-protection that lived a robust life in her family in that village. A child's emotional needs were irrelevant. Child-Maria's emotional needs had been irrelevant; child-Elena's had been.

Maria taught her children that they could trust no one outside the family, but the kicker was that they could trust no one inside the family either. Among siblings, there was intense rivalry. It was encouraged. Multiple betrayals could be had in an instant. Maria's children clung to each other; they clawed at each other. Here are Nancy, Ann, Vera, Alice and Margaret locked for a lifetime into reverberating accusations. There are Sam and George as young men, trying to escape to anywhere, fleeing separately into the bosom of Ivan and Elena. George's hostility becomes so legendary that in this day and age, one wonders if he might not have been capable of killing Maria, John and some of his elder brothers.[26] Maria's children, driven to aggress, to wrongfully accuse, to manipulate, to exploit, to retreat, to hide, to flee, in order to protect themselves. It was a fact of life at Soda Lake. Naturally, Soda Lake framed their lives long after what they learned there became counterproductive.

I actually met Maria. It was only once. Sam brought her to us for a visit. By then she was a widow in her seventies. (9.6) Our curious relationship intrigued me because it was, for the most part, wordless. Although this grandmother of mine knew how to speak English, she refrained from doing so on that first and last visit to our home. She spoke Ukrainian. I did not understand a word of it, although that is not exactly true. I did know the words for family dishes Mother would prepare for the holidays: *perohe* (пероги) dumplings, *holubtsi* (голубци) cabbage rolls, and *nachynka* (начунка) corn meal *soufflé*.

Showing off, I brought my sewing project to her. I wanted to make a connection—all part of my effort to discover exactly what it is that a grandmother does. Up until Maria's visit to our home, I'd had no experience with grandparents. I was suddenly proud to have a flesh-and-blood grandparent before me.

It was probably a doll's dress or some such thing that I was putting together. Mother would give me bits of fabric, scraps from the clothes she made for herself and for me. I would fashion these scraps into capes or skirts or such, tiny, lop-sided versions of the perfection that was Mother's sewing. This I would do with a needle and thread and my round-nosed scissors.

Because I knew that Maria did needlework—I'd seen it—I carried my workbasket to her to demonstrate that I too was a needlewoman. The window behind Maria gave us good light. I studied everything I could about her—how she sat in the big orange-and-yellow plaid armchair like a potentate, her thin white hair, her metal frame glasses, her snub nose, her pouty silence.

Ready to model my domestic prowess, I watched with dismay as my needle and thread parted company. For a child of eight or nine, threading a needle is an onerous task. Maria, sizing up the situation, wordlessly took the thread and the needle from me. Carefully, slowly, making certain that I was watching her, she trimmed the thread end blunt with my scissors, put the end in her mouth to moisten it, smoothed and sharpened the tip with her thumb and forefinger, sighted the needle's eye and expertly, effortlessly pushed the thread through it. Next she looked at me, her eyes sharp: did I understand what she had done, the steps of the procedure? Her eyes asked me this.

I did. I understood. This woman had just unlocked the secret of threading a needle to me.

I now have absolute confidence in that scantling thing. She had also communicated that her method was THE method to thread a needle. It was a gift, a wordless gift. For an instant, I was hers and she was mine, this exotic grandmother. When she was gone, I missed the excitement of her mystery. I was also relieved that she was gone, so that my mother—whom Maria churned into frantic activities to please her—could get back to normal.

Maria left behind another gift for me: a beadwork necklace—a geometric diamond pattern in blues, greens, golds, with a touch of orange and chartreuse. (9.7) The work of her hand, it was a long thin strip, about three-quarters of an inch (or two millimeters) wide. It had thread tassels with tied knots to secure the beads. There was no clear way to fasten the band around my neck. So I trimmed off the tassels, leaving the knots and basted the beaded strip to a length of black velvet ribbon that I could fix around my neck. A striking choker necklace. I wore it from time to time as a teen. I was proud of the beaded band, but it was not in vogue as something girls wore. Later I discovered that Maria had made the necklace for herself in Chornivka; there it was *à la mode* among her cohorts. It was a deeply thoughtful gift: a pretty feminine thing, a small treasure from her youth to my youth. I loved her for those beads.

Unquestionably, Maria had her strengths. Causing trouble is a form of power. Causing trouble in the greater world was one of Maria's strengths. The more unredeemable battles involve a fight against your family legacy or against your own nature. Of all the battles one can wage, the cleanest among them is to fight social or political injustice: us versus them. In Maria's case, she chose the bigger, cleaner mission. She would fight for justice in the abstract—Why do the teachers who come to the schools we've built speak not a word of Ukrainian? Why are the priests so intent on telling us women that we are unclean? The priests should get busy and teach my illiterate mother [Elena] how to read, how to understand the denominations of various coins.

Industry and stamina incarnate, Maria took on duties as Soda Lake postmistress. Attendant to her stamp-and-mail exertions, Maria acted as Registrar for births, marriages and deaths. In this latter role, neighbor Zelenko got her into trouble for a death she hadn't recorded. He had lost an infant and quietly buried it. She didn't know. The two of them were hauled before a judge who—to her chagrin—rebuked them. Being a Registrar had its unpleasant surprises. Technically, the job fell to John, but it was Maria who could read and write. Her official Registrar Book is now a treasured document guarded by the Provincial Archives of Alberta in Edmonton.

By speaking out about various deficits at the one-room Prut' school, Maria got herself elected to the school board. (9.9) "If you have so much to say, then you take it over"—her election was something of this nature. If that were not enough, when she could, she attended meetings about organizing a community hall for Soda Lake. Political activism was her strong suit; unhesitatingly, Maria wanted to get back at the injustices of the world. Soda

Lake would have a "National Home" (*Narodnyi Dim*, Народний Дім) or community hall.

An import from the Old Country, community halls were a big deal, a poke in the eye of the higher-ups. In them, the working classes learned what the aristocracy didn't want them to know. The concept and the institution began in Western Ukraine in the 1860s. Young populists (*narodnyky*)[27] created the Prosvita Society—*prosvita* (просвіта) means enlightenment—as a way to eradicate illiteracy, raise the educational and cultural level of the peasantry, and develop national consciousness.[28] The populists established branches—community centers or halls— in cities, towns and villages. Chornivka had one. These centers contained small libraries and reading rooms. In them, those who could read, read to those who had not learned how.

The *Narodnyi Dim* was used for theatrical performances, dances, elevating talks, courses—for example, the benefits of crop rotation and in time, political activities. Thus, the "national home" became a subversive center—certainly in Eastern Europe. In the "Dirty Thirties" in Canada, there were secular independent community halls (Soda Lake), Catholic halls—Ukrainians from villages close to Poland tended to be Catholic—and pro-Communist halls: the halls were a hotbed of international politics. Maria leapt in with both feet. By 1928, Soda Lake had its wood-frame hall (5.5)—tiny auditorium, hand-made wooden benches, elevated stage, painted canvas backdrops of an Old World country scene, advertisement-covered proscenium curtain (9.10)—"Third Bros. Drug Co., Prescriptions Filled Vegreville, Offices: Drs. Yak & Shandro," wood stove, gas lamps, bookcase and clothes closet.

It was an unexpected Community Hall connection my husband and I unearthed, when in the 1990s and at the end of a publishing conference in Chicago, we decided we would be tourists for a day. With me behind the wheel, we drove south into the town of Pullman. He, reluctant to travel in South Chicago, went on full "red alert." Here we were, a couple of middle-aged white folks doodling about the south side of Chicago, my husband nervously humming the verses of Jim Croce's "LeRoy Brown."[29]

Pullman is both famous and infamous for being a 19th century planned community, "a company town," designed to facilitate the builders of Pullman railroad cars. Handsome red brick townhouses and rows of more modest homes for Pullman's put-upon workers—former Croats, Czechs, Irish, Italians, Poles, Russians, Serbs, Ukrainians—lined the tree-shaded bricked streets. Thanks to Pullman, no one could afford the groceries or the rent; everyone was forced to live there. In 1894, the bloody Pullman railroad strike changed American labor policy and history, landed the pro-labor activist Eugene V. Debs in prison, rightfully turned Mr. Pullman into the most hated man in America and spawned Labor Day, at the time, a weak concession to America's workers.

As I slowly drove around the place studying the architecture—my husband certain of guns and active drug deals on every corner; mostly people smiled benignly at us—I spotted a limestone lintel over an arched entranceway with carved Cyrillic lettering—Український

Народний Дім (*Ukrains'kyi Narodnyi Dim*). The worn two-story brick structure had once been a "Ukrainian National Home," a community hall for self-improvement. Soda Lake and Pullman. Never would I have connected the two, but there it was. In the minutes leading up to the establishment of "The Yuriy Fedkowych Ukrainian Educational Society of Soda Lake," the designated secretary wrote, "Members who do not attend the meeting shall have no right to criticize."[30] I suspect this preemptive warning was directed at Maria, though there may have been other outspoken Soda Lakers.

Once the community hall was up and running, the determined Maria did not hold back. Favoring drama, she volunteered for evil stepmother roles. "It suited her," daughter Nancy said, "and she could be pretty mean to the family, to the children."[31] Maria's youngsters watched raptly as their mother made the lives of pretend-step-daughters miserable. Nancy remembered how, as a child, she would burst into tears feeling sorry for the little children being abused by Maria-the-stepmother on the stage. "Believe me, for what I understood then, she [my mother] was not a bad actress."[32]

The rise of Russian Communism—came to Maria via an assortment of Ukrainian-Canadian newspapers. When a proselytizer for Ukrainian nationalism who happened to be an Orthodox priest rolled into the area to speak at the community hall, Maria was at the ready. Out with the Russian priest! Out with the *Russian* Orthodox church! At the diminutive immigrant-built churches in the Soda Lake area, services were conducted by *any* Orthodox priest who was passing through. When, as a girl, she left Chornivka, Ukraine had nothing to do with her village. The village belonged to Austria. Ukrainian culture vs. Russian culture—the battle that grew at Soda Lake—caused bitter feelings among neighbors and not a few bruises and bloody noses among the small fry in the Prut' school yard.

In the end the community went both ways: half remained with their pioneer church, St. Demetrius. The other half—this included Maria and John—banded together to build a new church whose clergy answered to Ukraine, the Church of the Holy Ascension. Today, the cemeteries for the two churches face off across a dirt road (5.8), as do the churches though at further distance. Maria's two "Ukrainian" brothers—Gus and Bill, having died before all the partisan uproar, are buried in the "Russian" cemetery of St. Demetrius.

Pushed to excel, Maria's children carried subliminal messages from her to do so and some few of them—Nancy and Sam— involved themselves in politics and the "higher" battles to considerable success. Nancy ran for a seat in the Canadian Parliament on the Cooperative Commonwealth Federation ticket (3.10) and made a credible showing.[33] Businessman Sam became a committed environmentalist, helping to get the Indiana Dunes State Park designated "protected national lakeshore."[34] He also bought two rare peat bogs in northeastern Indiana, gifted them to ACRES, a conservancy organization, and hoped that the rest of us would enjoy these spaces in perpetuity.[35] Sam and Nancy took many pages from their mother's game book: it is more important to be a political javelin than a social butter knife. Even the "I'm not a part of *that* family" Margaret—post-demise— gave a whopping chunk of change to the American Civil Liberties Union.

They left Soda Lake, most left Alberta and Canada. As for their former playmates at Prut' school, the myriads of children of neighbors—each household seemed to produce eight to twelve children—a remarkable number of them stayed around home—that is, near Soda Lake, in Hairy Hill, in Vegreville, in Two Hills, in Mundare, in Edmonton, in Calgary, in Alberta. As for Maria's children, Maria was key to their unanimous flight. She sent them out, pushed them out, drove them out, until only she was left, stunned and saddened for her solitude.

These days, Soda Lake is characterized by absence—those who once populated the place are gone. The slough has disappeared too. Now Soda Lake, the slough, is a rim of salts drawn on the ground of what on occasion is a hollow filled with briny water. At a trash-strewn turn out along highway 637, there is a billboard put up by the Alberta provincial government. It acknowledges the pioneer settlers—from Ukraine and Romania—who once formed a community in the area.

Every mile or four on either side of 637 and around the non-slough there are clusters of buildings, farms that work, farms that don't—the latter are being taken over by scrub willow and black poplar. At Norma, now a non-hamlet, the one-room school building where my mother once taught stands forlorn—windows of gaping square holes, wood siding surreptitiously stripped off in the night, noisy interior shelter for families of swifts, blackboards clinging to the wall. In a few cases, the grandchildren or great-grandchildren of original homesteaders keep nearly-gone structures up as a reminder of their family's history. Or like Lena's farm near Andrew, the tatters are torn down, burnt up and smoothed over to make way for valuable Canola.

At the northwest corner of one of the intersections—two dirt roads that lead to Prut' school, the stone-slab stoup to Zelenko's private, onion-domed chapel is still in place. The inimitable Zelenko. His chapel disappeared long ago. Zelenko gave that intersection some thought. In the Old Country, crossroads were dangerous places, spiritually indeterminate; therefore, chances of encountering a devil were high. Putting up a cross, or better yet, a chapel was an excellent prophylactic. In winter, Zelenko's thick-timbered, thatch-roofed barn sags and leans under the weight of deep snow. (9.14) His house is gone, as is his garden of hemp—repeatedly and illicitly harvested by Ann on her way to Prut' school decades and decades ago.

At Maria and John's, the *burdei* and the *khata* have returned to the earth. The first Anglo house, the one that had no insulation because John heard some cockamamie story about a vacuum—an empty space, being superb insulation—has vanished. The well-insulated second Anglo house and most of the sheds are no more. Only the tall barn with its weather vane—the one that Sam fastened to the roof in 1919 while trying not to look down, the one I had so much trouble finding—is there. But the barn is much-compromised, its symmetrical wings either torn away or bashed away. The family that purchased Soda Lake farm from Maria was not a cracker-jack outfit when it came to keeping things up, not cracker-jack like John and Maria.

Maria the mountain, the volcano. Streams did not pool around her, they took their own direction away from her. She created the weather that swirled at her peak. She has driven the identity of her family for three generations now. It was ever Maria. In a grand sense, to try to fulfill herself, she helped to create and sustain institutions, but the intensity of her activism and narcissism had its price. She didn't want the family she got. What her children did and did not learn from her continues to trickle, ripple and course down those slopes.

"Bunny farmed sixty-three quarter sections of land, 160 acres in a quarter, pretty much the entire southeast corner of Saskatchewan."

9.1 *Farm equipment "Bunny style." Author at the Halyk Family Reunion, Birmingham, Saskatchewan.*

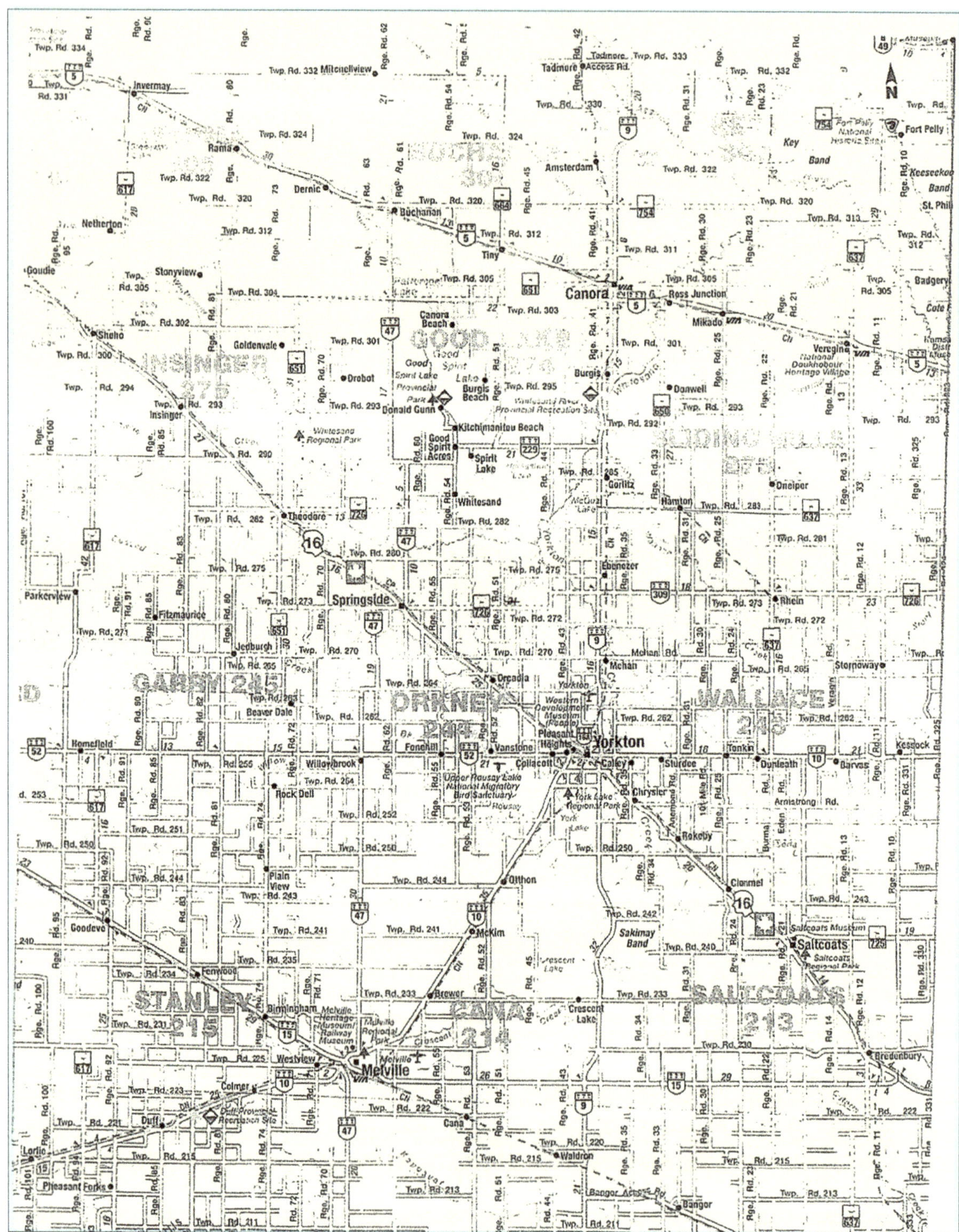

9.2 *Map (detail) of the southeast corner of Saskatchewan. Yorkton. Melville. Birmingham.*

9.3 *Commemorative rock on the site of the one-room school in Birmingham, where author's father did not learn to read or write.*

9.4 *Burning bales of hay on a melting flat-bed trailer. (above) Intersection of Highway 637 and Range Road 152, Soda Lake area near Willingdon, AB. (left) Truck cab and on-fire-flatbed with Highway 637 between the two.*

9.5 *Willingdon Fire Department douses the fire.*

9.6 (left) Photo of Maria Scraba Ropchan, ca. 1944. (right) Photo of Maria, ca. 1950.

9.7 Display of traditional Ukrainian beaded choker necklaces of the 19th century and the beaded chocker Maria made and gave to me.

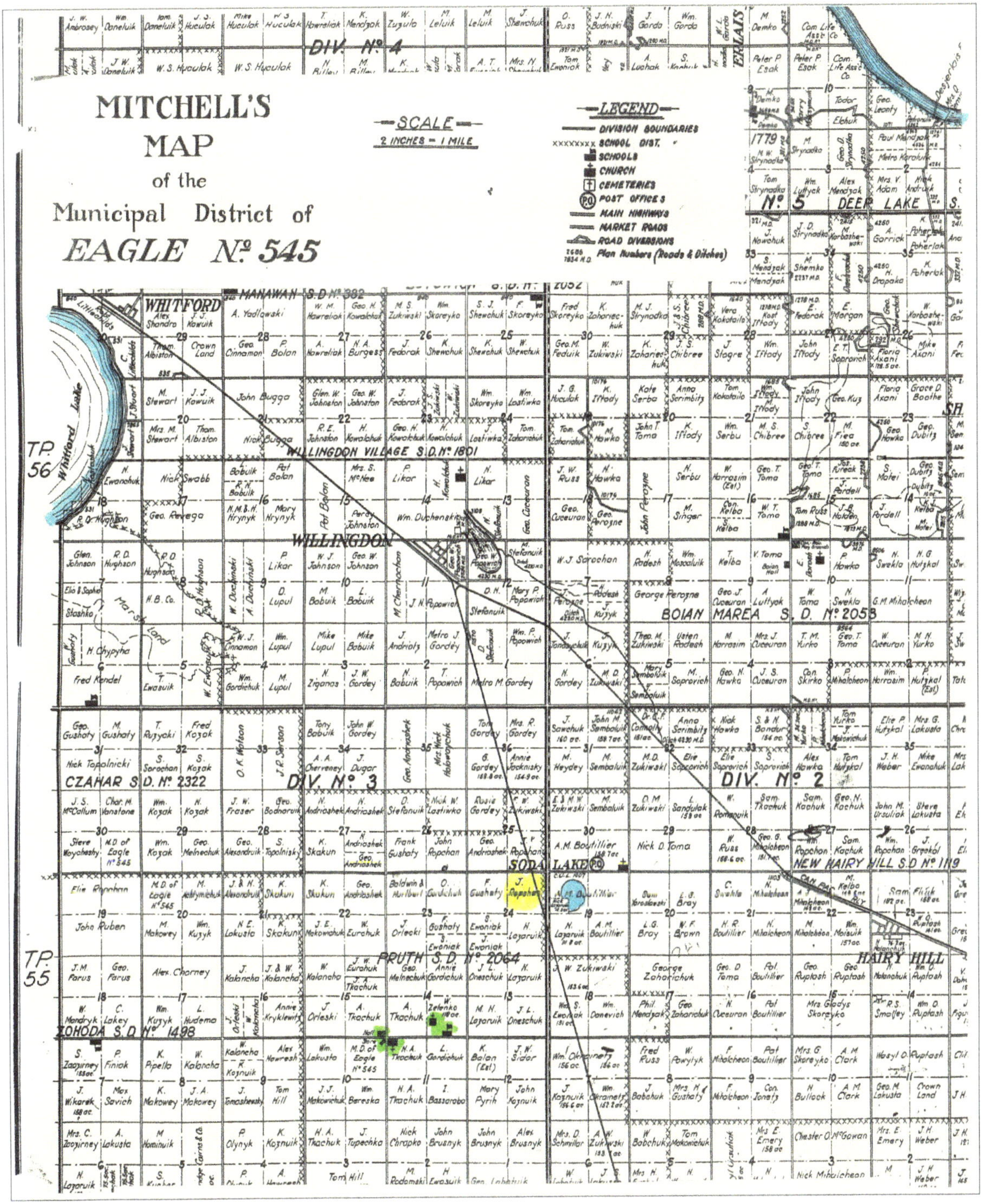

MITCHELL'S
MAP
of the
Municipal District of
EAGLE No 545
SCALE
2 INCHES = 1 MILE
LEGEND
DIVISION BOUNDARIES
SCHOOL DIST.
SCHOOLS
CHURCH
CEMETERIES
POST OFFICES
MAIN HIGHWAYS
MARKET ROADS
ROAD DIVERSIONS
Plan Numbers (Roads & Ditches)
DIV. No 4
DIV. No 3
DIV. No 2
No 5 DEEP LAKE
TP. 56
TP. 55
WHITFORD
Whitford Lake
MANAWAN S.D. No 382
WILLINGDON VILLAGE S.D. No 1801
WILLINGDON
BOIAN MAREA S.D. No 2058
CZAHAR S.D. No 2322
SODA LAKE
NEW HAIRY HILL S.D. No 1119
HAIRY HILL
PRUTH S.D. No 2064
ZOHODA S.D. No 1498

9.8 *Map (detail) of the Soda Lake neighborhood, 1932. The map is divided into quarter sections. The owner's name is in the center of the quarter.*

9.9 *Studio photo of Maria Scraba Ropchan, probably taken in the 1920s, when she was becoming more active in community affairs.*

"If you have so much to say, then you take it over" — her election was something of this nature.

9.10 *Interior of community hall at Soda Lake-Pruth—proscenium screen and screen detail, opposite page*

9.11 *Pause in the work at Soda Lake farm, 1913. (top, l-r) John Ropchan, Bill and Gus Scraba (Maria's brothers). The brothers would have recently returned from Colville, WA. (bottom, l-r) The Ropchan brood: Bill, Katherine, Maria with infant Ann in her lap, Nancy, Al and Sam.*

9.10 *Proscenium screen detail*

Maria and John

Maria Scraba

Born: 28 August 1884, Chornivka
Immigr.: 2 May 1897, Quebec, *S.S. Arcadia*
Married: 7 June 1903, Wostok, AB
Died: 24 September 1970, Estevan, SK
Buried: Riverside Cemetery, Vegreville, AB

John Ropchan

born: 27 August 1875, Molodiia
Immigr.: 1899, NYC, *S.S. Patria*
Married: 7 June 1903, Wostok, AB
Died: 13 March 1938, Vegreville
Buried: Riverside Cemetery

Al (Alexandr)
b. 11 March 1904, Soda Lake, AB
m. 29 June 1935, to Dorothy Canode
d. 1 May 2005, West Palm Beach, FL

Sam (Simion)
b. 6 September 1905, Soda Lake
m. 30 June 1951, to Adeline Beller
d. 6 April 1987, Fort Wayne, IN

Bill (Wasyl)
b. 14 February 1907, Soda Lake
m. 24 November 1931, to Katherine Humen
d. 8 May 2005, Surrey, BC, Canada

Nancy (Anastasia)
b. 3 July 1908, Soda Lake
m. 14 July 1926, to John Zaseybida
d. 15 June 2009, Calgary, AB, Canada

Katherine
b. 11 April 1910, Soda Lake
m. 11 April 1933, to Adolph Berger
d. 11 April 2007, Walnut Creek, CA

Ann (Anna)
b. 16 September 1912, Soda Lake
m. no
d. 14 June 2007, Cleveland, OH

George (Hrehoriy)
b. 29 November 1914, Soda Lake
m. 27 January 1951, to Vicki Kolasky
d. 2 November 2015, Toronto, ON, Canada

Vera (Veronia)
b. 8 November 1916, Soda Lake
m. 21 November 1937, to Peter Kindraka
d. 22 March 2004, Bloomington, IN

Alice (Lisovata)
b. 24 May 1919, Soda Lake
m. no
d. 14 February, 2021, Pullman, WA

Margaret (Margareta)
b. 24 October 1921, Soda Lake
m. no
d. 1 April 2017, San Francisco, CA

Walter (Volodymyr)
b. 13 February 1924, Vegreville (hospital)
m. 15 September 1967, to Jean Stieger
d. 6 May, 1955, Edmontonn, AB

9.12 *Maria and John Ropchan family tree.*

9.13 *Photo (detail) of Mrs. John Ropchan (Maria) in profile on the far right "looking at the ball game... at the first Boian picnic, 1919." Behind Maria, her 4-year old son, George who faces the camera.*

This photo is on page 161 of Never Far From Eagle Tail Hill: A Brief History of the Romanian Pioneers Who Settled in East-Central Alberta at the Turn of the Twentieth Century, *written by Michael G. Toma, n.d. George drew my attention to this photo. By the spring of 1919, Maria was pregnant with Alice, who was born in May.*

9.14 *Structures still standing on Zelenko's quarter section at Soda Lake, 2001.*

[1] One daughter, Margaret, adamantly refused to be interviewed.

[2] When in Chornivka, I observed that the one-room school had been absorbed into that prim grey and white building in which I'd discovered the photos of the Hurmuzaki luminaries.

[3] Taped interview with Nancy, Calgary, Alberta, Canada. 5 May 1995.

[4] Orest T. Martynowych, *The Ukrainian Bloc Settlement in East Central Alberta, 1890-1930: A History*. Historic Sites Service Occasional Paper No. 10 (Edmonton: Alberta Culture & Multiculturalism, 1985) 95. Martynowych quotes George M. Foster regarding "The image of limited good."

[5] Taped interview with Vera, Berkeley CA. 25 March 1995.

[6] Interview with Ruth Tkachuk, Edmonton, Alberta, Canada. 18 July 1997.

[7] The "Registration of Marriage" for "John Robchan" and "Marry Shkraba," Record No. 30 of 1903 in the Registration Division of Victoria, Canada/North-West Territories, is in the Provincial Archives of Alberta, Edmonton, AB, Canada. Accession Number 89.440/1740.

[8] Interview with Ruth Tkachuk, Edmonton, Alberta, Canada. 18 July 1997.

[9] Ibid., 25.

[10] Sarah Blaffer Hrdy, *Mother Nature: Maternal Instincts And How They Shape The Human Species* (New York: Random House Publishing Group, Ballantine Books, 1999) 9.

[11] Ibid., 21-22.

[12] Taped interview with Katherine, Walnut Creek, CA. 23 March 1994. Tape index #416.

[13] Alex Ropchan, "Al's Story: Memoirs of Alexander Ropchan," ed. Stacey Gutierrez (Unpublished manuscript, 2002) 21. Author's personal library.

[14] Taped interview with Katherine, Walnut Creek, CA. 19 February 1999.

[15] Taped interview with Vera, Berkeley, CA. 25 March 1995.

[16] Taped interview with Katherine, Walnute Creek, CA. 5 May 1994.

[17] Taped interview with Vera, Berkeley, CA. 25 March 1995.

[18] Sarah Blaffer Hrdy, 509.

[19] Ibid., 531.

[20] Taped interview with Katherine, Walnut Creek, CA. 14 March 1997.

[21] Sam Ropchan, *Pioneer Life on the Farm* (Unpublished manuscript, 14 February 1982) 8. Author's personal library.

[22] Taped interview with Katherine, Walnut Creek, CA. 23 March 1994.

[23] Taped interview with Katherine, Walnut Creek, CA. 28 April 1994.

[24] Taped interview with Katherine, Walnut Creek, CA. 28 April 1994.

[25] Sarah Blaffer Hrdy, 525.

[26] Ibid., 525.

[27] George recently passed (d. 2 November 2015) away having achieved the 100-year old mark. He became a respected educator and the father of three daughters, all very successful professional women.

[28] The word *narod*, [народ] means THE people. There is not quite an English equivalent. *Narod* carries the sense of the people as a collective national group. It has a touch of Manifest Destiny in it. The young populists—the *narodnyky*—are "for the people." And a *Narodnyi Dim* is both a "National" home and a "People's" home.

[29] There is a substantial literature on *Narodnyi Dim* in western Ukraine and in Canada. Orest T. Martynowych's *The Ukrainian Bloc Settlement in East Central Alberta, 1890-1930: A History*, Historic Sites Service Occasional Paper No. 10. Edmonton: Alberta Culture & Multiculturalism, 1985 is a good place to start reading.

[30] The song begins, "On the south side of Chicago…."

[31] *Ukrainians in Alberta* (Edmonton, AB: The Ukrainian Pioneers' Association of Alberta, 1975) 166.

[32] Taped interview with Nancy, Edmonton, Alberta, Canada. 26 May 1995.

[33] Taped interview with Nancy, Edmonton, Alberta, Canada. 26 May 1995.

[34] The election was in 1953. Nancy, a champion for farmers' rights, was politically active in the Vegreville district.

[35] Sam, in his role as President of the Ft. Wayne Isaac Walton League, was a very active member of the Save the Dunes Council. Save the Dunes played a major role in getting the Indiana Dunes State Park designated as a protected national lakeshore. It was a *battle royale* played out between Hoosier supporters of Burn's Waterway Harbor, less-than-lovingly called "Burn's Ditch"—a dreamed of industrial port, all business and industry—and environmentalists, those who wanted to save the last remnants of the bio-diverse sand-and-dunes shore on the Indiana edge of Lake Michigan. Attendant to the national lakeshore battle, Sam had two rare peat bogs in northeastern Indiana (Stuben County) saved and set aside.

[36] ACRES Land Trust is an active environmental organization serving northeast Indiana, northwest Ohio and southern Michigan. acres@acreslandtrust.org

"In winter,
Zelenko's thick-timbered,
thatch-roofed barn sags and
leans under the weight of deep snow. (9.14)
His house is gone, as is his garden of hemp—repeatedly
and illicitly harvested by Ann
on her way to Prut' school
decades and
decades
ago."

CHAPTER
::10::

SPEAKING OF FAMILIES: THE HURMUZAKIS
Owners of fields, forests, the village of Chornivka and my family

Бідний піт ллє, а багатий його кров п'є.
The poor man sweats, the rich man drinks his blood.
—Ukrainian Proverb

"Most of the time, the truth is different from the way things look."
—Stacy Schiff

MARIA and Elena knew the Hurmuzakis. About them, they gossiped and grumbled. They probably feared, contemned and hated them too. Perhaps Elena had empathy for what she'd heard about her namesake, Ilinka. Elena's mother would have spoken about Ilinka. Women tended to know about the infant mortalities of other women. It was a classless tragedy in a village such as Chornivka.

Thus, the saga of the Hurmuzaki family—somewhere between soap opera and *King Lear*—is modestly relevant to my ancestor-quest and reliably animated.[1] What the Hurmuzakis of Chornivka did, what happened to them affected the lives of Elena's mother and her family. Somewhat ironically, many of my ancestors carried Hurmuzaki names—Elena, Konstantyn, Alex, Hrehoriy (George), Nick— in hopes of gaining some advantage or connection with these overlords. (Illustration 10.1)

When my thirty-three year old great-great-grandmother—Elena's mother, one of Doksaki (Doxaki) Hurmuzaki's former serfs, stood silently with the other former serfs, and watched the *boyar's* remains committed to his resting place near the apple trees in the burial ground of Chornivka's church, I imagine that she heaved a sigh of relief and ruminated darkly about what would happen next. (10.2) It was 1857. When one of Doksaki's sons, speaking to others of his class, described his father as an "old guard *boyar*"—he meant it as an aristocratic compliment—it was not something that Doksaki's serfs liked to countenance.[2] Larger-than-life Doksaki riding his horse around estate lands with his riding crop—"a leather rod with a wood handle covered with gold decorations"—at the handy.[3]

Chornivka-the-Estate was controlled chaos from the beginning. It kept getting passed from hand to hand as a money-maker from 1412 on, a thoroughly typical situation. The estate consisted of the Big House, formal gardens, a church, various out-buildings, the farm and forest lands, a distillery, the village where the serfs lived and several pubs where the serfs paid for the alcohol distilled at the *boyar's* distillery. The entirety was a self-contained, self-supporting little factory of planting and harvesting; of fermenting and distilling; of dying and weaving; of grinding, picking, plucking and slaughtering—drying, pickling, salting, smoking; of chopping down and building. Anything that could be grown, made, bartered or sold, was.

During the fourteenth century, the Chornivka acreage was part of the territory cyclically ravaged by the Turks—these lands included Moldavia, Wallachia, Transylvania: Ottoman vassal states. Unguarded Chornivka in Moldavia was forced to pay tribute to the Sublime Porte, namely the Sultan in Istanbul. Now-crumbled Ottoman fortifications look down on Chornivka from the top of Berda Mountain and attest to those tenser days.

In the 18th century, the wealthy Greek Phanariot, Stefan Luca, unloaded the property onto his cousin, the first of the Hurmuzakis to own Chornivka.[4] It was 1765 when Constantin and his wife, Ruxanda became the owners. Nothing is ever simple. To take over what he had purchased, Constantin had to go to court against his brother Matei, who had insinuated himself into bogus ownership.[5] Matei was able to do this because another brother, Stefan lost the paperwork pertaining to the estate sale while fleeing invading Russians. As luck would have it, the purchase went through at the beginning of the Russian-Turkish War of 1768-1774. It was one of those wars that would go on for a bit, then stop, then fire up again. One hundred years later, Wasyl, Magdalyna's husband, got himself volunteered into the eleventh iteration of this conflict.

By 1782, Constantin and Ruxanda were resident master and mistress of Chornivka's 1500 hectares (3,706 acres) of arable land, 1500 hectares of forest, plus the village and its inhabitants. As if to inaugurate their arrival, a dispute broke out with the owner of a nearby, and logistically key village named Shireuts. Part fire ant, Giacomo Logotetti prohibited use of *the* road that linked Chornivka to its woods—a source for building material, food and fuel. The road also gave Chornivka access to an important market town, Sadahora.[6] (10.3-5) Constantin appealed to the Austrian courts; whereupon, Commissioner Baron Dik ordered Logotetti to unblock the road. After two years, the road was still a no-go. Chornivka's serfs, emboldened and angry, submitted a group claim to the commissioner: "The road is remembered by our fathers and forefathers as the old road, and Count Logotetti, the owner of the lands, blocks it unjustly."

It was one pitched cat-and-dog fight. When the hearing convened, chairs were hurled, threats were made, reputations sullied. The commissioner fled.[7] An *in-absentia* committee ruled in favor of Constantin and his serfs. But too soon, worn out by litigation and the travel required to hang onto his various estates, Constantin succumbed. It remained for Constantin's son, Doksaki to build a new road—using a different route—to Sadahora.

Constantin left no Will. No matter. His wife Ruxanda was more than up to the hostilities that followed. She handed the running of Chornivka over to her eldest son. Then because he would not give her enough of a cut of the estate's proceeds, she wrangled it away from him—litigation.[8] Her second son, Doksaki, took over, but he too did not provide her with the rental income she required.[9] Ruxanda tried to depose Doksaki and when this failed, she began to meddle with her daughter's portion of the estate—litigation.[10] Seven years of litigation—mother against son. Doksaki had to take out a loan to cover his mother's expenses. He put up Chornivka as security. His victory—that is, preventing Ruxanda from frittering away Chornivka— was pyrrhic.

Doksaki carried the debt forward. For the remainder of his seventy-five years, he borrowed, paid off, then borrowed again; distracted by ever-looming bankruptcy. In this manner, Doksaki, the new lord of Chornivka, emerged from his family's internecine conflicts as battle-hardened and economically challenged. His obedient, highborn wife, Ilinka (Elena) was already bearing him twelve children.[11] For a fourteen-year-old girl who wed a twenty-eight year old *mensch*, Ilinka had her job cut out for her. Later, she would be referred to as "a saint." She brought to Doksaki's home religiosity, the arts, elegance, French, German and good hostessing—this meant she knew how to spend money.

There is a grainy, nearly illegible photo of Doksaki and Ilinka. (10.6) A lace bonnet—it ties in a big bow at her chin, very *dégagé*—encircles the perfect oval of Ilinka's face. Unsmiling, she suggests weariness and *hauteur*. As for Doksaki, he is the *big guy*, he looks the part.[12] I picture him at ease on a riding mower, determinedly wheeling around *morgs* of unruly grass.

A contemporary describes the seventy-year old Doksaki in this way: "He wears expensive patriarchal (aristocratic) clothes—a long silk robe with an expensive sash from Baghdad wrapped around his waist and chest, a vest decorated with marten fur, a soft cloth shirt, a red Fez under which peeks his hair, white as milk. (10.7) In his hand he carries a riding crop—a leather rod with a wood handle covered with gold decorations. He rides a vigorous, fast horse, sturdy and strong. The horse, a canterer, makes small balanced steps and the… rider is a good rider."[13] Doksaki's costume leans east and south toward Ottoman-Phanariot styles. "Old-blood *boyar*," he is a fine mix of bespoke nobility and ferocity.

There is also a nearly illegible photo of the *boyar* residence Doksaki refurbished in Chornivka.[14] The photo shows a structure with multiple protruding porches and wrap-around decks on pylons. (10.8) If seen aerially, it would look like a Greek fret-work pattern. Next to this compound, we learn that Doksaki and Ilinka have created "a splendid English park" with plantings of lime (linden) trees, lilacs, jasmine and roses in a rose-alley. He imports grass seed from America—grass seed used for golf courses, only the best will do—and builds greenhouses. Depending on the source, a pond full of water lilies or fish graces this park.

Of Ilinka's twelve children, seven survive. They are packed off to good schools or educated by governesses. Constantin III, Eudoxiu, Gheorghe, Alexandru, Nicolae, Eufrosina, and Eliza—Chernivtsi, Vienna, Paris and Berlin. Doksaki insists that the five boys study for law degrees. The girls, too, require their lifestyle perks. Meanwhile, Doksaki travels among the estates that remain to him in Austrian-controlled Bukovyna and Ottoman-controlled Moldavia—battling in the courts to keep them.

When Romanian-speaking intellectuals and aristocrats try unsuccessfully to break away from Moldavia, Wallachia and the Austro-Hungarian Empire to form their own nation—in 1821 and 1848—they find refuge with Doksaki and Ilinka in Chornivka. Doksaki's allegiance is to his Moldavian-Romanian *boyar* roots. It is pleasant for the crowd of failed revolutionaries: some stay with the Hurmuzakis for years at-a-time.[15] "Saint" Ilinka puts on her good-hostess face and the debt ratchets-up.

Doksaki calls for his sons, all five of them, to return home from law school and Vienna to help him manage Chornivka. They write lovely letters to their mother, but avoid the issue at hand. They don't want to come home, and for the most part, they succeed. Eudoxiu spends his life traipsing about Europe, from library to library, living off of the hand-outs from aristocratic friends, copying out documents that seem to prove that Romania has always been a nation. Constantin III—probably the best lawyer among them—returns home only to be humiliated by Doksaki for the young man's bride-choice.[16] Constantin banishes himself to Moldavia, where he becomes a successful lawyer for other estates—not his father's, and tops out late in his life as Romanian Minister of Jurisprudence.

As for the other Hurmuzaki brothers, Gheorghe and Alex—persuaded by secessionist talk at home—gravitate to publishing the revolutionary gazette *Bukovina*, which is all for breaking from the Austrian-Hapsburg Empire; after a brief scrape with authorities, Alex becomes a theater critic; Nicolae, who is of a "different temperament," is somehow out of the circle. In the twentieth century, Doksaki's five boys will be considered great Romanian patriots, for indeed they have served on commissions and in legislative groups and have been ministers and have encouraged Romanian nationhood and culture.

That year of revolutionary unrest across the Empire—1848—when Franz-Joseph emancipates the Empire's serfs, my great-great grandmother serf is twenty-four years old and the mother of two daughters—one four, the other three. She and her husband, like the rest of Doksaki's laborers, "received title to the land they worked…and no longer had to pay the tithe or perform labor services for a landlord."[17] The deal does not work in their favor. And upstairs? Doksaki's financial troubles multiply—even before "emancipation," he is besieged by debt collectors and lawsuits. (10.9) By 1850, Doksaki has written his will: Chornivka goes to his seven children. He and Ilinka move to their home in Chernivtsi,[18] where they had once hosted the musical genius Franz Liszt. After seven year's residence, Doksaki dies in the city, then is buried in Chornivka under the apple trees. No one in my family is graced with his name.

From enserfment forward, the day-to-day management of the serfs and the Chornivka estate was "outsourced" to contractors, middlemen usually of Jewish extraction. Their charge was to make Chornivka profitable above-all-else. It put them at odds with the serfs and later the freed serfs. With the inter-family battles over estate ownership, the battles between neighbors, the several generations of *boyars*, lawyers and commissioners hired to straighten things out, the insistence on aristocratic appearances—Chornivka and its serf-workers would never catch up to equal the expenses of the Hurmuzakis. Surely everyone felt the pressure. In truth, the very ground seethed in Chornivka.

During Doksaki's tenure, one free-loading revolutionary ensconced in the Chornivka Big House wrote that this "quiet, patrician residence" is "in a sea of foreignness"... surrounded by "the same peasants with the same faces, bowing down deep towards the earth."[19] What choice did my faceless Ukrainian ancestors have—foreigners in their own land, but to countenance the sustaining earth with respect and show subservience to generations of usurping *boyars* who needed to take courses in money management?

When the "old blood *boyar*" died, his son Gheorghe immediately rented Chornivka out to Lazar Finkelstein and Jacob Skapir. Finkelstein continued to manage the place into Elena's girlhood. After ten years, Gheorghe sold Chornivka to his brother-in-law Petru Petrino, who refurbished the estate's church rather splendidly and passed on an intact property to his son Alexandru. By then, Elena's daughter, Maria—my grandmother— was studying arithmetic in the village school. She was eight when Alexandru sold Chornivka estate—this included the church—to Bernardt Rozenshtok for 655,000 florins. It was a last gasp measure, so that the Hurmuzaki-Petrinos could retreat to their gracious homes in Chernivtsi, Vienna and Dulcesti. Rozenshtok set about using the church grounds for haying.

Here was a fine tutorial for an eight-year old. It would be an understatement to say that the villagers of Chornivka were deeply attached to the church. It was there that they celebrated those myriad saints' days and Christmas and *Iordan* and Easter and on. Its succession of priests baptized, married and buried nearly every resident when the time came. Probably to a person, the small population of Chornivka considered the church's closing a spiritual, cultural and historical sacrilege. Setting aside their day-to-day hostilities, they turned to a high church official in Chernivtsi, who posthaste sent a lawyer. This was how to fight.

Rozenshtok vs. Chornivka, 1895 premiered in L'viv. Victory went to the villagers, but Rozenshtok appealed the case to Vienna. He lost. By then, Elena and Ivan, the thirteen-year old Maria, Gus (Konstantyn), Alex and Bill had steamed to the New World. Surely some word of the outcome, ten years in process, trickled all the way to Limestone Lake and Soda Lake. The villagers had won the right to their church. It had been just the sort of battle that Maria would relish—a heady and successful collective battle.

In August of 1914, Chornivka's Big House was reputedly destroyed by Russian troops. When Austrian troops regained the area, they paved the local roads with the pulled apart Big House. The church was not compromised.

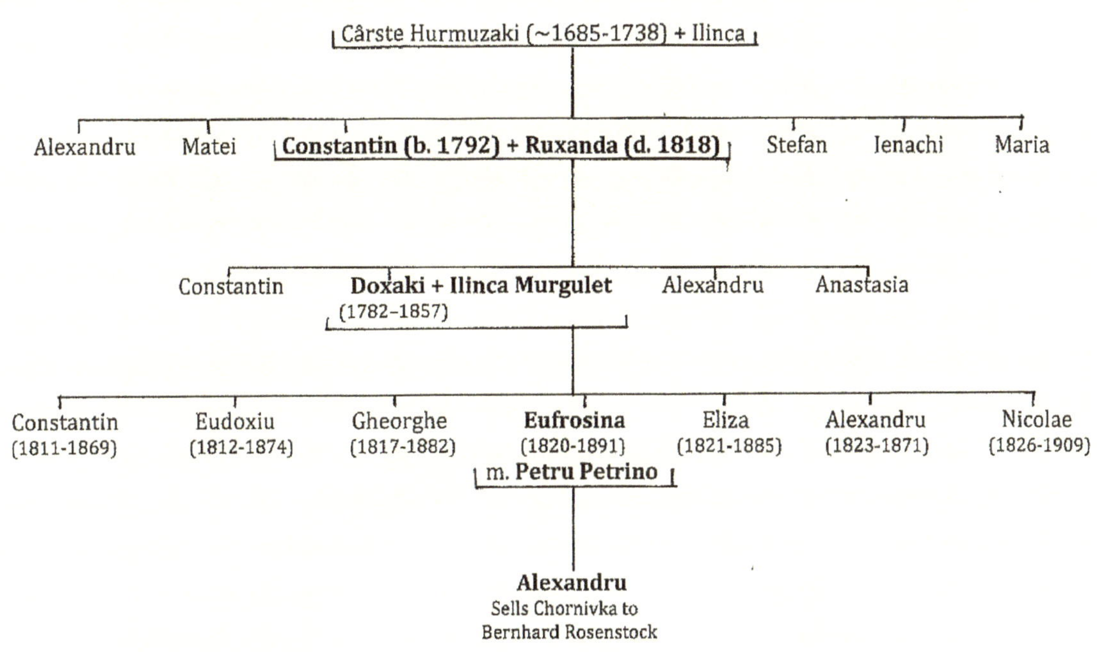

10.1 *Abbreviated Hurmuzaki family tree.*
For a beautifully researched and complete family tree of the Hurmuzakis, consult Ilie Luceac's Familia Hurmuzaki: între ideal şi realizare, 2000.

10.2 *Church of Saints Archangel Michael and Archangel Gabriel, Chornivka, Ukraine. The Hurmuzaki family church, located at the SE corner of their former estate. It was dedicated on November 8, 1825,*

10.3 Map (detail) of Northern Bukovyna, Austria-Hungary, 1914, village of Chornivka (German spelling: "Czernawka"). Czernowitz, Zone 12, Kol. XXXIV. Rutherford Library, University of Alberta, Edmonton, AB, Canada.

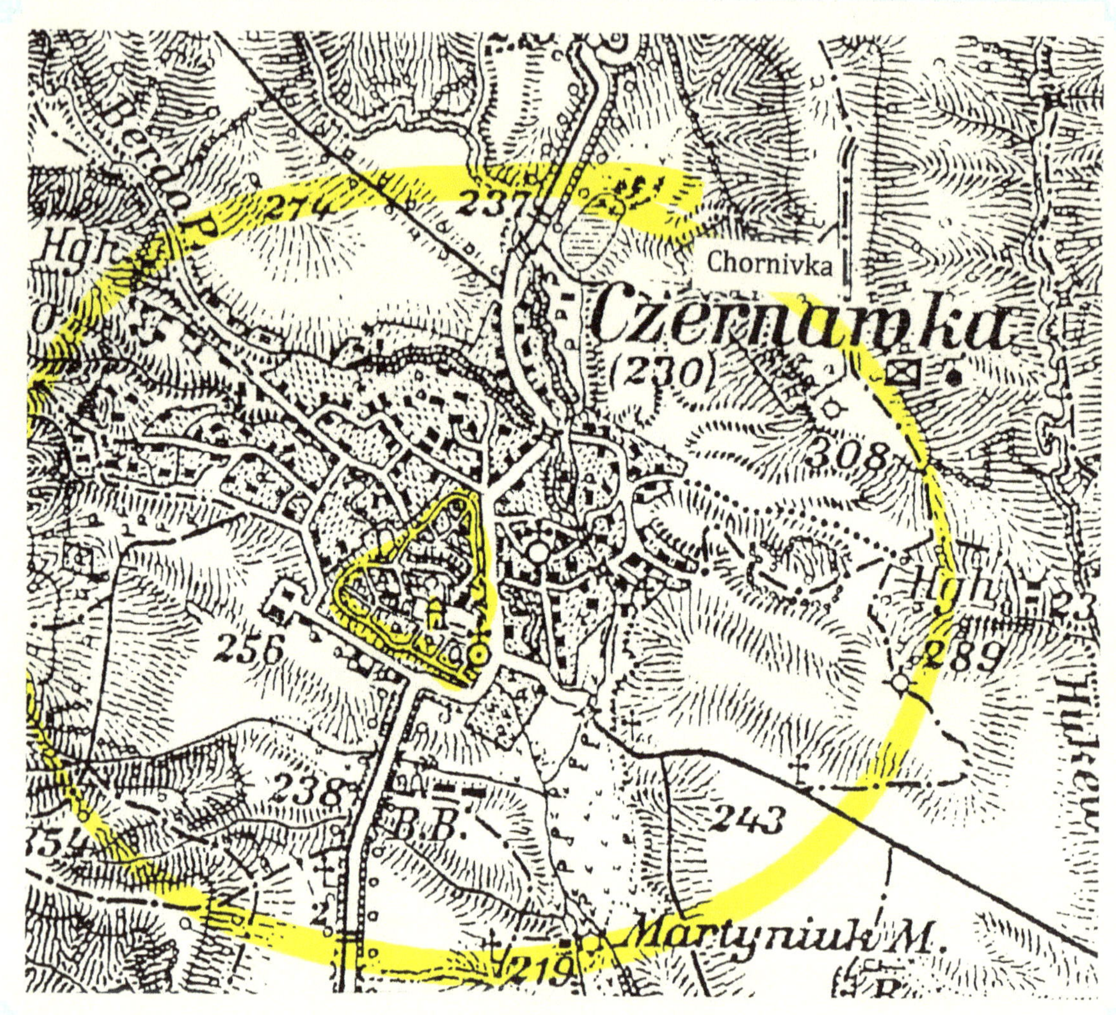

10.4 *Map (detail) of the village of Chornivka (Czernawka). The Hurmuzaki estate is clearly visible as a large triangle in the village's lower left. The Hurmuzaki church appears as a cross on top of a circle with a dot in it, at the lower right tip of the triangle. The estate's ornamental pond is a small oval immediately adjacent to the church. The manor house is visible slightly above the church.*

10.5 *Image of Doxachi (Doksaki) and Elena (Ilinka) Hurmuzachi (Hurmuzaki). From Petru Russindilar, 217.*

10.7 *Image of the Hurmuzaki manor house. From Petru Russindilar, 217.*

10.6 *An approximation of Doksaki's "aristocratic" garb. The red Fez cap and the wide silk sash hearkened back to Istanbul fashions of the 19th c.*

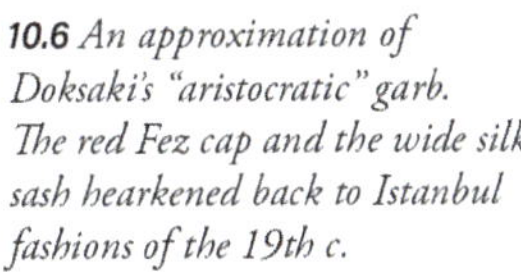

The sash, from Iran (17th c), of brocaded silk and metal-wrapped thread, may well have been the sort of sash that Doksaki sported. (Metropolitan Museum of Art, NY. Gift of George D. Pratt, 1933.33.80.18) Interwoven Globe, 269.

Economic Chronology of the Hurmuzakis
or Borrowing from Peter to pay Paul

1765 Constantin I pays Stefan Luca 1,000 lei for Chornivka, estate and village.

1792 Constantin I dies, leaving Chornivka to his wife Ruxanda and eldest son.

1796 Constantin II (Constantin I's son) rents the estate for 500 lei/year for 4 years to Dymitrashev Skraba (2,000 lei in all)

1800 Constantin II re-rents the estate to Dymitrashev Skraba, 500 lei/year for 4 years.

1804 Ruxanda complains to the Prince of Moldova that her son, Constantin II is "arrogant" and not sharing proceeds from the estate with her or with his other siblings.

1805 January 12, 1805. Estate divided between Constantin II and Ruxanda. Since Ruxanda refuses to allow her son—Constantin II—to do it, a boyar commission rules on the division. (She doesn't trust her eldest son.)

1806 February 22, 1806. Ruxanda leases *her part* of Chornivka to Doksaki, her younger son. She asks him to pay her 1,000 lei for it.

1807 Ruxanda borrows 340 German lei from her daughter's, Anastasiia's, prospective bridegroom, Iliia Sava. Doksaki nixes the deal and has Ruxanda return the money to Sava.

1808 Ruxanda tries to lease her part to Torosiievych for 210 gold coins (*zoloty*) plus the government tax, and succeeds with the deal for a brief time.

1811 Doksaki's father-in-law, Iordache Murgulets, gives the newlyweds half of the village of Mikhalcha and half of the village of Kamyana. Doksaki and his young wife, Elena (Ilinca), then trade properties with his sister Anastasiia and her husband, Vasile Vasilko. Thus Doksaki and Elena (Ilinka) get Anastasiia's part of Chornivka.

1812 The courts order Ruxanda to return Torosiievych's money + 5% = 310 *zoloty*. Doksaki buys a house in Chernitsi from Logotetti for 4,000 florins

1813 June 26, 1813. Doksaki borrows money from a lender—approx. 310 *zoloty*. He pays off Torosiievych on behalf of Ruxanda. Ruxanda owes Doksaki this amount. The result: Doksaki gets his mother out of the way of the creditors who are hounding her.

10.8 *Economic Chronology of the Hurmuzakis.(Continued)*

1815 Doksaki *finally* gets Ruxanda's part of the estate on September 13, 1815. He agrees to pay her an income of 200 Dutch ducats a year. Doksaki assumes all of Ruxanda's debts. Ruxanda owes money to Iliia Sava; Torosiievych; to a Jewish middleman; to government officials from Iasi, Chernivtsi and L'viv; to the Jewish woman, Tynia; to a Jewish man named Meilikh Iuster and to another Jewish man named Mikylia from Chernivtsi.

November 2, 1815. Doksaki takes out a loan to pay his expenses. He borrows 2,813 florins in Chernivtsi. He uses Chornivka as his security for the loan. Doksaki pays off this loan in 1828. He is late with this payment.

1818 August 12, 1818. Ruxanda dies intestate. She leaves behind clothing and 117 ducats.

1824 Doksaki is sued by Ion Mavromati—a builder (work on the church and house)—for 300 Turkish piastres. The suit is based on a contract between Doksaki and Mavromati dated December 7, 1823.

1828 Doksaki pays the debt of 2,813 florins that he borrowed in 1815.

1829 Doksaki pays 1,400 florins towards his other debts, but still owes large amounts to various shop owners in Chernivtsi.

1830 September 12, 1830. Doksaki's wife, Elena (Ilinka), turns her half-ownership of Chornivka over to him.

1833 Doksaki is sued for 1,104 florins by H. I. Sknirk.

1837 Doksaki borrows 67,436 florins from Sknirk. He owes Rozina Sknirk 1,656 florins. Doksaki borrows 2,715 florins from the firm of Liudovik and Anton Mikuli.

1840 Doksaki borrows 2,418 florins.

1842 Doksaki pays back the 2,418 florins.

1845 Doksaki pays back debts to Sknirk. Doksaki borrows 30,000 florins from a/the Bank of/in Vienna at 5% interest

1850s Doksaki's children—Constantin, Eudoxiu, Gheorghe, Eufrosina, Eliza, Alexandru, Nicolae—help with the debts he has incurred. Collectively, they pay back 28,047 florins, Doksaki's debt incurred during 1848-50. They pay some of his other debts.

10.8 *Economic Chronology of the Hurmuzakis.(Continued)*

10.8 *Economic Chronology of the Hurmuzakis. (Continued)*

1857	Gheorghe Hurmuzaki, Doksaki's son, borrows 60,000 florins from the religious fund in Chernivtsi, this, to help consolidate Chornivka at the time of his father's death.
1857-1863	Gheorghe rents out Chornivka to the Jews, Lazar Finkelstein and Jacob Skapir, for 16,000 florins a year, for six years (96,000 florins).
1858	Jacob Skapir withdraws from the deal
1867	Gheorghe sells the estate to Petru Petrino, his brother-in-law, that is, Eufrosina's husband. He buys two houses in Vienna: one at 787 Wollsels (worth 650,000 florins), the other at 15 Josefstadt (worth 880,000 florins). Total value is 1,530,000 florins.
1868	Petru Petrino refurbishes the *Church of Saints Archangel Michael and Archangel Gabriel* in Chornivka. The work takes two years.
1880	Petru Petrino again gives money to the church for its embellishment. His gift totals 18,000 florins.
1891	February 1, 1891. Petru Petrino dies. The estate—including the church—passes to his son, Alexandru Petrino.
1892	May 4, 1892. Alexandru Petrino sells the entirety to Bernardt Rozenshtock, a former Jewish estate manager who lives in nearby Sadahora.

[1] Stacy Schiff, Véra (Mrs. Vladimir Nabokov) (New York: The Modern Library, Random House, Inc., 1999) 125.

[2] The information in this chapter comes primarily from three sources—the Bota-Chornivka Manuscript which is based on the research of a number of Romanian scholars, Petru Russindilar's history of the Hurmuzaki family in Bukovyna and Ilie Luceac's broader study of Hurmuzaki contributions to the cause of Romania. My readings of Romanian and Austrian-Habsburg history have also added to the chapter.

[3] Petru Russindilar, Hurmuzachestii in Viata Culturala Si Politica A Bucovinei (Iasi: Editura "Glasul Bucovinei," 1995) 24.

[4] Ibid., 24.

[5] I came upon the Hurmuzakis as a result of Chornivka's mayor's generosity. He gave me a manuscript (Bota-Chornivka Manuscript), in part, about the Hurmuzakis. I was confused by the family name. Odd, that a thoroughly Slavic village sports a surname like Hurmuzaki in its venerable history. The name has no Slavic ring to it—no endings like -sky, -vych, -ov, -nyk, -enko. It is Greek. How did a dynasty of Greeks come to own considerable property at the furthest eastern end of the Austrian Hapsburg Empire? Well, it's all about that other empire a stone's throw across the Black Sea, the Ottoman Empire.

When cosmopolitan Constantinople fell and got renamed Istanbul, there were well-established families of Greeks living there. The Greek quarter of the city was near a lighthouse—phanar in Greek; thus those living in the vicinity of the lighthouse were referred to as Phanariots. Over time, Phanariot families—Greeks—acquired great wealth and influence. When the ruling currents changed direction, Phanariots took on high administrative posts in the new Ottoman Empire, serving as diplomats and provincial governors. A few were appointed Princes of the vassal principalities, for example swashbucklers like Grigory Ghica in Wallachia and later in Moldavia or Dimitri Cantacuzino and Ioan Sturdza in Moldavia.

The Phanariots "robed themselves in furs, velvet mantels, and diamond-studded turbans, and...equaled Turks in their ability to bleed the peasants"—this, according to Robert D. Kaplan in his Balkan Ghosts (page 91). Their positions were gained through big bribes, tended to be a game of musical chairs, and proved fatally treacherous. Phanariot princes routinely suffered exile, murder—sometimes at the hands of their own families—and execution. It was all rather malignant. The Phanariot Hurmuzakis were given a boost by their connections to the high-flyers. Constantin Hurmuzaki—the first of the Constantins and the Hurmuzakis in Chornivka— purchased the estate from a Luka, who was related to a Neculche who was related to a Cantacuzino. It was fair and clear.

[6] A commission was convened by Austria, because after Russia trounced the Turks for the moment and new treaties were made, Austria got the Bukovyna part of the Principality of Moldavia. Now, in the grander sense, Chornivka belonged to the Hapsburgs. As obdurate as Constantin, Matei sent a proxy to the Austrian commission. Constantin did not attend, because he had no proof-of-ownership documents. With neither of the brother-claimants present, on the 8th of June 1782, the commission ruled that Chornivka belonged to Stefan Luca—the Stefan who had been trying to divest himself of that patch of land for the past twenty-five years. This got Constantin's full attention; he made the very long journey to Vienna to insist that he was the true owner of Chornivka. According to historians, Constantin was a consummate orator; he convinced Vienna that he really had purchased the property from Luca. (*Bota-Chornivka Manuscript*)

[7] The village was also referred to as Sadhora, Sadahora, Sadgora and Sadagora.

[8] In his drawn out attempt to hang onto his estates—in Ottoman-held Moldavia and in Austrian-held Chornivka—Constantin was on the 18th century's version of the Frequent Flyer program. He was ever on the road. For this reason, he could not trust that he would be present in Chernivtsi when the hearing convened to unblock the disputed road. Therefore, he authorized a Toporivtsi *boyar*, Manoleia Potlog, to defend his interests in court. February 9, 1791, the day of the hearing, with Logotetti and Potlog facing off, Logotetti shouted "This man is my enemy. He ruined me, and all of my family and hurries to ruin me again. He is a damned peasant."

Potlog countered that Logotetti was not worthy to reproach him. Logotetti threatened, "If I had a knife, I would carve up your gut. I am a Count." To which Potlog replied, "Yes, you are a Count, but who knows what a hopeless huckster you are." Logotetti seized a chair and threw it at Potlog. The room erupted into a brawl. The table, where the two assessors of the Imperial Committee sat, pitched over. They abruptly adjourned the session. (*Bota-Chornivka Manuscript*)

[9] In 1792, Constantin Hurmuzaki left Ruxanda a widow with four children—twenty-year-old Constantin II, ten-year-old Doksaki, Alexandru at six and the baby Anastasia. Fast upon, she gave Chornivka, "in its entirety," to her eldest son; whereupon, Constantin II handed it over to one Dymitrashev Skraba to manage. Skraba was to pay him five hundred *zoloti* (gold coins) a year for the privilege of mowing "150 *falch* of hay," "producing fabric worth 12 zoloti a year," paying the taxes, guarding the forest and hosting Constantin II whenever he decided to visit his estate.

After eight years of this, Ruxanda had had it. She called for a commission of *boyars*. Here is Ruxanda: "Because of his arrogance, Constantin is taking all of the income from Chornivka....he is not sharing it with his brothers and sister." She demanded that Constantin pay her a share of the income for the past five years and that she be the manager of the estate. When Constantin agreed to divide the property into five equal parts, she demanded that he be removed from the partitioning process. As far as Ruxanda was concerned, her eldest could not be trusted. The boyar commission did the dissection, but Ruxanda remained unsatisfied.

She turned her attention to the remaining Hurmuzaki estates in Moldavia, horse-trading them among her children. Constantin II got Moldavian properties and Doksaki, Alex and Anastasia received Chornivka (Austria) and Horodishtea (Moldavia). The *boyars*, who clearly knew something, cautioned her that forthwith, "Ruxanda does not have the right to mortgage or sell the estates of her minor children." She retreated to Horodishtea with the three youngest, rarely visiting Chornivka. Chornivka was left to a manager to manage, until the twenty-two year old Doksaki rode in on horseback. It was 1804. (*Bota-Chornivka Manuscript*)

[10] Writing to Doksaki that she did not need any parts of the property, "especially since she has 'a woman's mind'," Ruxanda—in a rare fit of resignation—gave up her section of Chornivka. Doksaki was to pay her 1,000 Turkish lei for her parcel. But because he did not lease out her portion for two years, Ruxanda was without rental income. Infuriated, Ruxanda accused her son of being "a bad *hospodar*," dissolved the contract with Doksaki and signed a new contract with Hryhorii Torosiievych, a Polish gentleman. The fresh agreement stated that for three years, Ruxanda would hand over to Torosiievych "the rights of her serfs, the pub (*korchma*) and the forest, as well as the distillery (where alcohol is manufactured)" and Torosiievych would pay her 210 *zoloti* plus taxes a year. Doksaki would have none of it. The Hurmuzakis were back in court. (*Bota-Chornivka Manuscript*)

[11] It was 1812 when Ruxanda was ordered to cease her agreement with Torosiievych and return his rental monies plus 5% in two weeks time. Meanwhile, she meddled with her daughter's portion of the estate—using it to bargain for a husband for Anastasia, signing more agreements, borrowing from her future son-in-law. Doksaki tried to block her by dissolving the contract of marriage, but Ruxanda signed another agreement to sell Anastasia's portion of Chornivka to Torosiievych. Ruxanda-the-unstoppable. (*Bota-Chornivka Manuscript*)

[12] Ilinka (Ileana) Murguletz...The name "Ilinka" is an endearing Romanian form of the name "Elena." In her background, ancestors had sponsored the monastery at Sucevita and the Church of *Trei Ierarchi* (Three Wiseman) in Iasi.

[13] Petru Russindilar, *Hurmuzachestii in viata culturala si politica a Bucovinei* (Iasi: Editura "Glasul Bucovinei," 1995) 217.

[14] Petru Russindilar, 17.

[15] Ibid., 217.

[16] One describes the days of his stay in this way: "I was in great spirits the whole day, a beautiful and spacious garden that inspires with its shade, wide alleys for leisure walks and benches for resting. Comfortable house resembling a palace with bedrooms and the living room with a fireplace. There we would gather, read, learn new ideas, write and discuss, or simply chat and joke around." (Petru Russindilar, p. 60, fn 49.)

[17] The tall and elegant daughter of Baron Apostol Petrino and Ralu Venturi, Elena—not to be confused with Ilinka (Elena), Constantin's mother—captures Constantin III's eye. She loves to ride her horse through "the wide fields of the neighboring villages like the wind: people saw her riding in Sadahora and Chernivtsi, which shows what a brave girl she was." Doksaki frowns on her athleticism and wind-in-the-hair spirit: he calls her "*Amazonka*." Constantin falls in love with her.

Details of dubious authenticity tumble out of a 21st century "local interest" story, more *True Romance* than verifiable history. We read that "the old Doksaki liked his estate to be in perfect order, without any weeds or reeds. Besides fish, there was nothing else in his pond. If anything took root before fall, the gardener would swiftly remove the unwanted plants." The lovers' *rendez-vous* spot is, of course, the pond. There they meet, dream and ultimately part. Despite entreaties from the entire family, Doksaki will not consent to a marriage between Constantin and Elena—"the too emancipated, extravagant" and eternally in-motion girl.

Constantin banishes himself—he gallops off in the wee hours of a morning—to Moldavia. He never sees his father again. He never marries. We read that his "*Amazonka*" often returns to the pond, solitary and sad. In time, yellow lilies start to grow in the pond. "It has been one-hundred-and-sixty years since the lovers separated in Chornivka, yet the lilies—now an endangered species—are still blossoming every year, May until July. The gardener tried to destroy them year after year, yet they always came back." It is all rather tinny *Sturm und Drang*. (*Bota-Chornivka Manuscript*)

[18] Keith Hitchins, *Rumania*: 1866-1947 (Oxford: Clarendon Press, 1994) 231.

[19] The house is across from St. Paraskeva's church in Chernivtsi, Ukraine.

[20] Petru Ruşindilar, *Hurmuzăchestii in viaţa culturală şi politică a Bucovinei* (Iaşi: Editura "Glasul Bucovinei," 1995) 16.

CHAPTER
11

CHORNIVKA AND MARIA TURCHAK
Чорнівка і Марія Турчак

"Even when it isn't possible to completely defuse a mine—for these dilemmas are tough, sometimes truly irreconcilable—there are advantages to at least knowing where one is buried."
—***Sarah Blaffer Hrdy***[1]

"An autopsy showed that R.H. was stabbed 20 times, all over her body, including twice in the neck and three times in the heart. Green County Sheriff's Department Detective G.D. said in a report that he suspected the killer was someone with a close relationship to the victim because of the savage nature of the attack."
—***The Herald-Times, Bloomington, IN, 4 November 2014***

CHORNIVKA. The Old World. That's where the bad things began—all that familial abuse and mutual distrust. Thanks to the habitually begrudging Larysa, I got there and got it. In retrospect, I think that the one truly positive thing I derived from Larysa was the two days I spent in the village of my ancestors. Going to Chornivka was more of an afterthought for her. Our original destination had been the *oblast* archive in the city of Chernivtsi. Visualize the soft rolling green countryside of southwestern Ukraine along a river that flows into the Danube with an ancient city on the high side of the river bank. Larysa had an academic interest in the archive and I was ravenous for any information it might hold about the village of Chornivka just up the road.

Would the archive contain anything about Elena, her family? Was there retrievable history? Was it possible to find this great-great-grandmother serf of mine—Elena's mother? If she were the annihilating spirit Elena made her out to be, if she was the one who set the traumatized Elena on a life-course of not being present, if she was the one who mentored Elena's daughter Maria into her aggrieved position so that Maria in Soda Lake could pass it on to my mother and Katherine and the rest of *her* daughters, then who was she—this great-great-grandmother serf of mine?

So Larysa and I retraced our steps down the mountain from our Hutsul wedding misadventure, waited distractedly at grimy bus stations—Verkhovyna, Kosiv, Kolomyia, elbowed our way—and I mean elbowed!—onto little blue and yellow busses with lumpy seats and jostled and banged along the main semi-paved route to Chernivtsi—past the village of the Ukrainian-Canadian *wunderkind*, Peter Svarich, past villages whose names inform the now-closed one-room schools, community halls, churches and hamlets of the Ukrainian-Canadian settlement area in rural Alberta—Kitsman, Luzhan, Shipenetz, Sniatin. (Illustration 11.1) At some point, we came parallel to the River Prut'—a chocolate hued roiling affair after recent rains—and followed it to the burg.

With medieval wisdom, Chernivtsi had arranged itself along a steep hill above the river that we had to cross. When I first saw the river's name printed on a highway sign—in Cyrillic of course (Пруть, *Prut'*), my heart skipped a beat. My mother referred to her childhood days at Prut' school frequently enough that the word Prut'—or Pruth—was a viscerally basic part of my vocabulary, like "tree" or "house" or "dog." And here it was, applied to the real thing, the river for which the school was named. A thrill-tickle coursed through me: I was getting close to something.

The only hotel that seemed available and within walking distance of the *oblast* archive was the Hotel Kiev, a horrid Soviet left over. Larysa cringed at the expense even though I was paying. Once inside, I was outraged by the uncleanliness of our room and the noise emanating from a brothel bar on the first floor, just below. For fifty bucks, we had two single beds—emaciated mattresses on boards, questionable bed linens the color of sour milk, thin scratchy towels the same color, greasy water glasses—categorically I avoided all drinking water, a serviceable tea pot, no hot water, a defunct shower and Texas-sized cockroaches in the foul-smelling bathroom. Larysa shrugged her shoulders, "You want to stay in a hotel. Here it is."

In the morning, we walked five blocks to the archive. I assumed it would be housed in a drab office building—something square, grey, two-stories tall, that sort of thing. Instead, we walked through a high wrought-iron gate; edged a gracefully shaded and mostly abandoned patch of grass, flowers and shrubs; and ducked into a low, round-the-back doorway, the service entrance to a soaring limestone structure, modestly Gothic in style—a former Catholic church. I winced. The ex-Soviet Union had decommissioned this house of worship, and adding injury to insult, repurposed the building into an awkward research library. Fragile books, hundreds of years old, were crammed into the church's gables, spire and tower attics. To reach the archive office, one climbs a narrow spiral stairway—the stone steps dip in the middle from wear— up, up, around, around inside a steeple to the floor above the nave. I suppose the archive librarians have gotten used to supplicant patrons approaching them completely winded. At least the open study room benefits from the light of trefoil stained glass windows. (11.2)

The head librarian did not think my research proposal strong enough to allow me access to the collection. After hours of back and forth with explanations, qualifications and implorings that culminated in the gift of a box of Svitoch chocolate and a bottle of *champanski*, I finally had access; whereupon, I discovered that the records I sought were in the *raion* library in Novoselytsia, on the other side of the Prut'. The *oblast* archive, equivalent to a state or provincial archive is not to be confused with the *raion* library, which presides over county collections.

Without our own transportation, Larysa and I were not going to get to Novoselytsia, twenty miles further down the river. Furthermore, *raion* library hours can be whimsical: the library is open when the librarian is there. A year hence, I was to play the whack-a-mole game of "try to locate the librarian in Novoselytsia."

I tried to hide my disappointment at a nearby café with a fresh luncheon salad, but instead broke into hives and a rash. It was my off-and-on Ukrainian salad dressing allergy. Possibly because she herself was a researcher, Larysa took some pity on me, on my disappointment. She announced that we would use our allotted archive days to instead visit "my" village. All that remained was to figure out how to get to Chornivka, some fifteen kilometers—ten miles—north of the Prut' and of Chernivtsi.

By and by, a put-upon junior faculty member from the University of Chernivtsi appeared in his banged up Lada. He drove us precipitously down the cobblestone streets of the city, over the bridge, over the muddy river and up the rutted dirt road to the village. Appropriately, he unloaded us at the *tselorad's* (the mayor's) office at the edge of town center. Now we were the *tselorad's* problem.

Larysa knew the next part precisely. As an outsider, you introduce yourself to the *tselorad* and to his administrative assistant, show your papers, explain why you are in this-and-that village, indicate what you hope to accomplish, and so forth. Village mayors are less guardian-gate-dragons than librarians of *oblast* archives, and usually welcome you to town. Word goes out so that the inhabitants can say, "Oh yes, that's the nutcase from Kan-ah-da, looking for something that she won't find here."

Leaving our slight luggage at the *tselorad's* office, Larysa and I strolled the dirt lanes of Chornivka. The cherry trees were in furious bloom. Many of the fenced-in home compounds flaunted them. Family dogs, most often golden retriever-mixes trained to be vicious towards strangers, ravened when they saw us. Sunflowers and poppies brightened corners and fence edges. There were saucy-looking well-houses and out-houses. Homes were painted pastel colors or light grey. They looked sturdy and, I assume, were built of stucco over wood framing. (11.3) Many had shiny overhanging sheet-metal roofs with lacey-looking cut-tin decorations—gingerbread style. The closer to Romania you get, the more of these pretty, icing sugar, Hansel and Gretel structures you see.

Every so often, we would return to the village office, simply to sit in the shade. It was a sunny, +80°F day. There was no other place to seek respite. No coffeehouse, no restaurant, no pub, no hostel. The village was a collection of homes, two churches—the one of wood (boarded up), a school, a village-history-museum attached to the school, three youth centers, the *tselorad's* office and a World War II commemorative plaza. The memorial consisted of a paved square with a stuccoed back wall, tiled by oval ceramic portrait medallions—names lettered onto each medallion. There were lots of Scrabas. Sadly, many of the ovals had been used for target practice.

Tselorad Bota spoke Romanian and Russian. Larysa spoke Ukrainian, Russian and German. I spoke a smattering of Ukrainian, French, and, of course, English. About 5:00pm, when Bota was done with his official duties, he gave us a leisurely tour. At each stop, he would shout at me in Romanian and I would nod. Intermittently, a thought or a few words would leak through my various baffles. For example, when we stopped at the original village well, the one Elena would have known, Bota explained that proof of this being the oldest well could be seen in the huge stones that lined its walls deeper down. Sure enough, looking below the several feet of modern corrugated liner, one could see the Methuselah stones of which he shouted.

The pubs (*korchmas*) were long gone, transformed into youth clubs where the young people could dance to disco music. The *korchmas* were from the bad old days, when too many villagers bankrupted themselves by drinking on the credit extended by *korchma* managers. In the mid-19th century, this modest village supported three korchmas.[2] I thought immediately of my great-grandfather, who was forced to sell—land, possibly his house—in order to cover drinking debts. Ivan-the-Affable liked to buy drinks for all. When I asked *Tselorad* Bota whether there were Scrabas around, he fairly whooped, "Which ones?" Evidently, there were *eight clans of Scrabas*. Could I name an ancestor who might be recognizable? I couldn't. I only had Elena's name, and the mayor was awash in Scrabas.

We stopped to talk to random villagers who were working in their gardens. Bota would introduce me and then show them the photo I had of Elena. I expected nothing and got nothing; she had abandoned the village too long ago for any of them to remember her. One leathery old lady got started on the Jews of the village, how they had gotten rich and moved to New York City and gotten richer. She raged against the last *korchma* manager-owner, Leibik, Son-of-Etsko and another *korchma* manager named Duddia. It was depressing. So there it was. Anti-Semitism continued to reside in Chornivka, at least in the octogenarian and nonagenarian parts of it.

Bota avoided such talk. A modern civic leader, he was a genuine go-getter for Chornivka, nothing but spirited. Ambitious. He was directing his thirteen-year old daughter to medical school. She'd already written two children's books about her village. (11.4) His wife was a dietician and nutritionist who worked in Chernivtsi and spent the hours of our visit at the dining table pitting yellow cherries by the bowlful for jam-making.

To my surprise and relief, after our stroll-about, Bota invited us to his café, an occasionally-open-at-noon-or-in-the-evening situation, across from the bus stop. Indeed, little busses did ply the road from Chornivka to Chernivtsi and back. The stop in Chernivsti was so out-of-the way, that even the redoubtable Larysa could not find it, and thus our put-upon scholar in his well-worn Lada. The café was unmarked, so you just had to know about it. A modest open room of tables and benches, the café offered fresh tomatoes, cucumbers, bread, butter and *pivo* (пиво, wheaty Ukrainian beer, like *Obolon*). I mostly recall how cool and juicy the tomatoes and cucumbers were.

A storm was building. Thunderheads had been posing as mountains for much of the afternoon. The sky darkened and began flashing electric. Wind gusts swept away the heat and humidity of the day. Sufficiently exhausted, I could no longer follow the dialogue. It came as another surprise that we would be spending the night at the Bota residence. I was grateful for the invitation. We had no other place to go. Moreover, I sincerely liked Bota and his family.

It was a short walk—past the shrine commemorating the end of serfdom in 1848, past the town office, moving in the direction of the trim Orthodox church—to Bota's home. All the elements were there inside the gated compound: ravening dog, gabled gingerbread well-house, robust garden, light-grey stucco house, nondescript and necessary out-house, yellow and orange flowers, white-pink fruit tree. The place was quite close to the local stork, contentedly nesting in its over-sized mess of a pile of sticks atop a telephone pole. The village had electricity, but was not lit at night, nor for that matter were the streets of Kiev—with the exception of Хрещатик (*Khreshchatyk*), the central artery of the city. It saved money not to have streetlights blazing after dark. Village evenings were soot black. Such darkness is unique, something we've lost in North America. At night, even in remotest Death Valley, you can see the light pollution from Las Vegas glowing over the Funeral Mountains, and Los Angles, over the Panamints.

For both Larysa's sake and mine, the mayor invited his aunt-in-law over. Sugar beet field hand by day, in her off hours, Katerina established her reputation as a singer of traditional songs—what the peasants warbled around the old well or in the churchyard Easter afternoon or at a wedding, back eighty years or so. There she was in the mayor's *kylym*-lined living room, accoutered in a bead-encrusted blouse with a long embroidered skirt cinched at the waist. Olena, the thirteen- year old, had also donned a festive beaded costume.

The two of them began to sing very loud. It was a folk-vocal style in which a shouting voice is used. There were dancing songs, reflective songs, bawdy songs, mournful songs. And on it went. Katerina and Olena blocked out the considerable thunder. The rain came in a waterfall deluge. When the sky was lit, and it was mostly lit, I could see that the stork had not budged. It was determined to keep its storklet from drowning. Meanwhile, the sister-in-law was determined to sing every song she knew.

The next morning, my ears still ringing, I made a bee-line to the Orthodox church. There, walled within its apple tree-shaded grounds was a small cemetery with once-stately monuments to "Hurmuzaki" and "Petrino." Markers were leaning, broken or worn to near-illegible. There was no mistaking that these stones referred to formerly important people here.

Just outside the gate to the church grounds was a piebald grassy walkway that proceeded up a hill. At the wooded top was the outline of a formal circular drive, to the left a mucky, over-grown lily pond, in the distance an open meadow surrounded by a forest of massive linden, beech and alder trees—centenarians, all. The stately grace of the premises was there.

This was the site of the estate that had owned the land, the village and the serfs. Only a footprint of the Big House remained.

Hurmuzaki Museum. In the afternoon, the *tselorad's* daughter walked us through the village museum. It was set into a wing of the elementary school, charcoal grey trimmed with white, schoolgirl neat and prim. Here were faded photos of Hurmuzakis—grouchy-looking old guys, bushy beards. The Hurmuzaki family tree was a tangle of identical names. (10.1) In each generation, there were Constantins, Alexandrus, Gheorghes, Nicolaes and Eudoxius (Doxakis, Doksakis).

Meanwhile in the museum, there were shards of ceramic ware, decorated with red-yellow-green tulips conversing with one another—Hurmuzaki crockery, one was led to believe. (11.5) There was a framed copy of *Bukovina*, the partisan newspaper Gheorghe and Alex got in trouble for; a heavily embroidered woman's chemise—huge pink and black-fading-to-brown flowers from shoulder to cuff; a dark, moth-infested felted-wool overcoat; a vest expertly covered with *soutache* work. There were also weaving samples. In 1833, the *grande dam*, Ilinka, sent wool cloth made in the village to Emperor Franz-Joseph's wife, the Empress Elisabeth.[3] Reputedly, she was proud of the quality of wool woven under her direction. Reputedly, the Empress sent Ilinka an expensive gift as a sign of reciprocity. Then there were the usual complement of rusted scythes, wooden distaffs, wool carders, a skein of flax, a flax scutcher, clay jugs, wooden barrels, shallow bowls, a flail or two—the stuff of a peasant's everyday life. Upstairs, downstairs artifacts.

Back outside and strolling along the main street, quite by chance Larysa and I encountered the Orthodox priest. A youthful man in his late twenties, he wore a long black robe—it gave his stride a kind of majesty. He had an elfin dark beard and a ponytail. I must have expected *gravitas*, for I was caught off-guard by the priest's Johnny Depp sprightliness. Did we want to see the church, its interior? A miraculous invitation.

He unlocked the blue and yellow painted double doors. (11.6) On the left, inside the church's vestibule hung an unforgettable painting—large, graphic. Created by a devout and unschooled artist, *The Last Judgment* advertised the rewards of Heaven and the torments—"tortures" would be a better word— of Hell. Hieronymus Bosch, his *Garden of Earthly Delights* or his *Last Judgment*, came immediately to mind. Before us was a *tour de force* of Boschean fine-lined detail. (11.7) In Heaven, a circle of the holy floated—like synchronized swimmers— around God. Actually, there were circle-layers of those who had made it—kind of like vinyl records stacked on a God-spindle. A hierarchy of the holy. But in truth, not much was going on up top, just zen-ed out floating. Hell was lively a place teeming with action.

A parishioner closely studying The Last Judgment might break into a sweat over Hades' vicissitudes. The Last Judgment was purposefully placed so that it was the final image the worshiper saw upon leaving church after a service.[4] Vignettes were no-holds-barred:

all the usual instruments of torture—the stretching rack, the Catherine's wheel, branding irons—and then some. Tiny sinners were being burned, hung from butcher hooks, impaled, speared. Busy devils (чорти, *chorti*) creatively worked the crowd with sharp prodding implements, things that any 19th century Chornivka field hand might have. Each of the sins for which a torture evolved was labeled— in the local dialect of Ukrainian—in white paint above the being-tortured-sinner.

Recently one sunny Saturday morning, a Ukrainian colleague and friend, Svitlana, joined me in the seminar room of the Indiana University Fine Arts Library. For two hours, we played-and-paused my VCR tape of the Chornivka church interior, made at the time of my visit to the village. Fortified with cups of coffee, we were nothing but determined to code-break the crabbed white labels that defined the sins committed by the sufferers in Hell on *The Last Judgment*. It was an exercise in patience.

Right off, Svitlana observed that the list of deadly sins went quite beyond seven. Slowly, painstakingly, we counted twenty-five. (11.8) They ranged from "Satan blesses those who remain unmarried"—in the painting, a man in pantaloons and a women wearing a chemise are being married by a *chort*, to "Don't steal"—in the painting, a sinner, who has a large sack on his back and heavy metal balls attached to his ankles, is carrying and dragging weights and being forced by a *chort* to climb stairs. From the list, it seemed that the inhabitants of Chornivka faced numerous challenges—moral, social and religious. Orphans were not to be turned away; relatives were to be respected; wives and husbands were to be faithful; pagan practices were to be avoided; there was to be no lying, greed, gluttony or suicide; Christian practices, say fasting for Lent, were to be observed to the letter. In Elena's time and earlier, it would have been tough work.

Distracted by all the little *chorti*, I could barely believe my eyes when I entered the church proper. It was like being inside a tapestry-lined jewel box. Every surface was covered with frescoes, wall-to-wall, ceiling-to-floor, columns-to-domes. I could easily have been a tourist in Giotto's Arena Chapel—*Cappella degli Scrovegni*—in Padua, minus the press of other tourists. I was surrounded by a chorus of saints, angels, prophets, church fathers, the Holy family, the Holy Spirit, a heaven of stars, the sun and moon. This was an interior of surpassing beauty off a dirt road, in a seemingly unremarkable village, never mind that the great Hurmuzakis once owned it.

Such ethereal loveliness. As if the frescoes were not enough, portable painted-and-embroidered cloth banners stood against walls, here-and-there hung framed icons under glass, silver-incrusted icons were positioned on the altar and diminutive naïve-folk paintings of Biblical scenes were arranged around the nave. Nearly life-sized versions of St. Peter, St. Michael, St. Christopher, St. Basil the Great—the outspoken misogynist, St. Pantelemon, St. George, St. Nicholas, St. Barbara (*Varvara*), St. Paraskeva, St. Katerina, St. Evdokia the Nun, and the Virgin Mary extending her Protecting Veil—saint after saint, standing in painted *trompe l'œil* arches offered their compassionate gazes. Scenes from the life of Christ sparkled below the arches in *trompe l'œil* cartouches.

One or several folk artists contributed animated framed miniatures: Christ as the good shepherd herding his lambs into a protective pen as devils flap above, Christ with the woman at the well set off by clumps of wildflowers, the death of the Virgin Mary—she goes quietly to sleep, the resplendent crowning of the Virgin Mary by Christ and God. These miniatures were like a square dance to the waltz on the upper walls. If one thought to look up at the two dome interiors, there was Christ the Pantocrator (the Almighty, Ruler of All) wagging two fingers at you and God the wise old man with flowing grey hair accompanied by roundels of prophets, the four gospel writers, church patriarchs and tiny gold stars.

She knew this church. No wonder Elena clung to her saint's days and every ritual she had learned in Chornivka. It was hers for those feast days. It must have been the most beautiful interior she'd ever encountered. For Christmas, Easter, *Zeleni Sviata*, there would have been choral music sung *a capella*, a small forest of beeswax candles, incense, and—to use Poe's word—tintinnabulations of the church's iron bells, all the magic and majesty that an Orthodox service could provide, albeit on a modest scale.

SHORTLY before Larysa and I left Chornivka on another of those plucky blue and yellow busses, *Tselorad* Bota offered me a carbon paper copy of the village's history. "Would I like to have it?" he said offhandedly. It was another miraculous offer. Bota put fifty-some pages into my hands. It took several years to have the time to translate the document. (11.9)

Bota's manuscript, that's what I call it these days, is a series of essays, inventories, transcribed newspaper clippings, transcribed historical documents and letters, put together into a packet by village administrators. The essays were written by historians between 1923 and 1942—Mircha Pakhomi of Sucava, Teodor Balan and Silvia T. Belan of Chernivtsi. They tend to be flag waving and romantic in nature, an attempt to nail down the trajectory of the Hurmuzakis, who were, after all, Romanian patriots for several generations and a pain in Emperor Franz-Joseph's eastern side. Some of the inventories have the feel of one long dull day in the village—why not put together a list of all the village priests from 1772 to 2000, why not compile a list of all the owners of the estate and village from 1412 to 1940 (11.10), why not assemble a list of all the Heads of the Collective Farm (*Kolhosp*), this after 1940 when Russia took things over.

Out of the scramble of details in the manuscript, I began to piece together a better view of the way things were during Elena's time and earlier in the village. Here was a lush green thorp, adorned with flowering fruit trees, graced by a diadem of a church and apparently as old as the surrounding hills—historians repeatedly pointed to a document dated May 5th, 1412, Suchava, in which "Aleksandru the Good gives Iurko Drahozhesku Lower Chornivka, that is in front of Toporivtsi."[5] Eighty years before "Columbus sailed the ocean blue," serfs—among them, my ancestors— were working the lands for Drahozhesku at his Chornivka estate.

The first of the essays in Bota's manuscript is about the Church of Saints Archangel Michael and Archangel Gabriel. This is appropriate, since these days that church gives the village its star on the map. It was put up by a 17th or 18th century *boyar*. A modest affair of oak, with wooden walls and support columns, by 1804 it was falling down. When Doksaki, took up residence, he began a campaign to build a spiffier church.[6] He let the earlier wooden church fall to dust and changed the church site. Records indicate that on November 8th, 1825, Doksaki's new construction was blessed. My great-grandmother's father and uncles may well have been detailed to build the structure. She was nine years old when a second refurbishment—all those soulful frescoes— was consecrated. It was January 30th, 1870. Probably everyone turned out for that one.

Back when I was interviewing Julia on her mauve couch in Edmonton and she was sharing what Elena had told her, a second narrative about Elena's mother, my great-great grandmother serf, came up. Here is Julia speaking:

"Grandma Scraba's [Elena's] mother was still a slave [a serf]. During slavery, she was a slave. Let me get this straight, I remember that Grandmother was saying, that one day, she [the serf] decided to run away. And of course, if you decided to run away from one group of slaves, you went to another group of slaves, again into slavery. Anyway, she ran away.

And these people [the other serfs] knew that she would be found. They were making hay; it was during hay time. Of course, they made hay by hand. They put the hay in little haystacks. And they hid her in one of those little haystacks. When they saw two men coming on horseback, they knew that the men were coming for her. Of course, nobody saw her. Nobody knew where she was. But where would she run away? There was no place for anybody to run.

The men on horseback came and they asked, but nobody knew anything about her. So the horsemen took pitchforks and they started someplace and they put these pitchforks into the little haystacks. And they said, 'If you don't tell us where she is, we'll keep on, every one, and we'll find her.' And the people had to tell the horsemen where she was, because otherwise they would have killed her.

When they found her, they took her back to the place where she was before. They took her back and they said to her, 'Apologize to your landlord!' And she said, 'For what? What am I to apologize for?' She was stubborn. It didn't matter to her.

They put her on a bench, on a wooden bench. Put her face down. Lifted her skirts up and they whipped her. And they said, 'Apologize!' And she said, 'For what? You want to kill me? Kill me. Because you will anyway. I am not apologizing because I have nothing to apologize. You're beating me, and you want me to apologize.' It didn't matter to her. They let her go."[7]

Julia had insisted on two things. First, that my great-great grandmother serf was a youth.

Thus, if the beating occurred, it took place before 1843, before she was married. This would have been during Doksaki's time of debt-troubles, an unpleasant time. Punishing a run-away serf would have been a non-event.

Second, Julia was adamant that the point of the narrative, from Elena's perspective, was a young girl's nihilism. It had nothing to do with courage or heroism. She was trying to prove nothing. She wanted to end the misery. Doksaki's overseer and his men let her go because the depth of her darkness shocked them. Somehow the girl conveyed that she was absolutely ready to be whipped to death, hardened—as Elena communicated to Julia— by a life as a serf on Doksaki's Chornivka estate.

A year after the trip to Chornivka with Larysa, my young hosts and dear friends in L'viv, Lyuda and Andriy, decided to help me with my research-travels. (11.11) I'd spent the summer as their houseguest, really more a member of their family, while I plodded through conjugating Ukrainian verbs with a by-the-book tutor at Ivan Franko University. There was one week left in my stay. Since we were all going to visit Andriy's parents and grandparents in Striy (Стрий), an hour south, and since Andriy had a car, if I bought the petrol, he'd drive me further south and east to Chernivtsi and Novoselytsia. It would be a day trip.

In retrospect, it was a foolishly generous offer for which I am hugely grateful. The roads were terrible—some stretches barely paved, everywhere potholes, at one weedy roundabout a grazing herd spilled onto the highway. Andriy's car took a beating; I probably owe him a new car or at least a new muffler. We started out at 5am and reached Novoselytsia—where the Chornivka records were kept— at 11:00am. Then our adventure took on the feel of a Monty Python *schtik*. First, we couldn't locate the *raion* library. Then we found it. It was closed for a month of vacation. A group of locals who were enjoying a morning smoke together in the shade near the library told the inquiring Andriy where the librarian lived. We dashed to her home. The records had just been transferred to Chernivtsi, on the other side of the muddy river. Oh, no.

Without the crusty Larysa to run interference for me, I dreaded the librarians in Chernivtsi. And as I guessed, my access to village documents was blocked by obscure and absurd official protocols, in spite of my please-give-this-scholar-entrée file full of upstanding signatures and stamps. The Monty Python morning clung to us. As proof, from out of nowhere, Andriy and a random bird rescued the day.

While we sat in the gardens next to that cancelled-church-of-an-*oblast* archive, while we sat waiting for the head librarian to return from her lunch for the final "*tak* or *ni*," a smart-aleck black bird unloaded on Andriy's white shirt. Andriy was horrified. Several of the rank-and-file librarians were seated near us, lunching. They had warmed to the polite, willowy young man in the white shirt and tasteful tie who was trying to help a friend. Suddenly, he was tearing his shirt off, dashing back to the car for a fresh one. First a smile, then a giggle, then we were all laughing, Andriy, too. Birds!

The gates opened. There I was, sitting in front of four leather-bound volumes—"Births," "Marriages," "Deaths"—two for deaths. These were the records, begun in 1820 by the priest in Chornivka. I slipped into shock. So little time. Where to begin? I knew Elena; I had her dates, so I began with her. She was there in "Births" and "Marriages." The librarian with us helpfully noted that #175 was Elena's house number, so we back-tracked through the volumes to find others in her family living in *khata* #175. In this way, we came to her sisters, her brothers, her father, and finally her mother, my great-great-grandmother serf. (11.12)

Maria Turchak. That was her name. She was born just before Doksaki's new church was consecrated and probably stood near the altar with the village priest, nineteen years later, for her marriage to the twenty-two year old Ivan Koropets'kiy. It was November 11th, 1824—the post-harvest time of courtship and marriage— and, Maria Turchak was five months pregnant. Fortunate girl; the guy married her. With her marriage, she would have moved into the Koropets'kiy *khata* #175, the home of Ivan's parents. The Koropets'kiy clan would have been eager for the advantage of a daughter-in-law's muscle. The nineteen-year-old Maria's ultimate reputation would be based on how many sons she had and how well she subordinated herself to her female elders in the household.[8] All this, until she became the senior female herself.

As for premarital pregnancy, I assume Ivan grabbed Maria and had his way with her in some meadow or threshing shed on that humid July night, or the two were flirty-tussling and one thing led to another. How long Maria was able to conceal her condition from her not-pleased family, we'll never know.

MARCH. Maria Turchak Koropets'ka gave birth to Anna—the infant's namesake was Saint Anne, protector of women in childbirth, not to mention the Virgin Mary's mother. Perhaps that first birth for Maria Turchak had been difficult enough for St. Anne to be summoned into it. The saint did her miracle work. A year later, Maria Turchak had another girl, Varvara, named after the exceptionally beautiful St. Barbara.

St. Barbara—Варвара, *Varvara* in Ukrainian—a second-century Roman virgin, was also exceptionally devout. To protect her from the inevitable, Barbara's wealthy father contracted for "a strong, two-windowed tower" to be built in order to install his daughter there.[9] But while the tower was rising, Barbara secretly converted to Christianity. Then, "she convinced the workmen to add a third window, so that she might meditate on the Trinity."[10] Furious for her failure to remain faithful to the pagan gods, her father turned her over to the authorities. The tortures—scourging, burning, hammers, knives—began, but Barbara just wouldn't die. Finally, Dad took things into his own hands. Dragging Barbara by the hair up a mountain, he lopped off her head, presumably when he got to the top. From out of nowhere, ZOT! He was struck dead by lightning.

It is that bolt of lightning that secured St. Barbara's reputation or, rather, her power. She became the patron saint of—quite sensibly and over the passage of time—stonemasons, architects, prisoners, electricians, artillery gunners, miners, and more expansively, anyone in danger of sudden death. Ukrainians believe that her bones lie under the golden domes of St. Michaels-of-the-Golden-Domes in Kiev—newly rebuilt.[11] (11.13) The Russians—who seem to be attracted to demolition—blasted the original monastic complex to rubble, a kind of sudden death in itself, during the Second World War. I have no idea how St. Varvara's bones got to Kiev or whether any of them are still there. The faithful—Orthodox and Catholic—continue to pray to St. Varvara-Barbara to protect them from sudden death and to help them in case it should occur.

But to return to little Varvara in Chornivka, the infant was aptly named, but the saint's power did not protect her.[12] A second female birth would not have pleased the Koropets'kiy family or Ivan. It would have opened Maria up to ridicule. If she had been Doksaki's runaway serf, humiliated and punished by his men, an angry girl who refused to give in, then her uncomfortable life as a daughter-in-law giving birth to less-valued girls would have set her jaw.

Summer, fall, winter, spring. There was field work and work in the *khata*. Revolutionary ideas swirled above, not among, the serfs of Chornivka. When Emperor Franz Joseph emancipated her, Maria Turchak was a twenty-four year old mother. Now she and Ivan would be working for themselves. But they no longer had free-access to Doksaki's forests and the charges and taxes they were paying to Doksaki and the Emperor for everything from matches to mushrooms, made them poorer, more desperate with every passing day.

Another two years and Maria Turchak had *another* girl, Domnika. Three girls, no boys. Ivan, too, must have been taking flak from village cohorts: "What? Not able to father a boy." But beginning at the ripe age of twenty-eight, Maria hit her stride with Dmytro, then Hrehoriiy, then Konstantyn. A year after Konstantyn's birth, and twenty-three days before Doksaki died, March of 1857, Maria delivered a stillborn child. The priest, who was recording her births in the village register, indicated that the infant was "not baptized." This, of course, had spiritual implications. The child could not be buried in consecrated ground. It would have been quietly buried on the grounds of *khata* #175 or in the woods. A stillborn birth also suggests that Maria was in poor shape—exhausted, overworked, undernourished, perhaps subject to beatings.

Of all her sufferings in 1857, I imagine this—Maria Turchak standing like a stone, watching at Doksaki's burial, grieving for her just-lost babe. Impassive. Like the women of the Brazilian *favella*, she knew that birth and infancy were uncertain, chancy for both mother and child. But the thought of an un-baptized stillborn child, its spirit an innocent frantic butterfly beseeching her at her window, would have weighed heavily. Years later and in a different land, her daughter Elena would bear this same weight.

Without recourse, she conceived again in December of that year and the next August, delivered a girl, Vasylka. *Khata* #175 was full: Ivan and Maria; Anna and Varvara and Domnika; Dmytro and Hrehoriiy and Konstantyn. Vasylka did not last. She was four years old—the priest noted this in his tome—when she "died from cold or chill." For children, cramped unsanitary quarters and access to cholera, diphtheria, measles, scarlet fever, smallpox, typhus and a susceptibility to infection were the rule, not the exception. Those who made it past the first four or five years, were fortunate beyond measure, possibly born in a month—say, December, January or February— when their mothers could devote themselves more completely to child care. The rate of child death was highest in the summer months, when mothers were involved in fieldwork, away from their nursing babes.

Maria Turchak was not yet finished with childbearing. At thirty-seven, she delivered the last of her nine children, another girl. This one she named Elena, possibly in some whiff of solidarity with Doksaki's wife, Ilinka (Elena), who bore twelve children and lost five of them. Maria's "Elena" is the Elena who should have married the prince, the Elena who reluctantly immigrated to a multitude of slough-y outposts in Canada with her will-o'-the-wisp husband, the Elena who sat at Julia's table and spoke of her mother-the-serf.

The baby of the bunch, got mothered by a covey of elder sisters—Anna, Varvara and Domnika. Maria Turchak, Ivan and the boys would have been consumed by fieldwork. Perhaps Elena spent the lion's share of her infancy and childhood with Domnika, eleven years her senior. It was Domnika whose name Elena reputedly favored when it came to naming her own daughters.[13]

When Elena was three, her sister Anna married and left *khata* #175 to move to her husband's, Ivan Pascal's, home—#65. This first marriage in the family must have been joyful. Traditionally coinciding with harvest time, the October wedding featured a twenty-year old bride and a thirty-year old groom. The intra-family meetings to agree on property exchanges, the myriad ritual pre-nuptial events, the brief church ceremony, the wedding food, the songs, the dancing, the villagers gathered in cheer must have left child-Elena wide-eyed and delighted. (4.8-4.10) Meanwhile, in the Big House, the transition from Doksaki to his son Gheorghe had been quiet and the desperate business of extracting value from estate lands continued.

Varvara did not leave *khata* #175, at least not in the way that her sisters did. When Elena was ten and Varvara twenty-six, Varvara had a son. The priest recorded the name of the boy's father—Tanaciia Chornei—and made a special note in the register that Varvara and Tanaciia were "without service" (без шлиб, *bez shlyb*), meaning that they were not married. They were like that tiny couple in *The Last Judgment* painting getting blessed by a *chort*. The village's spiritual advisor wanted all of posterity to know of Varvara's transgression, having entered it thus in the church's holy records. It was a condemnatory act to pen those words. Official shaming. It did not raise Varvara's family's currency in Chornivka.

As for Tanaciia, he was the guy next door, in *khata* #174. Why Tanaciia did not marry

Varvara, we will never know. Perhaps he simply did not want to live with the woman. Perhaps his family did not approve of the match—for economic or dynastic reasons. Perhaps it was a Romeo and Juliet situation, whereupon the Koropets'kiys and the Chorneis mixed like oil and water. Perhaps, the Chornei side did not want to be stuck with one more mouth to feed. At least Varvara had the fortune to have a boy-child, who would ultimately be a strong worker for the Koropets'kiys.

Thus, little Sava Chornei was embraced.[14] He prospered: indeed, as the record also revealed, he lived to be a venerable seventy-one. But no one could have been happy with Varvara. She brought dishonor, disgrace, scandal to the Koropets'kiys and pushed them towards an economic (and social) precipice. With less and less land to feed more and more mouths, hunger was ever an issue. Varvara was supposed to leave home, not to bring other mouths-to-feed into it. Pregnant, she also weakened the family's fieldwork muscle.

During a six-month period at the impressionable age of thirteen, Elena had the experience of a funeral—surely this was her introduction to keening—and of a wedding. Her brother Dmytro died in January, then in June, Domnika married and left home. A wedding celebration tinged with grief. The "Births" register indicates that Domnika had a son *four months* before she married the boy's father, Ivan Bodnar. Undeniably her mother's daughter, Domnika was another fortunate bride. It is hard not to think that there was some untoward problem in the Koropets'kiy home, that the girls either were seeking refuge in the arms of their male cohort or were being victimized by them. The sheer volume of their pre- and extra-marital births points to something.

Then in 1877, when Elena was sixteen, the thirty-two-year old Varvara had another out-of-wedlock child, this time a daughter. The little girl was christened "Elena." According to the priest's register, Tanaciia Chornei was again the father. This birth was exponentially bad for the Koropets'kiys, for Varvara, for the infant. Misfortune not squared, but cubed. Was Varvara helpless? Was she unable to resist Tanaciia's charms, in spite of the fact that he had put her into a very difficult situation? Was she a devil-may-care daughter? Be that as it may, the six years between the births of Sava and infant Elena seem to indicate restraint on someone's part. What was going on?

Questions abound. Did Elena speak the truth to Julia years and years later? As an octogenarian with her memories, there was nothing to be gained by making up tales. She was not going to win Julia's favor with narrative feats. Nor was Elena a talkative fabulist. Except for her repeated claim about a prince—considered a fabrication by all, she was remembered principally for her silence. Her grandson Al called her "taciturn."

What Elena told Julia was that "her mother went and got a rope, soaked it in water, and came and beat her [older sister] to death."[15] The written records suggest that that daughter would have been Varvara. The priest's notations about Varvara come closest to Elena's narrative. Maria Turchak beat her daughter while "she was having these contracting pains, giving birth to the baby." She died. The story shook Julia. Rarely pensive, she mused, "This is her *own* mother, who killed her *own* daughter."

The horror of the situation certainly settled into my heart. I could not shake the specificity of Elena's description. That rope, wetted to extract an extra dollop of delivery. When later I immersed myself in peasant studies, I found 19th century observers who commented that "Older women [peasants] are very ruthless and cold-blooded about the killing of an illegitimate 'whelp,' whom they view as a nuisance and a burden."[16] But I was looking at something else. If Maria, in her fury and frustration beat the offending Varvara so severely during or after birthing that she died, that was second-degree murder. Even in a culture of brutality, such an act would not be condoned, not by the church, or the priest, or the village or the Big House elders. No. But committed within the walls of *khata* #175, with only the eyes and ears of the family, silence—enforced silence— would bury the act. Such a murder would be impossible to prove to any outside authority.

So on May 22nd, Varvara delivered a daughter, whom she named Elena, and on May 23rd, Varvara was dead—any number of complications could be written into a church ledger, save "severely beaten by her mother so that she died." It was a situation not unlike that "Asthma" written on Magdalyna's death certificate twenty-eight years later at Whitford Lake.

Varvara's namesake saint did not keep her from the danger of sudden death. As for her infant daughter, the tadpole Elena was not embraced as Sava had been. According to octogenarian Elena, Maria Turchak would carry the babe to the cemetery and ask Varvara's spirit to take it. After four months, her exhortations worked. That was that.

Imagine being sixteen, aware of the fact that your mother has mortally injured a dear sister—a sister who has named her first girl-baby after you? Or perhaps you have gathered up the baby-sprite and named her protectively after yourself and then watched as she struggled to survive in a home that did not want her. Your mother has her way. You can't cry out. You can't inform. You must remain loyal to family, but what a family— that so-called cohesive unit, a facade of peasant normalcy barely concealing terror, rage and a homicidal matriarch. Put another way, your family illustrates the complete absence of love. One big black hole. You attend services at the church; you study the images of the saints; you kiss the icons; you listen to what the priest has to say. But you have no center. It has been corrupted. And you too are complicit in innocent death.

At twenty-one years, Elena married Ivan. Given her family's propensity and propinquity, she was a near-anomaly: the girl who succeeded in avoiding an out-of-wedlock surprise. When Elena did finally begin to have her children, she seems not to have known how to keep them alive. Perhaps off-and-on, she didn't care. Then again, Ivan was more of an afterthought. It was the fairy tale prince who had captured Elena's fancy. She knew she was an uncommon beauty and perhaps the prince might see it.

I do not have a death date for Maria Turchak.[17] I assume she lived long enough to have made an impression on her eponymous granddaughter, Maria Scraba, Elena's only surviving girl. The two bear no small resemblance in their ferocity. If Maria Turchak passed away before her granddaughter's birth, Maria Scraba would have pieced together a sense of her grandmother from whispered family stories and village gossip. As for Elena, she drifted by her husband's side and never quite earned her daughter's respect. When Elena left for Canada, the ties she had with her sisters were severed. But the ties to family history or the reality of a murder were not.

So I returned to Canada and then to the United States, with these women in my soul. Every so often, I would rummage around in the great catalog of the Indiana University library, hoping for the perfect book about Chornivka. I didn't find one, but I did stumble upon a book about the Hurmuzakis in Chornivka. An odd little volume published in Romania and naturally written in Romanian. It is not a language I speak or read. This led me to Mihaela, a graduate student—quick, sparkling and Romanian—who labored through this text, with me taking notes next to her.[18]

In an old-fashioned way, our *Hurmuzachesti în Viata Culturala si Politica a Bucovinei* (*Hurmuzakis in the Cultural and Political Life of Bukovyna*) was very rah-rah-Romania, and hugely flattered the Hurmuzakis for their contributions to Romanian nationhood. We both grew bored with the flowery language of the text and began to focus on the scarce footnotes. And there it was, footnote #97. In the spring of 1879, the twenty-one-year-old Prince Gustav, later King Gustav V of Sweden, visited Chornivka. He was brought there by his Romanian host, Ion Bratianu, to meet the Hurmuzaki-Petrinos and presumably to see a Romanian estate at work.[19] Elena was an eighteen-year-old maidenly beauty that day-month-and year. She had spoken the truth all of her life: the prince was real. No one believed her.

It is more than possible that Elena spoke the truth about Varvara. If so, who could fault Elena for trying to avoid her own life? What a hell the matriarch's—Maria Turchak's—life had been. Excruciating. Ruinous. It is entirely possible that she was driven to an act of ravening madness by her circumstances. Who could fault Elena's daughter, Maria-of-Soda Lake, for going at the wrongs of the world—never mind that this included half of her children? Had she not been wronged by village innuendo, by a psychologically absent mother, by a lackadaisical father, by poverty, by colossal ignorance? Nothing but broken women in every direction—daughters and mothers, mothers and daughters. Maria Scraba's offspring took their mother to heart and launched their own raging campaigns against injustice—in whatever form they construed injustice to be. Up and down the line, it has ever been anger and injustice— prime movers, eclipsing all else. Eclipsing empathy, encouragement, support—love. A clan cannibalizing itself.

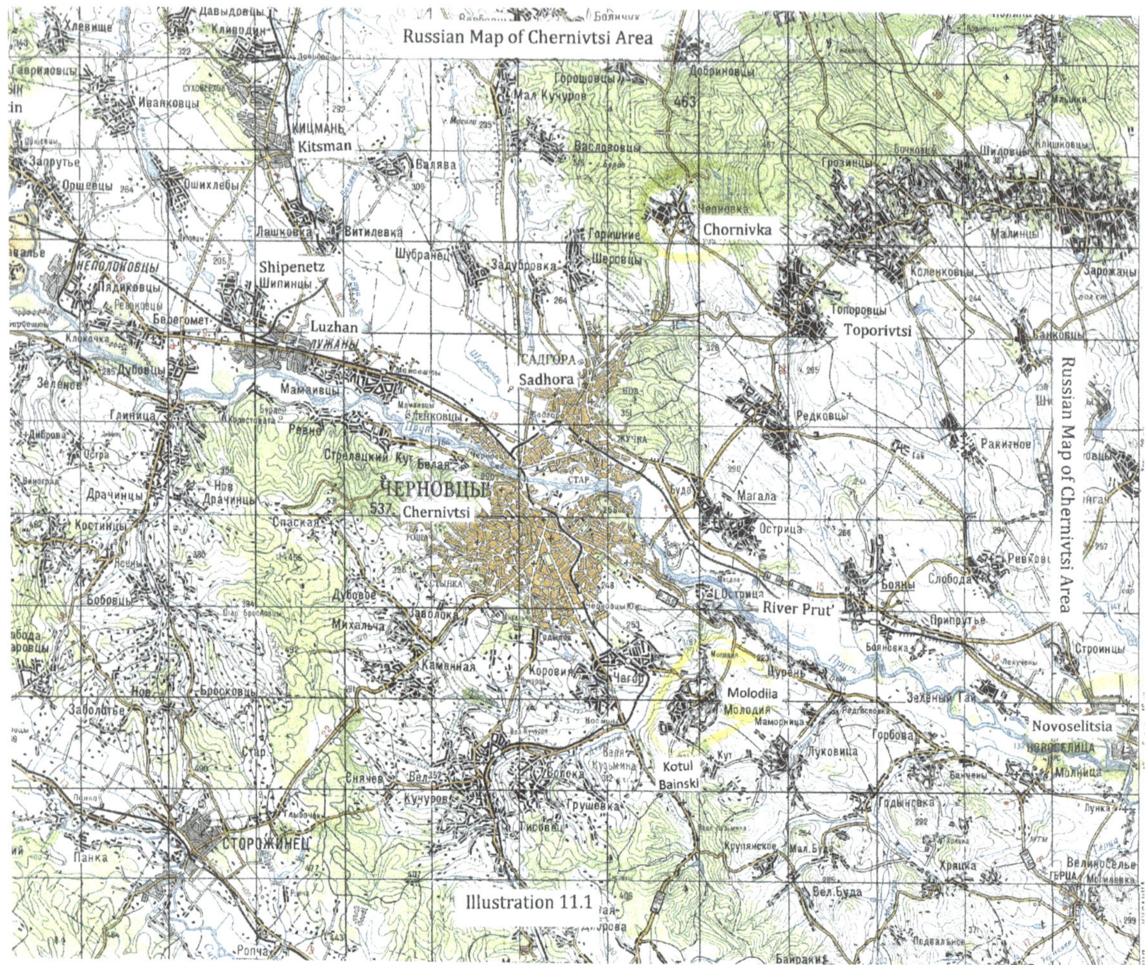

***11.1** Russian map of Chernivtsi Area (detail)*

"Visualize the soft rolling green countryside of southwestern Ukraine along a river that flows into the Danube with an ancient city on the high side of the river bank."

"After hours of back and forth with explanations, qualifications and implorings that culminated in the gift of a box of Svitoch *chocolate and a bottle of* champanski, *I finally had access . . . "*

11.2 *Trefoil shaped stained-glass windows in reading room of Chernivtsi Oblast archive, formerly a church.*

11.3 *Private homes in Chornivka. Pastel colors and decorative stenciling. July 2001.*

11.4 *"The Black Eyed One & Her Friends." Children's book about Chornivka written by Olena Bota (11 years old).*

11.5 *Chornvika village museum, 19th c. ceramic ware.*

***11.7** Church of Saints Archangel Michael and Archangel Gabriel in Chornivka. The church that Doksaki built and Petro Petrino redecorated.*

***11.6** Light blue and yellow entrance doors to the Church of Saints Archangel Michael and Archangel Gabriel in Chornivka.*

"The Last Judgment" *painting in the church, Chornivka.*

Painting of "The Last Judgment"—Tortures of Hell
Church of Saints Archangel Michael and Archangel Gabriel, Chornivka

1) Невінчених вінчає сатана.* *(Nevinchenikh vinchae satana.)*	Satan [not God] blesses couples who remain unmarried. (+Man & woman being blessed by a devil/чорт/*chort.*)
2) Не чаруй. *(Ne charyj.)*	Don't practice magic!
3) Не п'янствуй. *(Ne p'ianstvyj.)*	Don't drink! (Чорт pouring a thick black oily drink down sinner's throat.)
4) Хто не святкує [у] свята. *(Khto ne sviatkyie [y] sviata.)*	Those who don't honor saints' days, holidays and religious holidays.
5) (Illegible)	
6) Не скривджуй сиротів. *(Ne skrivdzhyj sirotiv.)*	Don't offend or hurt orphans! (Sinners tied to a large wheel.)
7) Не суди нікого. *(Ne sydj nikoho.)*	Don't judge others! (Sinner stands at foot of stairway; judge sits at top. Behind the чорт-judge is a pile of skulls.)
8) Хто не постить піст. *(Khto ne postit' pist.)*	Those who don't observe Lent. (Sinner lies on bed of hot coals with fire in піч-like oven burning below.)
9) Illegible	
10) Не пожадай смерти. *(Ne pozhadnj smerti.)*	Don't wish for death! (Sinner being hung from a gallows by a чорт.)
11) Не будь скупим. *(Ne byd' skypim.)*	Don't be miserly! (Tiny wheel attached to sinner's waist, feet and arms tied to a post. The wheel is being ratcheted tighter, pulling the limbs tauter.)
12) Не пожадай жени ближнього. *(Ne pozhadni zheni blizhn'oho.)*	Don't desire your neighbor's wife! (Sinner hangs upside down on a vertical rack. Hands & feet are tied, each to one of the four rack corners. The sinner is suspended in an X-shape.)
13) Не завидуй. *(Ne zavidyj.)*	Don't be jealous! (Sinner is on a spit. The spit rod pierces his chest. His hands, extended behind him, are tied to his feet. A fire burns below.)

11.8a *Working through the captions and images in "The Last Judgment" painting.*

14) Не свідчи фальшиво. *(Ne svidchi fal'shivo.)*	Don't give false witness! (Sinner is tied to a pole/stake, and is poked with a pitchfork by a чорт.)
15) Не зводи. *(Ne zvodi.)*	Do not seduce! (Sinner is hung from a lintel-like system over a fire. A rope ties the sinner's neck to its knees—the knees are brought up to the head. It is the private parts of the sinner that are closest to the fire.)
16) Хто робить перелюб. *(Khto robit' pereliub.)*	Those who commit adultery. (Sinner has its hands in a cauldron of boiling water or oil.)
17) Не убивай. *(Ne ybivaj.)*	Don't kill! (Sinner, lying extended above the ground, legs and arms tied to four posts, faces the ground as a чорт beats its torso with a large baseball bat-like object.)
18) Не бреши. *(Ne breshi.)*	Don't lie! (Using metal tongs, a чорт is pulling out a sinner's tongue.)
19) Хто не шанує своїх родичів. *(Khto ne shanyie svoiikh rodichiv.)*	Those who do not respect their relatives!
20) Не кради. *(Ne kradi.)*	Don't steal! (Sinner is carrying and dragging weights. Big sac on its back and heavy metal balls attached to its ankles, as it is forced to climb stairs.)
21) Не об'їдайся. *(Ne ob'iidaisia.)*	Don't be a glutton!
22) Хто божиться задармо. *(Khto bozhit'sia zadarmo.)*	Those who speak the name of God in vain. (Sinner sits on hot coals, its head in a cloud.)
23) Не шукай собі іншого Бога. *(Ne shykaj sobi inshoho, boha.)*	Don't seek out other gods! (Sinner sits on chair, nails protruding from its back & seat.)
24) Не будь гордим. *(Ne byd' hordim.)*	Don't be arrogant!
25) Будь вірна своєму мужу. *(Byd' virna svoyehmy myzhy.)*	Be faithful to your husband!

* *Caption lettered—in white— onto the painting above each image of torture.*
\+ *Description of the image—rendered by the artist—of a particular torture.*

11.8b *Working through the captions and images in "The Last Judgment" painting.*

ДОКСАКІ ГУРМУЗАКІ ПРИКРАЩАЄ ЧЕРНАУКУ

Багато різних страждань та нервових потрясінь переніс Доксакі Гурмузакі, щоб нарешті стати власником цілої Чернауки. Навіть його
брати, бачучи які важкі судові процеси з мамою Руксандою несе Доксакі, добровільно віддають йому свої частини маєтків. Важче було з
сестрою Настасією, яка ще тримала I/3 маєтку своєї частини та I/I2
Чернауки, яка належала її після смерті матері. Настасія була одру-
жена в I8I0 році з бояром Васілем Васілко з Луковіце/ Луківці/.
Вона свою I/3 маєтку віддає у власність свому чоловіку. Цей,
I3 квітня I8II року дає в адміністративне ведення I/3 частину Чер-
наукі Штефану Васілко, мотивуя тим, що останній має більше знань і
зможе краще "дбати про Чернауку, яке майже знищене самовільними та
неправомірними діями Дорофтея Гурмузакі." Вказано ще на те, що Васі-
ле Васілко живе далеко від Чернауки і не може керувати нею.
Після одруження сестри, одружився і Доксакі. Його дружина була Ілінка, дочка столніка Іордакія Мургулец, володаря-маєтку Міхалча.

Він 8 листопада I8II року пише листа до Чернауки де
віддає пів.села Міхалчі / а саме I/2 села Камяна, що складає I/4
частини всієї Михалчі/ своїй дочці Ілінці та зятю Доксакі.
Через деякий час Доксакі та Єлена / іноді зустрічаємо ім"я Єлена
замість Ілінка - це одна і та ж людина/ віддають своє право на власність стосовно маєтків Камяна та Михалча подружжям Васілю та Наста-
сії Васілко. Взамін вони віддають свої частини Чернауки I/3 та
I/I2.
Після смерті матері Руксанди Доксакі стає повноцінним володарем Чернауки, якщо не рахувати, що дружина Єлена була записана, як співвлас-
ниця. Але і вона I2 вересня I830 року передає право власності на
свого чоловіка Доксакія.
Село Чернаука висловлює велику вдячність Доксакію Гурмузакі.
Він подарував мешканцям чудову церкву, побудував боярську садибу,
навколо яких посадив розкішний парк. Раніше була у селі церква /вона
існує і сь[illegible] ю села в сторону Топо-
руец. Під [illegible] див Іохім Войуцкі про-
топросвіти[illegible] 1820 року констактував,
що стара ц[illegible] тара та маленька" з це-
ревяними [illegible] покриття теж старе, а
навколо церкви огорожа була в поганому стані. Цвинтар не мав ніякої
огорожі лише був загороджений плотом з верби. Сторож, що сторожував
боярську садибу [illegible]

Sample page of Bota-Chornivka Manuscript.

Illustration 11.9

***11.9** Sample page of Bota-Chornivka Manuscript.*

Volodari (Owners) of Chornivka, 1412 to 1940s

	Owner	Date / Acquisition
1.	Aleksandru Dobriy (Alexandru the Good) Voivode (Prince) of Moldavia, betw. 1400 and 1432	5 April 1412. Rec'd as Gift.
2.	Iurko Drahozhesku	5 April 1412. Gift from Aleksandru the Good
3.	Petreskul Baldeskul	17 March 1636. A sale
4.	Mateiash Havrilash	17 March 1636. Purchased
5.	Ileana Andriiash, wife of Mateiash Havrilash	4 March 1652. Inheritance
6.	Aleksandra Cantacuzino, a Havrilash	4 March 1652. Inheritance
7.	Katrina Neculche, a Cantacuzino	1670. Inheritance
8.	Mariia Luka, a Neculche	11 April 1723. Inheritance
9.	Toma Luka, son of Stefan and Mariia Luka	1738, probably. Inheritance
10.	Mykhalako Luka, son of Stefan and Mariia	1738, probably. Inheritance
11.	Konstantin Hurmuzaki, I	1765. Purchased
12.	Matei Hurmuzaki, brother of Konstantin I	1772. Unlawful owner
13.	Konstantin Hurmuzaki I. Owner of Chornivka	1765 – 1792. Owner
14.	Ruxanda, wife of Konstantin I	1792 – 1796. Owner
15.	Konstantin Hurmuzaki II, son of Ruxanda and Konstantin I	1796 – 1804. Owner
16.	Ruxanda and Konstantin II	1805. Division of Chornivka
17.	Ruxanda, Konstantin II, Doksaki — sons of Ruxanda	1806. Division of Chornivka
18.	Ruxanda, Doksaki, Vasile Vasilko, husband of Anastasiia, daughter of Ruxanda	1811. Division of Chornivka
19.	Ruxanda and Doksaki	1811. Division of Chornivka
20.	Doksaki Hurmuzaki and Ilinka, his wife	1818 – 1830. Owner
21.	Doksaki Hurmuzaki	1806 – 1850. Owner
22.	Konstantin III, Eudoxiu, Gheorghe, Aleksandru, Nicolai, Eliza, Eufrozina — Doksaki's children and heirs.	1850. Will of the father
23.	Gheorghe Hurmuzaki	Feb 16, 1854–Dec 31, 1867, A sale.
24.	Petru Petrino, husband of Eufrozina H.	Dec 31, 1867–May 4, 1891
25.	Alexandru Petrino, son of Petru Petrino.	1891 – 1892. Inheritance.
26.	Bernardt Rozenshtok of Galicia Estate manager in nearby Sadahora.	May 4, 1892–1937. A sale.
27.	Mariia Rozenshtok, Bernardt's daughter and F[ery] O[tto] Rostots'kiy, Bernardt's son.	1927–1940. Inheritance.
28.	Nicolae Hurmuzaki Great grandson of Doksaki & Elena.	1944 or 1942 — transferred from N.H. to Collective Farm ownership.

11.10 *List of Owners of the village of Chornivka, from 1412 to 1940s.*

My young hosts and friends in L'viv.

11.11 *l-r: Author, Andriy and Lyuda standing in front of the L'viv-to-Kyiv train car. The car is painted in Ukraine's national colors: blue/sky and yellow/wheat.*

Maria and Ivan

(Марія і Іван)

(House #175, Chornivka)

Maria Turchak
(Маріа Турчак)

Born: 1824, Chornivka
Married: 11 November 1843 (o.s.)*
Died: ?

Ivan Koropets'kiy
(Іван Коропецький)

Born: 1821, Chornivka
Married: 11 November 1843
Died: ?

Anna Koropets'ka (Анна)
b. 30 March 1844, Chornivka
m. 4 October 1864, to Ivan Paskal, House #65
age at marriage, 20 years
d. ?
Children: Deceased at birth, 9 June 1881
Deceased at birth, 6 March 1889

Varvara Koropets'ka (Варвара)
b. 3 December 1845
m. "Without service" (без шлюб),
to Tanaciia Chornei, House #174
d. 23 May 1877, "From childbirth"
age at death, 32 years
Children: **Sava** (a son) Chornei
b. 21 May 1871
d. 1942, age at death, 71

Elena Chornei (Єлена)
b. 22 May 1877, "Weak when born"
d. 20 August 1877, age at death, 4 month

Domnika Koropets'ka (Домніка)
b. 12 January 1850
m. 26 June 1874, to Ivan Bodnar, son of Andriy Bodnar
d. ?
Children: Sava Bodnar
b. 28 February 1874

Maranda Bodnar
b. 1876
m. 1897

Dmytro Koropets'kiy (Дмутро)
b. 27 September 1852
m. ?
d. 24 January 1874, age at death, 21 years

Hrehoriiy Koropets'kiy (Григорій)
b. 21 July 1855
m. ?
d. ?

Konstantyn Koropets'kiy (Константин)
b. 11 June 1856
m. ?
d. ?

Stillborn child. "Not baptized"
b. 7 March 1857
d. 7 March 1857

Vasylka Koropets'ka (Василка)
b. 19 August 1858
d. 14 March 1862, age at death, 4 years
"Died from cold or chill"

Elena Koropets'ka (Єлена)
b. 29 August 1861
m. 24 January 1882, to Ivan Scraba
(Settled in House #175)
Immigr.: 2 May 1897, Quebec, S.S. Arcadia
d. 28 November 1947, Edmonton AB, Canada

All dates are "Old Style" dates. This information comes from the "Birth," "Marriage," and "Death" registers kept—from 1820 on—by the priests of Chornivka village. The four registers now reside in the Oblast Archives in Chernivtsi, Ukraine.

11.12 *Maria (Turchak) and Ivan Koropets'kiy family tree.*

11.13 *St. Michael's-of-the-Golden-Domes, Kyiv. Final stages of reconstruction. Hanging the bells in the bell tower. 2000.*

"Ukrainians believe that Saint Varvara's bones lie under the golden domes of Saint-Michael's-of-the-Golden-Domes in Kyiv."

1 Sarah Blaffer Hrdy, *Mother Nature: Maternal Instincts And How They Shape The Human Species* (New York: Random House Publishing Group, Ballantine Books, 1999), 26.

2 According to Bota, one korchma was established in the early 1840s—it later burned down, another was established around 1847, and a third, from 1852, which was built in front of the schoolhouse and was still operating in the 1890s.

3 Ilinka's son, Eudoxi, refers to the gift exchange in a letter to his mother dated March 3, 1833.

4 Liliya Berezhnaya and John-Paul Himka, *The World To Come. Ukrainian Images of The Last Judgment* (Cambridge: Harvard University Press for the Ukrainian Research Institute, Harvard University, 2014) ix.

5 Bota-Chornivka Manuscript, page 26.

6 Sixteen years later in 1820, the Protopresbyter of Chernivtsi, Ioachim Voiutski, on a quarterly inspection of church properties grumbled that, " the Chornivka church is old and small, with wooden walls whose pillars have started to rot. The roof is also old and the fence around the church is in bad condition. The graveyard has no enclosure and is surrounded by a willow (wicker) fence. The watchman who guards the boyar compound at night, also takes care of the church."

Clearly, the pressure was on for Doksaki to do better for the Orthodox faith, or at least its buildings. He let the earlier wooden church fall to dust and changed the church site. Records indicate that on November 8th, 1825, the honorable Bishop of Bukovyna planned to be in Chornivka to bless Doksaki's new construction. And in 1826, Protopresbyter-the-grumbler Voiutski returned—on another of his quarterly inspections—and joyfully declared the church "to be new inside and out."

By the time Petru Petrino married Doksaki's daughter and settled on the Chornivka estate as its new *boyar*, Petru was refurbishing the church. He hired an artist from Vienna [Iobet?] to work on the frescoes. Whether this was touch-up work for the frescoes or additive probably doesn't matter. The point is, that Elena learned her saints by studying the walls of that church. Her father and uncles may well have been detailed to build the structure. She was nine years old when Petrino's "refurbishment" was consecrated. It was January 30th, 1870. Probably everyone turned out for that one. [This information comes from the *Bota-Chornivka Manuscript.*)

7 Taped interview with Julia, May 2, 1995. Edmonton, Alberta, Canada.

8 Christine D. Worobec, Possessed. Women, Witches And Demons in Imperial Russia (DeKalb: Northern Illinois University Press, 2003), 204.

9 Kathleen Norris, *The Cloister Walk* (New York: Riverhead Books, 1996), 197.

10 Ibid., 197.

11 The massive undertaking of reconstructing St. Michaels was completed ca. 2000.

12 "Varvara" is the one name Elena avoided when it came to naming her own daughters.

13 Family stories have it that Elena gave birth to two "Domnikas," but I could find records for only one. The sense of it is that she hopefully and repeatedly named her baby girls "Domnika." This would indicate that Elena favored this sister's name for some (good) reason.

14 Concurrent with Sava's birth, in the manor house, Doksaki's son Gheorghe gave up on Chornivka. He extricated himself from the financial mess of the estate by selling it to his brother-in-law who passed it on to a grandson, who then sold Chornivka to Bernard Rozenshtok, an estate manager and Galician Jew from near-by Sadahora. After that, it got collectivized, turned into the sugar-beet plantation where Tselorad Bota's aunt-in-law developed her biceps.

15 Taped interview with Julia, 2 May 1995, Edmonton, Alberta, Canada.

16 David L. Ransel, editor, Village Life in Late Tsarist Russia by Olga Semyonova Tian-Shanskaia, translated by David L. Ransel with Michael Levine (Bloomington and Indianapolis: Indiana University Press, 1993), 99.

17 This omission is not for lack of trying. The Oblast Archive in Chernivtsi, Ukraine has repeatedly ignored my (repeated) written requests for this information.

18 Doctoral candidates at Indiana University, Mihaela Petrescu and Alexandra Cotofana were each readers for the two separate books about the Hurmuzaki family—resources for this text.

19 Prince Gustav's Romanian travel companion, Ion Bratianu, took him to the Hurmuzaki estate in Chornivka to see the place and to meet part of this influential family, namely Baron Petru Petrino and his wife Eufrosina (Dosaki's daughter). They may have made a stop in Chernivtsi, where the Hurmuzaki-Petrinos also had an elegant home. Then they journeyed on to the Dulcesti estate of Eliza Hurmuzaki. She had married Gheorghe Sturdza, a politically powerful Romanian. He was deceased. Eliza's eldest brother, Constantin, also deceased (d. 1869), an influential lawyer, confidant of Carol I, King of Romania, and for a brief time Minister of Justice, had managed and lived at Eliza's estate in Dulcesti. Gustav and Bratianu were probably making a kind of pilgrimage to the former Sturdza-Constantin Hurmuzaki estate, as well as using it and Eliza's hospitality as a high-end rest stop.

CHAPTER 12

WHAT REMAINS . . . ?

"I could never peer into my soul and find nothing, for my soul is not entirely my own; nothing of mine is. . . . I had peered into my soul by peering into my ancestral past."

—In My Blood[1]

FILICIDE, the murder of a daughter by her mother, informs everything in the preceding pages. It happened. It continues to blight—metaphorically— the women to whom I am related by blood. Maria Turchak ravaged her daughters. Elena ravaged hers, albeit in a different manner. Elena's daughter, Maria, was ruinous. And so it goes. They were abusers. They were victims. They were all worthy of being cared for, of being cared about, of lives of grace, of being loved. It didn't happen.

Where there is profound fear, there is no trust.

Each of my predecessors learned that a mother's love will betray you. How they interacted, how they influenced each other, what they inadvertently passed on—they didn't treat each other well. They were not treated well. They were an air-tight system of apprehension, despondency, intimidation, distrust, despair, dread, terror and horror . What they had learned, they kept carrying forward without ever stopping to understand the consequences. No one had a moment to stop.

Katherine got me to Soda Lake. Larysa got me to Chornivka, my ancestral village. Veronica, Magdalyna, Elena, Maria Turchak, Anna, Varvara, Domynika, Maria Scraba, Nancy, Katherine, Ann, Vera, Alice, Margaret. They are part of me. They inhabit my head and my heart. Those I knew personally, I can hear them speak. I see them in their homes with their potted Peperomias or bowls of hand-dyed yarn or embroidered throw pillows gathered around them. Those I never met, the ones who died decades and decades, even centuries before I was born, I have found the places they lived, studied the contours of the lands they knew and tried to imagine them in it. Larysa, Oksana, Liuda, Andriy, the Hurmuzakis helped to lead me to them.

I never expected to find documents and narratives regarding "my" women. I never expected to ride those busses and airplanes as far as I did in search of family threads. I never expected to find them—nearly whole cloth. I never imagined that so many of their lives were compromised by violence and a profound absence of love. I did not expect to write what I have written here.

In the 20th century, almost to a person, "my" women sought escape, each doing her best to avoid other women. Flight didn't work; the further they fled from the center—Chornivka or Limestone Lake or Whitford Lake or that other slough-y expanse at Soda Lake, the more it oozed into their lives. Nothing got resolved. It rarely does in these kinds of family things. No one found freedom. If you transmit little love and less support, if no one feels safe generation after generation, the infrastructure begins to crack, crumble, fracture, rupture, separate, splinter, unloosen, disintegrate, and disperse on the wind like so much Milkweed fluff.

Would there be any recognition of connection among them? Of this congress of females, my mother and her sisters knew only their maternal grandmother, and glancingly at that. So in four generations of women, in spite of profound influences from one to the other—habits of mind, practical folkways, oral sharings, a tendency to dry skin and thick, dark eyebrows—these kinswomen were strangers to the rest and to themselves. Talk about being alone in the world. No hands got held. As for my own experience among "my" women, I have found no "exaltation of female relatives."[2] No crowd to gladly come to a recital or a graduation or out for a lowly shopping spree. At least they have given me the wherewithal to write.

I cherish the putatively "noble" goal of bringing them into the light, particularly those like Magdalyna. With my research axe, picking away I've struck a few veins in the rock. Each of my antecedents has more than earned the right to be recognized, acknowledged, remembered—each had her place in the fabric of daily life, the life of her family, the life of THE family and beyond. But no pedestals. My Ukrainian *materfamilias* persevered against great odds and carried the line on—nine children here, eleven children there.

IN her *Mother Nature: Maternal Instincts And How They Shape The Human Species*, Sarah Blaffer Hrdy writes that the 18th and 19th century's association of "motherhood" with "charity and self-sacrifice" is fictive.[3] In the real world of mothering, costs and benefits are attached to each child; maternal commitment is contingent on circumstances.[4] The compromises and tactics a mother must make to manage her reproductive effort are not automatic, nor will they necessarily "result in nurturing behavior."[5] The women of whom I write, had trouble in the grander sense, when it came to nurturing their young—both physically and psychologically. They lived in a world of *real politik*, beyond notions of "charity." As for "self-sacrifice," it carried the day; although here and there, a daughter was sacrificed instead.

The circumstances of a mother like Maria Turchak were devastating. Coming from a culture in which degradation and de-humanization were the norm, she hung on. According to Elena, she even fought back. She did not win. The suffering she endured did not ennoble her; it did irreparable damage. I surmise that the depredations of serfdom and of being a female in a rabidly misogynist society got burnt into her psyche.

It would be wonderfully simple to attribute all the family demons, mine included, to one woman who was born in 1824 and resided in a benighted village—once owned by a bunch of well-to-do Greeks from Istanbul who lived beyond their means—in what is now Eastern Europe. More sensibly, it would be foolish to assign problems to any one cause or person: there are myriad factors at play among five generations of females. But Maria Turchak is a marker for what was going on and the level of her destructive activity affected generations. Maria Turchak's experience of life in Chornivka left wounds so deep, fractures so serious, they would not heal. Those wounds and fractures left a trail of broken emotional attachments that got paved over with the stress of immigration and acculturation. The roads, lousy in Ukraine, were worse in Canada and not so good in the United States either.

Few in my family seem ready or willing to forgive the world and the people in it. No amnesty. Swift to smell the smoke of a threat, lightning-fast to feel injustice, we are quick-draw specialists. It is a defensive position. It circumvents responsibility and the need to change. My sad, angry mother developed arthritis in that finger she used to point accusatorily. Her sisters, too, had the same arthritis. "My" women wanted to distance themselves from what frightened and hurt them —all that internecine cruelty blithely commerced because of things from the past, a disquieting past that is no longer useful.

How to let go of the accumulated wrongs, perpetrated across centuries? Is it possible? When is "drip-feeding the pain forward" finished?[6] When will we stop relegating ourselves and each other to solitary confinement—to protect ourselves? When will we flee from the well-hidden fortress of family legacies? At least women-being-cruel-to-women is now an accepted subject—except among a few hold-outs in the academic feminist camp. I now see Alice, Ann, Katherine, Margaret, Mother, Nancy, the Marias, Elena, Magdalyna, Veronica, Anna, Varvara, Domnica, even Larysa as vulnerable creatures clinging to giant ice floes of grief adrift in a great annihilating ocean. Would that we could all embrace each other.

I propose no answers. I write as truthfully as I know how, as a woman and a scholar, born of troubled females, and troubled by them still. I so wish I could trust women. I have no choice but to try to be among them and at times to stand aside.

✣

"Each of my antecedents has more than earned the right to be recognized, acknowledged, remembered—each had her place in the fabric of daily life, the life of her family, the life of THE family and beyond."

✣

[1] John Sedgwick, *In My Blood. Six Generations of Madness and Desire in an American Family* (New York: Harper Perennial 2007), 373.

[2] Alexandra Fuller, *Leaving Before the Rains Come* (New York: Penguin Press, 2015), 156.

[3] Sarah Blaffer Hrdy, *Mother Nature: Maternal Instincts And How They Shape The Human Species* (New York: Random House Publishing Group, Ballantine Books, 1999), 12.

[4] Ibid., 31.

[5] Ibid., 29.

[6] Alexandra Fuller, *Leaving Before the Rains Come* (New York: Penguin Press, 2015), 176.

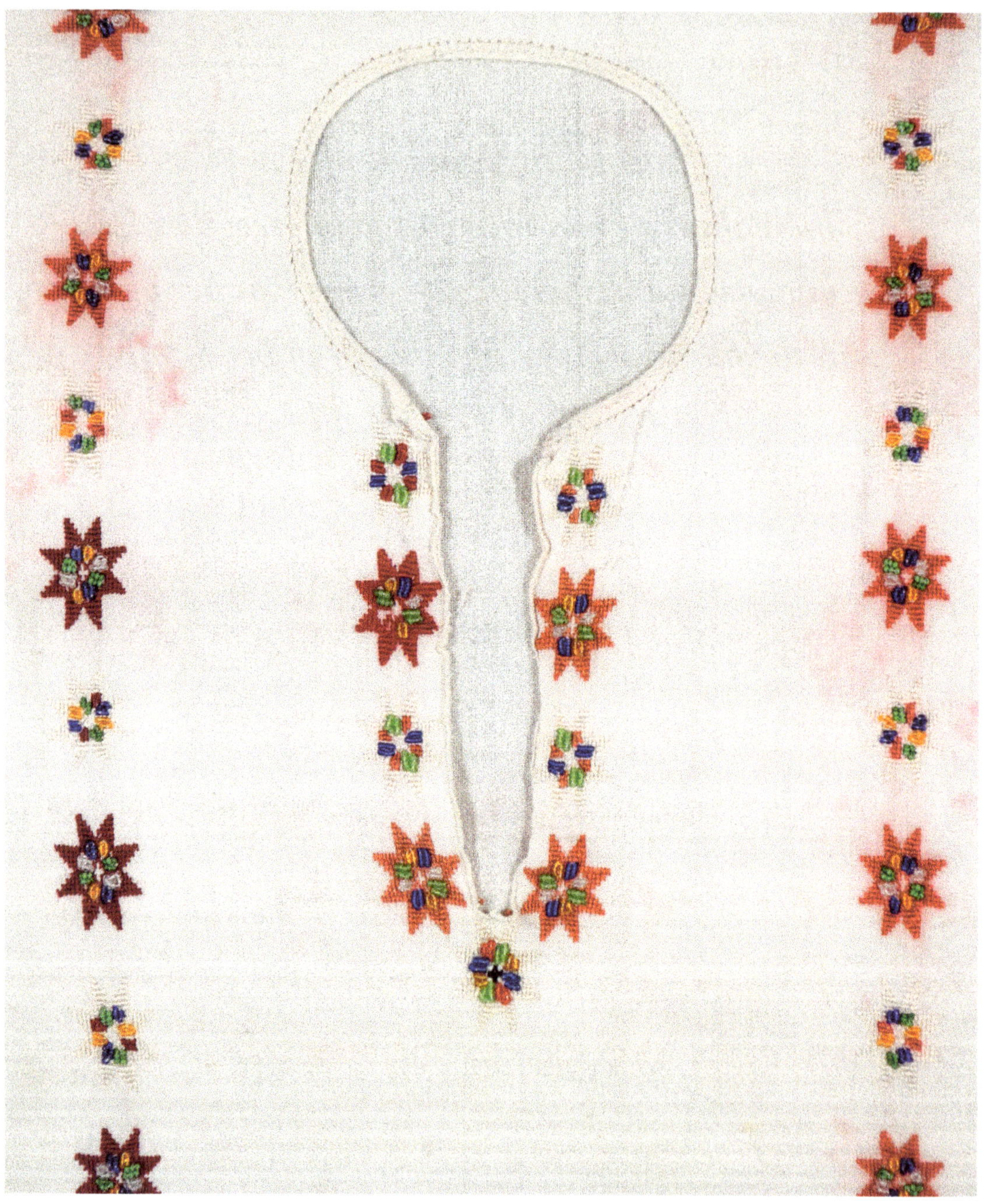

***Chemise**. Photo (detail) of a Ukrainian peasant woman's chemise (sorochka), 19th century. Village of Chornivka, (Bukovyna) Ukraine. Hand-spun linen (flax), woven into cloth by village weaver. Hand-sewn. Keyhole neck. Running stitch at neck opening. Satin stitch below neck circle. Embroidered eight-point stars around neck line (and across bodice). Aniline dyes. Blue, green, yellow and white beads embellishing the stars. Unfortunate use of Chlorox bleach has stained the garment and faded some of the intense reds. Originally floor-length, the chemise is now cut off at the waist, probably to lighten weight and ease movement—what with the hard work of pioneering in Alberta.*

Quilt Design. *Author's template for the Ropchan Family quilt hand-sewn and quilted by her mother, Vera. Each of the eight-pointed stars—its colors taken from a woven wool belt (family heirloom from Chornivka)—represnts one of Maria's eleven children. Each star, a psychological portrait. The template has yellowed. For the actual quilt, the background is a muslin-white to suggest the traditional cloth of a Ukrainian peasant girl's chemise.*

Top, row 1 (l-r) Al, Sam, Bill

Row 2 (l-r) Nancy, Katherine, Ann

Row 3 (l-r) George, Vera, Alice

Row 4 (l-r) Margaret, Walter, a hope for balance.

BIBLIOGRAPHY

Berezhnaya, Liliya and John-Paul Himka. *The World To Come. Ukrainian Images of The Last Judgment.* Cambridge: Harvard University Press for the Ukrainian Research Institute, Harvard University, 2014.

Blum, Jerome. *Lord And Peasant In Russia From the Ninth to the Nineteenth Century.* Princeton: Princeton University Press, 1961.

Bota-Chornivka Manuscript. Short essays, transcribed newspaper articles, lists of notables and functionaries, legends, letters—about Chornivka village's history by anonymous 20th century writer-compilers. Forty-two pages of text in Ukrainian. Original version in the mayor's (Bota's) office, Chornivka, Ukraine. Copy, in the possession of author, 2001. Transl. Dr. Maryna Bazylevych and Dr. Monica Kindraka Jensen.

Bruhn, Wolfgang and Max Tilke. *A Pictorial History of Costume.* New York: Frederick A. Praeger, 1955.

Charuk, Myrtle, ed. *The History of Willingdon: 1928-1978.* St. Paul, Alberta: St. Paul Journal, 1978.

Cisneros, Sandra. *The House on Mango Street.* New York: Vintage Books, A Division of Random House, Inc., 1991.

Coffey, Timothy. *The History And Folklore of North American Wildflowers.* Boston & New York: Houghton Mifflin Company, 1993.

Curran, Harold. *Fearful Crossing. The Central Overland Trail Through Nevada.* Las Vegas: Nevada Publications, 1982.

Engle, Barbara Alpern. *Between The Fields And the City: Women, Work and Family In Russia, 1861-1914.* "Patriarchy and Its Discontents." Cambridge: Cambridge University Press, 1994.

Figes, Orlando. *A People's Tragedy. The Russian Revolution. 1891-1924.* New York: Penguin Group, 1996.

Foster, George M. "Peasant Society and the Image of Limited Good," pp. 300-323. *Peasant Society: A Reader.* Eds. Jack M. Potter, May N. Diaz, George M. Foster. Boston: Little, Brown and Company, 1967.

Frank, Stephen P., and Mark D. Steinberg, eds. *Cultures In Flux. Lower-Class Values, Practices, And Resistance in Late Imperial Russia.* Princeton: Princeton University Press, 1994.

Frank, Steven P. "Popular Justice, Community and Culture among the Russian Peasantry, 1870-1900," *The Russian Review*, vol. 46, 1987, pp. 239-265.

Fuller, Alexandra. *Leaving Before the Rains Come.* New York: The Penguin Press, 2015.

Don't Let's Go to the Dogs Tonight. An African Childhood. New York: Random House, 2001.

Gallagher, Dorothy. *How I Came Into My Inheritance: And Other True Stories.* New York: Random House, 2001.

Geisel, Theodor Seuss ("Dr. Seuss"). *Bartholomew And the Oobleck.* New York: Random House, 1949.

Gilmore, Mikal. *Shot In the Heart.* New York: Doubleday, 1994.

Graydon, Charles K. *Trail of the First Wagons Over the Sierra Nevada (A Guide).* St. Louis, Missouri: The Patrice Press, 1986.

Gushaty, Nick, ed. *Forty Years of Memories: History of Pruth School S.D. 2064 in Words and Pictures.* Edmonton: Priority Printing Ltd., 1990.

Himka, John-Paul. *Galician Villagers and the Ukrainian National Movement in the Nineteenth Century.* Edmonton: Canadian Institute of Ukrainian Studies, University of Alberta, 1988.

Himka, John-Paul and Andriy Zayarnyuk, eds. *Letters from Heaven: Popular Religion in Russia and Ukraine.* Toronto: University of Toronto Press, 2006.

Hitchins, Keith. *Rumania: 1866-1947.* Oxford: Clarendon Press, 1994.

Hong, Sogu. "Ukrainian Canadian Weddings as Expressions of Ethnic Identity: Contemporary Edmonton Traditions," dissertation. Edmonton: University of Alberta, 2005.

Hrdy, Sarah Blaffer. *Mother Nature: Maternal Instincts And How They Shape The Human Species.* New York: Random House Publishing Group, Ballantine Books, 1999.

Jensen, Monica Kindraka. *Personal Narratives and Ritual Observance: How Personal Narratives Based on Ritual Observances Shaped the Family Identities of Two Groups of Second Generation Ukrainian-Canadian Sisters.* Unpublished dissertation. Modern Languages and Cultural Studies, University of Alberta, 2005.

Kelly, John. *The Great Mortality: An Intimate History of the Black Death, the Most Devastating Plague of All.* New York: HarperCollins Publishers, 2005.

Kligman, Gail. *The Wedding of the Dead. Ritual, Poetics, And Popular Culture In Transylvania.* Berkeley: University of California Press, 1988.

Klymasz, Robert B. *Sviéto: Celebrating Ukrainian-Canadian Ritual in East Central Alberta Through the Generations.* Edmonton: Historic Sites and Archives Service, Occasional Paper No. 21, Alberta Culture & Multiculturalism, Historical Resources Division, 1992.

Kononenko, Natalie. *Slavic Folklore: A Handbook.* Westport, Connecticut: Greenwood Press, 2007.

Kostash, Myrna. *All of Baba's Children.* Edmonton: Hurtig Publishers, 1977.

Krawchuk, Peter, ed. *Our Stage: The Amateur Performing Arts of the Ukrainian Settlers in Canada.* Trans. Mary Skrypnyk. Toronto: Kobzar Publishing Company Ltd., 1984.

Lehr, John C. *Ukrainian Vernacular Architecture in Alberta.* Historic Sites Service Occasional Paper No. 1, Edmonton: Alberta Culture, Historical Resources Division, 1976.

Luceac, Ilie. *Familia Hurmuzaki: intre ideal si realizare.* Cernauti: Editura Alexandru cel Bun, Editura Augusta Timisoara, 2000.

Lupul, Manoly R., ed. *Continuity and Change: the Cultural Life of Alberta's First Ukrainians.* Edmonton: Canadian Institute of Ukrainian Studies, University of Alberta and Historic Sites Service, Alberta Culture and Multiculturalism, 1988.

A Heritage in Transition: Essays in the History of Ukrainians in Canada. Toronto: McClelland and Stewart Ltd., in association with the Multiculturalism Directorate, Department of the Secretary of State and the Canadian Government Publishing Centre, 1982.

MacGregor, Greg. *Overland. The California Emigrant Trail of 1841-1870.* Albuquerque, NM: University of New Mexico Press, 1996.

Martynowych, Orest T. *The Ukrainian Bloc Settlement in East Central Alberta, 1890-1930: A History.* Historic Sites Service Occasional Paper No. 10. Edmonton: Alberta Culture & Multiculturalism, 1985.

Ukrainians in Canada: The Formative Period, 1891-1924. Edmonton: Canadian Institute of Ukrainian Studies Press, University of Alberta, 1991.

Norris, Kathleen. *The Cloister Walk.* New York: Riverhead Books, 1996.

Peck, Amelia, ed. *Interwoven Globe: The Worldwide Textile Trade, 1500-1800.* Exhibition catalog for "Interwoven Globe: The Worldwide Textile Trade, 1500-1800," on view from September 16, 2013, through January 5, 2014, The Metropolitan Museum of Art, New York. New Haven: Yale University Press, 2013.

Raban, Jonathan. *Bad Land: An American Romance.* London: Picador, 1996.

Ransel, David L., ed. *Village Life in Late Tsarist Russia,* by Olga Semyonova Tian- Shanskaia, translated by David L. Ransel with Michael Levine. Bloomington and Indianapolis: Indiana University Press, 1993.

Reid, Anna. *Borderland. A Journey Through the History of Ukraine.* London: Phoenix, a division of Orion Books, Ltd., 1998.

Robbins, Chandler S., Bertel Bruun and **Herbert S. Zim**. *A Guide to Field Identification—Birds of North America.* Illustrated by Arthur Singer. Produced by Western Publishing Company, Inc. in Racine, Wisconsin. New York: Golden Press, 1983.

Ropchan, Alex. "Al's Story: Memoirs of Alexander Ropchan." Stacey Gutierrez, ed. Unpublished manuscript. West Palm Beach, Florida, 2002. In the Bohdan Medwidsky Ukrainian Folklore Archives in the Ukrainian Folklore Centre, University of Alberta, Acc. No. 2005:001.

Ropchan, Bill. "Bill's Recollections." Unpublished manuscript. Vernon, British Columbia, 1981. In the Bohdan Medwidsky Ukrainian Folklore Archives in the Ukrainian Folklore Centre, University of Alberta, Acc. No. 2005:001.

Ropchan, Sam. "Pioneer Life on the Farm: Early Days." Unpublished autobiography. Fort Wayne, Indiana, 1982. In the Bohdan Medwidsky Ukrainian Folklore Archives in the Ukrainian Folklore Centre, University of Alberta, Acc. No. 2005:001.

Rușșindilar, Petru. *Hurmuzăchestii în viața culturală și politică a Bucovinei.* Iași: Editura "Glasul Bucovinei," 1995.

Scheper-Hughes, Nancy. *Death Without Weeping: The Violence of Everyday Life in Brazil.* Berkeley: University of California Press, 1992.

Schiff, Stacy. *Véra (Mrs. Vladimir Nabokov).* New York: The Modern Library, Random House, 1999.

Sedgwick, John. *In My Blood. Six Generations of Madness and Desire in an American Family.* New York: Harper Perennial, 2007.

Shteyngart, Gary. *Little Failure: A Memoir.* New York: Random House, 2014.

– Continued

Slomka, Jan. *From Serfdom to Self-Government. Memoirs of a Polish Village Mayor. 1842-1927.* Translated from the Polish by William John Rose. London: Minerva Publishing Co., Ltd., 1941.

Stewart, Amy. *Wicked Plants. The Weed that Killed Lincoln's Mother & Other Botanical Atrocities.* Chapel Hill, NC: Algonquin Books, 2009.

Stewart, George R. Ordeal By Hunger: The Story of the Donner Party. Lincoln and London: University of Nebraska Press, 1960.

The California Trail. Lincoln and London: University of Nebraska Press, 1962,

Svarich, Peter. *Peter Svarich Memoirs, 1877-1904.* Translated by William Kostash. Edmonton: Ukrainian Pioneers' Association of Alberta, Huculak Chair of Ukrainian Culture and Ethnography, 1999.

Ukrainians in Alberta. Edmonton: The Ukrainian Pioneers' Association of Alberta, 1975.

Wilkinson, Kathleen. *Wildflowers of Alberta. A Guide to Common Wildflowers and Other Herbaceous Plants.* Edmonton: University of Alberta Press and Lone Pine Publishing, 1999.

Worobec, Christine D. *Peasant Russia. Family and Community in the Post-Emancipation Period.* DeKalb: Northern Illinois University Press, 1995.

Possessed. Women, Witches, And Demons In Imperial Russia. DeKalb: Northern Illinois University Press, 2003.

"If you transmit little love and less support,
if no one feels safe generation after generation,
the infrastructure begins to crack, crumble,
fracture, rupture, separate, splinter,
unloosen, disintegrate, and
disperse on the wind
like so much
Milkweed
fluff."

ADDENDUM—ALEX SCRABA

By James "Jim" Alexander Kindraka

I had run out of time to pursue all the leads that research into Among Women *afforded. Alex Scraba was high on that list. My brother, Jim, after reading an early draft of the book, was particularly interested in the gaps of Chapter 8—"Elena." Because there was a photo of a train locomotive that could be linked to Alex, he thought he might be able to find out more about him. Jim knows about trains. The following essay is the result of Jim's superior train-wise sleuthing abilities. It helps to close a circle.*

—Monica K. Jensen

WHAT happened to Alex Scraba? He disappeared and was never heard from again. He had deep-set thoughtful eyes and, in 1907, was one of the four surviving sons of Elena and Ivan Scraba—Konstantyn (Gus), Alex, Wasyl (Bill) and Nick. The boys accompanied their parents to Colville, Washington where work was to be had. Alex was fifteen. The Scrabas labored there from 1907 to 1913. When Elena and Ivan left Colville in 1913 to return to Canada with three of their boys, Alex stayed behind. The understanding seems to have been that he would soon re-join the family at Soda Lake, Alberta. But Alex never returned home. He simply vanished. He was 21 years old.

Photo of Alex Scraba, possibly used on a flyer or in a newspaper ad to advertise his disappearance.

His father put ads in the Pacific Northwest newspapers, posted a photograph (8.13) of his son—"about 6 feet; weight 170 pounds; black hair and eyes," in order to seek news of Alex's whereabouts. Ivan doubled back to Washington state, retraced steps, but Alex was gone. A mystery. He was a loved son and brother. His loss hurt.

The family's work in the Colville area had been at a lumber camp (8.12) near Orin, Washington, owned by the Winslow Lumber Company. One photo (8.10) shows the family posed politely in front of the lumber camp's cook house. Needless to say, logging provided many opportunites for injury or death. Back home in Alberta, gradually,

Photo of Winslow Lumber Company, ca. and a two-truck 'Shay' engine, 1910.

Ivan, Elena, Gus, Bill, Nick and Maria, Alex's sister and her family, came to believe that Alex had met death in an accident or in foul play. They said little about him and grieved. Around the cemeteries of Soda Lake, every spring after Easter during Provody, the ritual blessing of the graves, Alex—graveless—was blessed by the priest as a "Victim." Ivan and Elena would not forget him. They listed Alex as "victim" in the small black book of the deceased-to-be-blessed that they handed to the priest for Provody.

AFTER my sister Monica completed Among Women, we had a "what if" conversation. It went something like this: what if Alex had decided not to return to Alberta for more years of hard farming labor under the control of his father? "Hand over the money"—that sort of thing. What if he quietly decided to strike out on his own? I decided to follow some of the leads that beguiled me.

There was a tantalizing photo in our family collection of men in their soiled bib-overalls standing on or around a Winslow Lumber Company locomotive. Neither of us could identify Alex or any other Scrabas in the photo, but I could identify the locomotive with great exactitude. I love trains and am deeply connected to research, writing and the enthusiastic model railroad community. Thus, I decided to give the Alex-query a try.

With a bit help from my railroad cohorts, I found that the locomotive in question was a two-truck "Shay" engine, built by the Lima Locomotive Works (Lima, Ohio) in April 1910, Shop Number 2299. The locomotive was built as Winslow Lumber Company #5 and shipped through a distributor in Seattle.[1] This would make the time of the photo late 1910 at the earliest. I had no way to identify the individuals on and near the locomotive, but the photo led me to Ms. Jodie Roberts, Chief Historian, and Ms. Linda Terry, researcher for the Stevens County Historical Society in Colville. They were interested in the photo and I was interested in anything these researchers could find.

Who would have suspected that there was a Scraba paper trail! Ms. Roberts and Ms. Terry found documents showing that in May of 1909, Ivan (John) Scraba filed for and received a 160-acre homestead tract east of Colville, near Park Rapids, Washington. What he intended to do with the quarter section is not clear. Even now, the land presents itself as hilly and heavily wooded, not appropriate for farming. Although, as Monica pointed out to me, early Ukrainian immigrants favored woodland. Trees meant resources for building and fuel, never mind the quality of the soil under the forest.

In August 1911, Ivan (John) Scraba was paid an amount by the Stevens County Board of Commissioners for his work helping to construct a road past a property that would link two secondary roads. That same August, John's name appeared on a list of applicants granted naturalization. However, Ivan's (John's) financial fortunes floundered and in 1913, his 160-acre property was attached and foreclosed. It was the year that the Scrabas, sans Alex, returned to Soda Lake, Alberta, where they knew they had a resource in daughter Maria (my grandmother) and the farm she had built with her husband.

As for Alex, his last post to the family was a playful note to his sister Maria (8.14), postmarked January 16th, 1914 and mailed from the Post Office in Napoleon, Washington, which was permanently closed in 1915 and now ceases to exist. The post came after Alex's parents and brothers had returned to Canada. It reads [as is] "Hello sister, I have received welcome card and was glad to hear from you. that is me on the picture. I have a cape [cap] and my friend has a hat. Your Brother Alex Scraba." The postcard was addressed to "Mrs. Marry Ropchan, Soda Lake, Alta." Somehow, the card arrived to her. Ah, those ancient days before five and six-digit postal codes.

On the verso side of Alex's card was a photo in which Alex was seated with an unnamed male standing behind him. The two appeared to be friends, relaxed and comfortable together. Coincidentally, on January 10th, 1914, The Coleville Examiner printed a one-sentence social note—"Ray Lindley and Alex Scraba were down from Bossburg the first of the week." Bossburg, now a ghost town, was a small community on the Columbia River, twenty miles north of Colville. It sported a sawmill and a ferry to cross the Columbia.

That Alex sent his last communication to his only sister, was probably due, not only to their fondness for each other, but also to the fact that Maria, unlike Elena and Ivan, was literate, established and geographically nailed down. Alex signaled to all that he was fine. One wonders if, by then, he had decided to break from his family, for the postcard suggests connection.

According to our Coleville researchers, in June of 1917, Alex's name resurfaced when his World War I military registration card was completed. The card listed him as "single" and "an Alien," born in and a citizen of Austro-Hungary. At that time, the western portion of Ukraine where Alex was born (in Chornivka), was part of the Austro-Hungarian Empire. His home was recorded as "Colville." No street address. Alex's employment was inscribed as "laborer" for the Rutledge Timber Company in Fernwood, Idaho, about 150 miles from Colville. It was in Fernwood where the registration card had been filled out and signed. An aside, in a jarring sign-of-the-times, tiny lettering in the bottom corner of the card had the instruction—"If person is of African descent, tear off this corner."

August 18th, 1917, two months later, Alex Scraba's name, along with 150 others, was listed in a Spokane newspaper. These fortunates were being called for induction into the US Army's 91st Infantry Division, nicknamed "The Wild West Division." It had been formed in early 1917 and headquartered in Tacoma, Washington. Alex completed basic training in Tacoma in the fall, 1917. In February of 1918, he, along with thirty-six other recruits was discharged. This was just before the 91st was deployed to Europe and saw combat action in France.

Military documentation gave no reason for Alex's discharge. He was still a citizen of an "enemy" country. He was an "Austrian" from Austro-Hungary. Could this have been a factor? Then again, perhaps the Army's enrollment quotas were met; or it's possible Alex had some medical condition that disqualified him.

Alex had completed basic training, but his "Army Veteran" status was unclear. Although

Form 1 — REGISTRATION CARD 271

1. Name in full: Alexander Scraba — Age: 25
2. Home address: Cirile, Washington
3. Date of birth: April 5 1892
4. an alien
5. Where were you born? Austria
6. If not a citizen, of what country are you a citizen or subject? Austria
7. What is your present trade, occupation, or office? Laborer 30
8. By whom employed? Rutledge Timber Co. Where employed? Fernwood Idaho
9. Father
10. Married or single (which)? Single Race (specify which)? Caucasian
11. What military service have you had? Rank ; branch ; years ; Nation or State
12. Do you claim exemption from draft (specify grounds)?

I affirm that I have verified above answers and that they are true.

Alexander Scraba (Signature or mark)

11-1-1-A

REGISTRAR'S REPORT

1. Tall, medium, or short (specify which)? Tall Slender, medium, or stout (which)? [illegible]
2. Color of eyes? Dark Color of hair? Dark Bald? No
3. Has person lost arm, leg, hand, foot, or both eyes, or is he otherwise disabled (specify)?

I certify that my answers are true, that the person registered has read his own answers, that I have witnessed his signature, and that all of his answers of which I have knowledge are true, except as follows:

B. S. Walker (Signature of registrar)

Precinct Fernwood
City or County Fernwood
State Idaho

June 5 1917 (Date of registration)

Copy of Alexander Scraba's US Army Registration Card.

STANDARD CERTIFICATE OF DEATH
STATE OF OREGON
BOARD OF HEALTH—PORTLAND
U. S. PUBLIC HEALTH SERVICE

LOCAL REGISTRAR'S NUMBER 20 — 45-8001
STATE FILE NO. 6338
DATE RECEIVED JUN 2 1955

1. NAME OF DECEASED (TYPE OR PRINT) a. (First) Alexander b. (Middle) c. (Last) Scraba 4201
2. PLACE OF DEATH a. COUNTY Umatilla b. CITY OR TOWN Hermiston c. LENGTH OF STAY (in this place) 1 month d. FULL NAME OF HOSPITAL OR INSTITUTION Good Shepherd Hosp.
3. USUAL RESIDENCE (Where deceased lived. If institution: residence before admission). a. STATE California b. COUNTY Shasta c. CITY OR TOWN Redding d. STREET ADDRESS Sacramento Street
4. DATE OF DEATH (Month) (Day) (Year) May 6, 1955
5. SEX Male
6. COLOR OR RACE White
7a. MARRIED, NEVER MARRIED, WIDOWED, DIVORCED (Specify) never married
7b. NAME OF HUSBAND OR WIFE -----
8. DATE OF BIRTH April 5, 1892
9. AGE (In years last birthday) 63
10. BIRTHPLACE (State or foreign country) Turkey
11. CITIZEN OF WHAT COUNTRY? --
12. FATHER'S NAME Unknown
13. MOTHER'S MAIDEN NAME Unknown
14a. USUAL OCCUPATION Lineman
14b. KIND OF BUSINESS OR INDUSTRY Electrical Const.
15. IF VETERAN, NAME WAR none
16. INFORMANT'S OWN SIGNATURE P. W. Perryman
17. SOCIAL SECURITY NO. 526-07-9956
18. CAUSE OF DEATH — MEDICAL CERTIFICATION — I. DISEASE OR CONDITION DIRECTLY LEADING TO DEATH (a) Coronary occlusion, acute — INTERVAL BETWEEN ONSET AND DEATH 5 minutes
ANTECEDENT CAUSES — DUE TO (b) — DUE TO (c)
II. OTHER SIGNIFICANT CONDITIONS
19a. DATE OF OPERATION
19b. MAJOR FINDINGS OF OPERATION
20. AUTOPSY? YES ☐ NO ☒
21a. ACCIDENT, SUICIDE, HOMICIDE (Specify)
21b. PLACE OF INJURY
21c. (CITY, TOWN, OR TOWNSHIP) (COUNTY) (STATE)
21d. TIME OF INJURY
21e. INJURY OCCURRED WHILE AT WORK ☐ NOT WHILE AT WORK ☐
21f. HOW DID INJURY OCCUR?
22. I HEREBY CERTIFY THAT I ATTENDED THE DECEASED FROM —, 19 TO —, 19, THAT I LAST SAW THE DECEASED ALIVE ON — 19, AND THAT DEATH OCCURRED AT 2:30 P.M., FROM THE CAUSES AND ON THE DATE STATED ABOVE.
23a. SIGNATURE Milton J. Johnson, M.D.
23b. ADDRESS Hermiston, Oregon
23c. DATE SIGNED 12 May 1955
24a. BURIAL, CREMATION, REMOVAL (Specify) Burial
24b. DATE May/12/1955
24c. NAME OF CEMETERY OR CREMATORY City
24d. LOCATION Hermiston, Oregon
DATE REC'D BY LOCAL REG. 5-21-55
REGISTRAR'S SIGNATURE Vera Thomas
25. FUNERAL DIRECTOR'S SIGNATURE Joseph E. Burns — ADDRESS Hermiston Ore.

AGE SHOULD BE STATED EXACTLY. PHYSICIANS SHOULD STATE CAUSE OF DEATH IN PLAIN TERMS, SO THAT IT MAY BE PROPERLY CLASSIFIED. EXACT STATEMENT OF OCCUPATION IS VERY IMPORTANT.

Copy of Alexander Scraba's death certificate.

the US Army likes to hold on to "paper," records needed to verify Alex's discharge and veteran status were lost in a July, 1973 fire that destroyed millions of documents at the military's National Personnel Records Center in St. Louis, Missouri.

When Alex again appeared, it was in a 1930-census report. By today's standards, the report is a bit invasive. He was now thirty-eight years old. Alex was living in the Union Hotel in San Mateo, California—he listed it as "home." Ironic that he was nine-hundred miles from Colville and many more miles from Soda Lake, Alberta—previous and alternative "homes." There were twenty other males listed as "Roomer" at the San Mateo Union Hotel. The place appeared to be more a boarding house, than a "hotel."

Alex was still recorded as "Single" and "Alien." Reputedly he spoke "Polish," which is questionable. What is the difference between Polish and Ukrainian? Who, at the time, knew? Alex answered "yes" for "Reads, Writes, Speaks English." He was clearly literate. His occupation, unchanged was that of "Laborer," but he was paid a "Salary," so that he was possibly a tradesman and not an hourly day-laborer. He worked just north of San Mateo at the site for the new San Francisco airport—currently and colloquially known as SFO—which began construction in 1927.

By clan standards, Alex passed away at a youthful 63. His nephews, nieces, sister, brother, parents, grandparents slipped away in their 80's, 90's and 100's. A life of physical labor—farming—and simple food contributed to longevity among the Scrabas. But Alex bore the additional burden of being alone, a solitary radical. It was by choice, but that didn't make his life easier.

The cause of his death was a sudden heart attack, officially a "coronary occlusion." Alex died on May 6th, 1955. He was buried in the Hermiston Cemetery in Hermiston, Oregon, thousands of miles from Chornivka, Bukovyna (Ukraine); Limestone Lake, Alberta; Soda Lake, Alberta and 235 miles south of Colville, Washington.

Stevens County Historical Society's chief historian, Ms. Roberts, was able to provide me a copy of Alex's Death Certificate and a photo of his cemetery marker. He died in Oregon, yet the certificate lists Redding, California as Alex's "home." Mysteries abound. He was working in electrical construction, possibly as a lineman—in my mind, I can hear the mournful refrain of "Wichita Lineman" sung by Glen Campbell in 1968—"I am a lineman for the county, and I drive the main road, searchin' in the sun for another overload...." Moving from place to place as he was needed, Alex had been in Hermiston for only a month, likely hired for electrical work during the final construction phase of the McNary hydroelectric dam on the nearby Columbia River.

His death certificate noted that Alex was "Never married" and that "Turkey" was his birthplace. Amusing. Painful. Appalling. Turkey?! At Alex's death, Chornivka, his birth-vil-

[1]In an ironic twist, the twenty-mile logging railroad for which the Winslow Lumber Company's "Shay" engine was built lay within what is today the Little Pend Oreille National Wildlife refuge in Washington state. Given our family's deep personal and financial dedication to environmental protection, It seems somehow fitting.

lage once in the Austro-Hungarian Empire, became part of the Soviet Union. Well, none of that is Turkey. There is a whole Black Sea between the two places, but nevermind. At least, in 1955, Alex was not considered a citizen of the U.S.S.R. and therefore he was not a Communist! For Alex, it was a small grace to be considered Turkish.

Many questions remain. Who handled Alex Scraba's interment after his death? He left no next of kin to contact. His burial could have been handled by an employer or a labor union. It is also plausible a partner, obviously unknown to the family, took care of things. Alex's remains could have ended up unmarked or in a pauper's grave. Instead, the condition of Alex's headstone would indicate it was placed with consideration and well-cared for.

More profoundly, I wonder why Alex chose to absent himself from the ones who loved him? Did he understand that if he returned to Alberta with Elena and Ivan, his life would be one of unremitting and unrewarding labor for a questionable cause—his distracted, floundering parents? Of Alex's brothers, Gus died in 1918 of the Spanish influenza and Bill died in 1920 of typhoid. These were young men.

Editorial note:

Elena, Alex's mother, suffered unimaginable loss. Of the ten children she bore, only two—Maria and Nick—survived into adulthood. She knew nothing of Alex. And thus, Alex added another stone to her soul, to the grief that she carried. What does it say about a family whose future flees from it?

ACKNOWLEDGEMENTS

First of all, my sincere thanks go to all those in my (matrilineal) Ropchan-Scraba family who generously shared their narratives: Alex, Sam (in manuscript form, for that is all that I had of him), Bill, Nancy (Zaseybida), Katherine (Berger), Ann, George, Vera (Kindraka, my mother), Alice, Walter, Julia and Alberta (Scraba). In my (patrilineal) Kindraka family, thanks go to Pete (my father), Jack, Annie (Palmer), Kay (Mitchell), Pauline (Suydam), Alex and Nellie, Olga Kindrake and Harry Halyk, uncle to them all! My Canadian first cousins Hazel and Julian Ulan, Beatrice Kindraka Koss, Betty and Lawrence Tymko, Marie Gordon and Jim Kindrake and their daughters Maya and Renata—all added depth, humor, artful hospitality and joyful year-round-bbq grilling to my research and writing travails. In Edmonton, they were my home away from home.

I owe thanks to Soda Lake homestead neighbors: George and Lily Hill who showed great forbearance when I naively trespassed onto their farm looking for the family barn; Harry and Medoria Zukiwski who were an encyclopedia of Soda Lake lore; and Myrtle Lazaruk in Vegreville who was a school chum of my mother's sisters. Thanks as well go to far-flung family members in the Andrews, Alberta area—the Tkachuks, Semeniuks and the elder George Ropchan clan.

To my faculty mentors and graduate colleagues at the University of Alberta in Edmonton—Bohdan Medwidsky, Andriy Nahachewsky, Frances Swyripa, Natalie Kononenko, Alla Nedavkivska; Anya Kuranicheva, Nadya Foty, Brian Cherwick, Roman Shiyan, Sogu Hong—from whom I learned worlds and shared pizza at Pharoh's, thank you.

To my faculty mentors and graduate colleagues at the Russian and East European Institute [REEI] at Indiana University in Bloomington, Indiana—Sarah Philliips, Maria Bucker, Steve Franks, Svitlana Melnychuk, Alexandra Cotofana and Mihaela Petrescu—thank you for the encouragement, for the opportunity to further my Ukrainian studies, to teach and for the hours and hours of translation work from Ukrainian to English and from Romanian to English—this last, regarding the history of the Hurmuzaki's in Chornivka, Ukraine.

In Ukraine, there were the helpful, focused librarians at the Oblast Archive in Chernivtsi; the delightful Tselorad (Mayor) of Chornivka, Mr. Bota; the inimitable Larysa; and the marvellous Lyuda and Andriy Irynyshyn, my young hosts, for summer months of research and of family friendship, salubrious bread, beet salad and champanski. Without them, little would have been possible as broadly as it was.

To my brother, James Alexander Kindraka, who after reading a rough draft of this book, decided to do a bit of research on his own. His Addendum is a welcome and invaluable addition. Thank you Jim!

To Don McCartney, award-winning artist and graphic designer. I have been uniquely fortunate to have him working on my behalf to put the jumbled files of Among Women—text, maps, photos, into sensible visual order.

And how to acknowledge the vital input, the critical improvements and the profound support I have received from my editor and husband, Edwin Pennfield Jensen? It was no secret that, from the start, I wanted to write a book about the women in my family. After listening to my whining about it for years, it was Penn who insisted I interview elderly family members in Canada and the United States and school myself in Alberta, Saskatchewan, and perhaps most importantly in Ukraine, and get down to the business of writing. So, dear Penn, you could see this narrative much more clearly than I and, over the years, wrestled me into it. This book is ours.

—Monica Kindraka Jensen, May 6, 2024

CONCLUDING NOTES

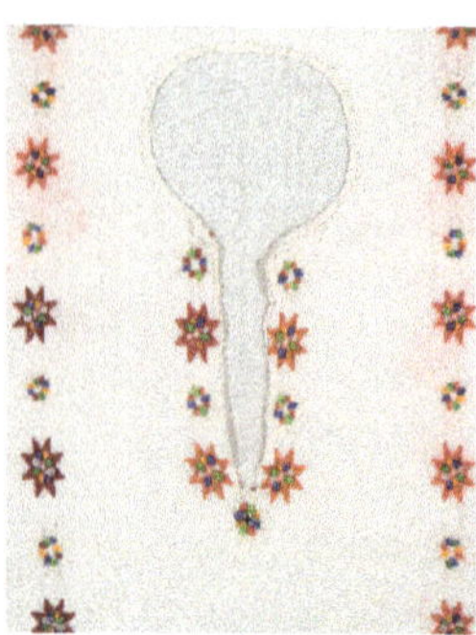

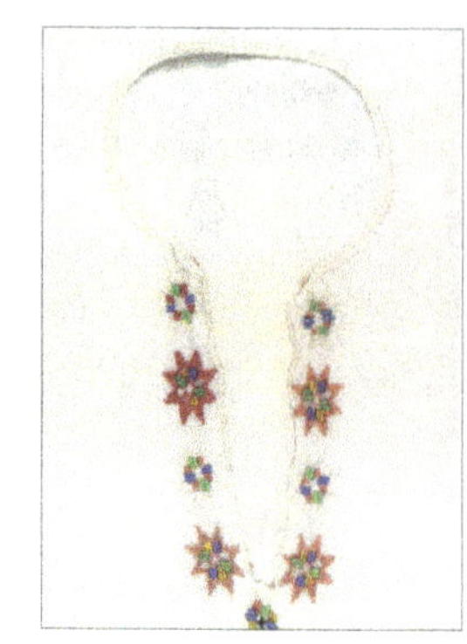

Ukrainian peasant woman's chemise (Сорочка/Sorochka). 19th century. Village of Chornivka, Bukovyna. Scraba family heirloom (worn).

Hand-spun flax (linen), woven then hand-sewn and embroidered into floor length garment, later cut off at the waist, probably to lighten weight and ease movement—to facilitate the hard work of pioneering in Alberta.

Keyhole neckline. Running stitch at circle opening. Buttonhole stitch below neck. Inside, quarter-inch seams—the fabric is precious. Embroidered eight-point stars around neckline. Aniline dyes—thus the garment was made after 1860. Blue, green, yellow and white beads embellishing the stars. Unfortunate (later) use of Clorox bleach.

Schematic for Ropchan Family quilt. Designed by the author. Hand & machine pieced, appliquéd and hand quilted by Vera Ropchan Kindraka as a wedding gift to her daughter, the author. Each of the 8-pointed stars (save one) represents a psychological portrait of Maria Scraba's eleven children, beginning with Al and ending with Walter. The star colors were inspired by a family heirloom—a man's wide, woven wool belt (poias) that originated in Chornivka, Bukovyna. The stars, which also appear in the Bukovyna chemise, are set against a linen-white to suggest the chemise's color.

Poias (Пояс). Bukovynian (Ukrainian) man's wide woven wool wrap-around belt. The traditional belt girded a linen-white tunic worn over linen-white pantaloons. Its colors were specific to the area—think township, county, province—around Chornivka village. The magenta, purple, green & red would have identified the man who wore the belt as someone from Chornivka. Aniline-dyed wool yarn, woven by a village expert into intricate geometric patterns; a weaving tour-de-force, as well as a cultural identifier. Scraba-Ropchan family heirloom.

Childhood Friend – Wild Crocus

Quilt. 30" x 30". 2023

By Monica Kindraka Jensen; Border calligraphy by Patricia Callison

The Blackfoot and Cree paid homage to this modest wild crocus. It grows on native northern prarie lands. My Ukrainian-Canadian mother grew up there, in Alberta. These lavender blossoms are welcome in April snows. Mother clung to the crocus's soft beauty as her singular joy in a gray landscape.

Common names: Pasqueflower, Pulsatilla patens, Easterflower, April Fools, Hartshorn plant, Lion's Beard, Old Man, Windflower, Quiverer, Stone Lily, Wild Crocus, Prairie Crocus.

www.ingramcontent.com/pod-product-compliance
Ingram Content Group UK Ltd.
Pitfield, Milton Keynes, MK11 3LW, UK
UKHW050136280726
14058UKWH00006B/674

9 798985 807943